A Personal Journey... devotional and journal

365 days of
Refining,
Renewal
And Restoration

# LIVING *Life* ABUNDANTLY

### Dare to Believe ~ Devotional and Journal

LARENE SANFORD

WESTBOW
PRESS®
A DIVISION OF THOMAS NELSON
& ZONDERVAN

Copyright © 2018 Larene Sanford.

All rights reserved. No part of this book may be used or reproduced by any means, graphic, electronic, or mechanical, including photocopying, recording, taping or by any information storage retrieval system without the written permission of the author except in the case of brief quotations embodied in critical articles and reviews.

WestBow Press books may be ordered through booksellers or by contacting:

WestBow Press
A Division of Thomas Nelson & Zondervan
1663 Liberty Drive
Bloomington, IN 47403
www.westbowpress.com
1 (866) 928-1240

Because of the dynamic nature of the Internet, any web addresses or links contained in this book may have changed since publication and may no longer be valid. The views expressed in this work are solely those of the author and do not necessarily reflect the views of the publisher, and the publisher hereby disclaims any responsibility for them.

Any people depicted in stock imagery provided by Getty Images are models, and such images are being used for illustrative purposes only.
Certain stock imagery © Getty Images.

ISBN: 978-1-9736-3262-7 (sc)
ISBN: 978-1-9736-3263-4 (hc)
ISBN: 978-1-9736-3261-0 (e)

Library of Congress Control Number: 2018907702

Print information available on the last page.

WestBow Press rev. date: 7/10/2018

Scripture taken from the New King James Version®. Copyright © 1982 by Thomas Nelson. Used by permission. All rights reserved.

Scripture taken from the New Century Version®. Copyright © 2005 by Thomas Nelson. Used by permission. All rights reserved.

Scripture quotations marked (NIV) are taken from the Holy Bible, New International Version®, NIV®. Copyright © 1973, 1978, 1984, 2011 by Biblica, Inc.™ Used by permission of Zondervan. All rights reserved worldwide. www.zondervan.com The "NIV" and "New International Version" are trademarks registered in the United States Patent and Trademark Office by Biblica, Inc.™

Scripture quotations marked (AMP) are taken from the Amplified Bible, Copyright © 1954, 1958, 1962, 1964, 1965, 1987 by The Lockman Foundation. Used by permission.

Scripture quotations marked (NLT) are taken from the Holy Bible, New Living Translation, copyright ©1996, 2004, 2015 by Tyndale House Foundation. Used by permission of Tyndale House Publishers, Inc., Carol Stream, Illinois 60188. All rights reserved.

Scripture quotations marked (TLB) are taken from The Living Bible copyright © 1971. Used by permission of Tyndale House Publishers, Inc., Carol Stream, Illinois 60188. All rights reserved.

Scripture quotations marked MSG are taken from THE MESSAGE, copyright © 1993, 1994, 1995, 1996, 2000, 2001, 2002 by Eugene H. Peterson. Used by permission of NavPress. All rights reserved. Represented by Tyndale House Publishers, Inc.

The Holy Bible, English Standard Version® (ESV®) Copyright © 2001 by Crossway, a publishing ministry of Good News Publishers. All rights reserved. ESV Text Edition: 2016

Scripture quotations marked (CEV) are from the Contemporary English Version Copyright © 1991, 1992, 1995 by American Bible Society, Used by Permission.

Scripture quotations marked (GNT) are from the Good News Translation in Today's English Version- Second Edition Copyright © 1992 by American Bible Society. Used by Permission.

Scripture quotations marked RSV are taken from the Revised Standard Version of the Bible, copyright © 1946, 1952, 1971 by the Division of Christian Education of the National Council of the Churches of Christ in the USA. Used by permission.

Scripture quotations marked KJV are from the Holy Bible, King James Version (Authorized Version). First published in 1611. Quoted from the KJV Classic Reference Bible, Copyright © 1983 by The Zondervan Corporation.

Scripture quotations marked HCSB®, are taken from the Holman Christian Standard Bible®, Copyright © 1999, 2000, 2002, 2003, 2009 by Holman Bible Publishers. Used by permission. HCSB® is a federally registered trademark of Holman Bible Publishers.

I dedicate this book to my grandchildren, Caleb, Noah, Elizabeth, Luke, Rocky and Scotland. My grandbabies have been an inspiration to me. Many times, I've learned how to love others by watching the purity of their love and interaction with others. Each one with their unique personality, and the way they show character has made this world a better place—especially in my little world.

# Contents

Preface ..................................................................................................xi
Introduction ........................................................................................xv

January      I Am a Child of God .................................................... 1
February    Be Renewed ............................................................... 41
March        Be Still Know I Am God ............................................. 77
April          You're Beautiful Treasured One ................................ 121
May          Holy Spirit Rain Down ............................................... 157
June          Joy in the Mourning .................................................. 203
July          Restored ..................................................................... 239
August       Rejoice! ...................................................................... 275
September  Restored to Believe ................................................. 309
October     Live the Life of Faith ................................................ 345
November  Look Up! ................................................................... 385
December   It's All About Jesus ~ Believe ~ ............................... 423

Endnotes .......................................................................................... 465

# Preface

Do you ever feel you are up against the same wall that hindered you before? When you are reminded of God's presence, and remember how you witnessed His power to set you free, God wants you to revere Him and know how powerful He is. Remembering what God has done in the past as you saw His power unfold, should not cause you to fear He will never move as mighty as to match such an experience again. Do not become frozen in fear; but, instead His presence and knowledge of His power can give you the courage to step out in faith, and trust God to lead you through again—through whatever rapid rivers of circumstances you face, that are keeping you from moving forward. He parted the way before; He'll do it again.

God will restore us when we are broken—whether by loss of a marriage, a loved one or a home; He will either return to you that which was lost, replace that which was lost, or remove the need for that which was lost.

"Living Life Abundantly Devotional and Journal" is about living the life we were meant to live—a journal to help readers to be transformed throughout the year into a life of hope and peace, living life abundantly as Jesus promised. There are 365 days of devotional reading to allow your heart to be refined through holy fire, removing anything that does not belong; renewing the mind and restoring the soul.

In *Living Life Abundantly, Dare to Believe, Devotional and Journal,* Larene shares a journey she traveled where she learned of God's grace, realizing that brokenness is not what defines a person. She offers to take you along memory lane.

Letter from the heart of the author

I would like to share a story with you—one that has changed my life. I first met Jesus when I was a young girl. I heard about His love and wanted to do my part in following Him. There came a point in my teenaged years, that I realized I wasn't living the life of one who was following Jesus. "How did I ever allow my life to end up this way?" I thought to myself. I sat in the sanctuary, at Beaumont First Assembly of God, and listened to Pastor Brewer, Sr. speak of the salvation of the Lord. He told of a God who could forgive and make your life brand new. He told us to come and lay our burdens down at the altar and not to pick them up when we left that place.

My heart was pounding so severely that I thought it might burst out of my chest. I hadn't realized it at the time, but the Holy Spirit was calling me so powerfully that my entire body couldn't contain it. As the psalmist wrote, "His grace has taught my heart to fear, and grace, my fears relieved," I understood the fear of denying Him, and once I answered that call, my fear was gone.

I was determined to live the life God had sacrificed His son for, and dedicate myself to His purpose.

Then, when I thought I had it all figured out, my world crumbled. I didn't understand why. And I didn't realize how fear had crept in and taken hold of my heart. Fear crippled me. I knew my only hope was to cry out to my Father. And that, I did.

I prayed for God to change the circumstances that seemed to be destroying me, my family, and my future. He did something greater. He gave me the peace that only comes from Him that would be sufficient to see me through any storm. Through this peace, He showed me what it meant to live—really live the abundant life He spoke of. It wasn't about status. It wasn't about popularity, or anything else I had placed such value. It was about Jesus. And He was enough. He was all I needed to survive this crazy world we call *life*.

God will use the weak, the broken, the unexpected, the uneducated, the young and old to confound the wisest. Society will claim that the fittest, strongest, most wise and educated, and most beautiful will succeed—that these are the people to listen to when you need good advice. Be careful not to place God in a box—God can work in the small details and in the storms.

Others say, "Who is she to think she can tell others how to live? Look at her!" Ridiculed by others as being the wrong choice to speak on His behalf, and yet God chose me and you! Be strong and brave.

I would like to share this journey with you in a daily devotion, just the way He laid it out for me, as He took my heart and transformed it. He showed me that restoration began before I was born, and my life would be restored to show His incredible restoring power. He will restore us when we are broken—whether by loss of a marriage, a loved one or a home; He will either return to you that which was lost, replace that which was lost, or remove the need for that which was lost.

I pray that you will find Him; see His great love; experience the incredible restoring power of the Lord; and learn to live the abundant life that He intended for you.

—Larene Sanford

# Introduction

Living Abundantly ~ Dare to Believe
A Personal Journey
Devotional and Journal
By Larene Sanford

This book is inspired by author's books, "Railroad Crossings to Restoration ~ A Child's Cry for Help", "Living for Jesus ~ Restored to Believe", and "Railroad Crossings to Restoration ~ Looking Back and Pressing Forward" where I took readers on a personal journey from rejection, through renewal and onto a new hope, restoration and faith sure based on the truth that withstands all storms of life—God is faithful.

We live in a time where the interest in prolonged life and better life is increasing. Magazines, products, internet articles and books about good diet and exercise programs promise a higher quality of life and living a long life.

This is natural. We are built to desire long lives and live abundantly; but, the answer isn't found in products, programs and promises to live long and well on earth alone. We were made to live forever; and with the eternal perspective, we will live our lives abundantly—the true quality of life. We will be able to find identity and security in God and realize the abundant life comes by living the life of faith—believing that what God said is true.

I pray the scriptures and encouraging thoughts will touch your heart, whether broken, hardened, or strong in the Lord. And my hopes are that they will bring you to a new place with God that you will never forget.

Each day, allow the words to resonate with you throughout the day. Read God's Word and heed His guidance. I encourage you to journal your thoughts, your prayers and commitments each day, so that you will be able to see the transformation throughout the process. Begin this journey with me as your heart cries out to the living God and, as you do, you will find rest for your soul, and find life abundant.

> The thief does not come except to steal, and to kill, and to destroy. I have come that they may have life, and that they may have *it* more abundantly. (John 10:10 NKJV)

# January

God is our refuge and strength, an ever-present help in trouble.
—Psalm 46:1 (NIV)

# I Am a Child of God

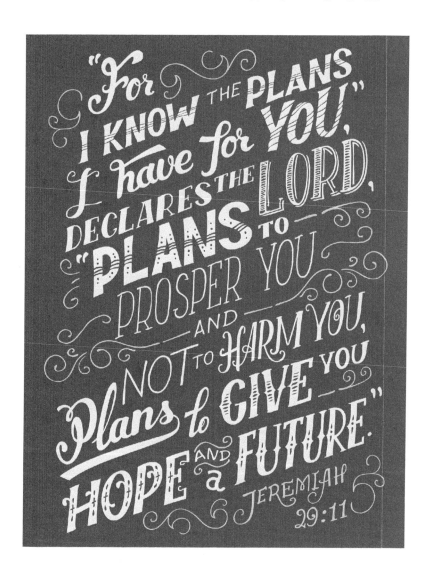

# January 1

"Come to Me, all you who are weary and burdened, and I will give you rest."
—Matthew 11:28 (NIV)

Before you start your journey in this new year, take a moment of rest. Allow God to work in you, His peace and comfort. You may anticipate great things this year, and some things you are committed to achieve may seem overwhelming. This may even seem contradictory to most messages for New Year's Day and resolutions—this is not your normal New Year's motivational speech. However, the first and most important thing you need to do is to wait. The God of peace loves you. He cares about you and wants you to commit all of your plans to Him as He unfolds the mysteries of tomorrow in the most appropriate time.

You may be anxious to start fixing everything that needs fixing. You might be thinking about all of the things wrong in your life that you want to change for the better. Too often, we try to fix things our own way before consulting with God as to how we should go about it.

Ask the Lord what He wants as a priority in your life. Let your plan, your resolution, your hopes, and your dreams be created in you by the God who formed you so that you can be the person you were meant to be.

> Therefore, humble yourselves under the mighty hand of God [set aside self-righteous pride], so that He may exalt you [to a place of honor in His service] at the appropriate time, casting all your cares [all your anxieties, all your worries, and all your concerns, once and for all] on Him, for He cares about you [with deepest affection, and watches over you very carefully]. Be sober [well balanced and self-disciplined], be alert *and* cautious at all times. That enemy of yours, the devil, prowls around like a roaring lion [fiercely hungry], seeking someone to devour. But resist him, be firm in *your* faith [against his attack—rooted, established, immovable], knowing that the same experiences

of suffering are being experienced by your brothers and sisters throughout the world. [You do not suffer alone.] After you have suffered for a little while, the God of all grace [who imparts His blessing and favor], who called you to His *own* eternal glory in Christ, will Himself complete, confirm, strengthen, and establish you [making you what you ought to be]. To Him be dominion (power, authority, sovereignty) forever and ever. Amen.

—1 Peter 5:6–11 (AMP)

# January 2

> See what great love the Father has lavished on us, that we should be called children of God! And that is what we are! The reason the world does not know us is that it did not know Him.
>
> —1 John 3:1 (NIV)

Consider that thought for just a moment. Who is God? The Creator of all things. The Beginning and the End. Almighty God. Bread of Life. Great Shepherd. Messiah. Cornerstone. Deliverer. Everlasting Father.; Holy One. King of Kings. Lord of Lords. Lamb of God. Light of the World. Lion of the tribe of Judah. Master. Great Physician. Prince of Peace. Redeemer. Refuge. Rock. Ruler of all creation. Savior. Truth. The Life. The Way. Wonderful Counselor. The Word. The Vine. These incredible descriptions are just some of the names of God. And we are His children! What a powerful Father we have who loves us and wants to lavish His love on us!

---
---
---

# January 3

> I can do all things through Christ who strengthens me.
> —Philippians 4:13 (NKJV)

Believe ~ with childlike faith, believe with no predetermined ideas or ulterior motives, and without requiring physical proof. Trust that the Father loves you and will guide you. Our heavenly Father is strong in us; He is able to accomplish things that we cannot do alone. In our relationship of active faith in Christ, we have the strength with Him we would not have any other way. We are able to persevere in the most difficult circumstances. The key is Jesus. He is the one who will give you the strength through these moments that may seem unbearable.

> Now faith is confidence in what we hope for and assurance about what we do not see. By faith we understand that the universe was formed at God's command, so that what is seen was not made out of what was visible.
> —Hebrews 11:1, 3 (NIV)

The next time you begin to fret, look with your heart and not your eyes. Look to the almighty, powerful God and remember that He cannot be matched in His power. We cannot even begin to understand God's ability and intelligence; yet He chooses to bend low to the earth and speak peace into our hearts—like a mother bending low to her little boy, speaking words to him so that he can understand.

Think about what you could not do without Him. Is there truly anything that we *can* do, without God giving the ability to do so?

_____
_____
_____
_____

# January 4

Even if my father and mother abandon me, the LORD will hold me close.
—Psalm 27:10 (NLT)

The eyes of the LORD are on the righteous, and His ears are attentive to their cry.
—Psalm 34:15 (NIV)

You are not abandoned. You are not an orphan. You are not alone. Reach out and take hold of His hand, child of God. He is reaching down to hold yours. He will save you!

Whatever you are facing, God will stay by your side. You may not be able to see an answer to your situation that could result in anything good. But God hears your cry. He knows your pain. Joy comes from the assurance that God is in control—in control of the storms, and the flood, and in control of the details of our lives. This peaceful confidence that we will survive the storm convinces our hearts that we can surely praise Him in all things. In the midst of the storm, it's difficult to see clearly. Don't let the chaos create fear. Stay close to the one who will not leave you.

What are you afraid of that keeps you from being confident and full of joy?

_____
_____
_____
_____

# January 5

> Trust in the LORD with all your heart, and lean not on your own understanding; in all your ways acknowledge Him, And He shall direct your paths.
> —Proverbs 3:5–6 (NKJV)

The Lord restores the heart that is broken. He brings life and hope. Jesus has already restored your soul. Restoration took place on the cross. He is not bound by time; therefore, what He did then on the cross has accomplished restoration in me and you in this very moment, in the now, just as you and I will be restored when we enter heaven. He rescues, reaffirms, reassures, renews, and restores. There is nothing He can't fix.

The Bible doesn't say we are to acknowledge God in circumstances where you can find no other way. It says, "In all your ways, acknowledge Him." We cannot rely on our own insight. Instead, recognize and know God will make your way straight, with purpose and meaning. Lean on God; trust in God; and be confident in God with all your heart and mind. God has given us the ability to do what we are able to do, even in the simplest of daily tasks.

Give reverence to the Lord God and worship Him. Your future is laid out on the map God holds in His hands. He has a good plan for your life.

# January 6

> And after you have suffered a little while, the God of all grace, who has called you to His eternal glory in Christ, will Himself restore, confirm, strengthen, and establish you. To Him be the dominion forever and ever. Amen.
> —1 Peter 5:10–11 (ESV)

Are you hurting today? Do you wonder how you arrived where you are today? Has life worn you down to a point where you feel empty, exhausted, overwhelmed, or worthless? Life here on earth will bring pain, sorrow, and struggles in ways that, sometimes, appear unbearable. This world is decaying and everyone in this world will be affected by its decay. The first sin of Adam and Eve began a decay of this world, and the suffering will continue until we enter heaven. But don't let that news discourage you. There's good news. In a little while, God will restore you, He will confirm you, He will strengthen you, and He will establish you.

Key thought: God will restore you. He will make you strong and ground you securely. He will settle you. Though you may feel weak now, He is made strong in you, and though you may struggle now, He will make you everything you ought to be.

There will be times of drought in our lives. We find ourselves at a loss for words or action at times. Whatever you have lost, whether it be a job, relationship, health, home, or anything of worth, God is the one who can restore. Do you need a miracle today? If God determines what you have lost is what you need, then He will bring back what was lost, or replace what was lost. God may even remove the need for what was lost; and He will help you live without it. Those who dedicate themselves to following God's will for their lives have that promise of restoration. He would not bring you to this place, where you are today, without a way to keep you moving forward. And if it takes a miracle, then, that is what He will do.

What is it that you need God to do? Believe that God will provide what is needed. Then, accept whatever that may be.

_____
_____
_____
_____

# January 7

Do not be anxious about anything, but in every situation, by prayer and petition, with thanksgiving, present your requests to God. And the peace of God, which transcends all understanding, will guard your hearts and your minds in Christ Jesus.
—Philippians 4:6–7 (NIV)

Let God reside in the core of your heart. As you allow Him to take that place of authority over all things, you will find that He is able to meet all of your needs, and that He will guard all else you place in your heart—then you will have peace.

You will no longer be afraid—instead you will trust God is in control of all things; for He is rich in love; His grace is sufficient; and He is the creator of all things, and therefore, is in charge of all things. He is more powerful than what ails you. He is stronger than that which intends to harm you.

Search your heart today. Do you need courage, hope, faith?

_____
_____
_____
_____

# January 8

Do you not know that your bodies are temples of the Holy Spirit, who is in you, whom you have received from God? You are not your own; you were bought at a price. Therefore honor God with your bodies.

—1 Corinthians 4:19-20 (NIV)

Your body—Your body consists of body mass (structure with head, neck, trunk, two arms and hands, two legs and feet); inner body systems (such as a skeletal system, muscular system, cardiovascular system, digestive system, endocrine system, nervous system, respiratory system, immune lymphatic system, urinary system, female or male productive system, and integumentary system such as skin, hair and nails.

Wow!

There's so much more to our bodies than we realize at times. From time to time, I have had some issues with one or more of these systems requiring medical attention. At times, I needed to develop a plan to manage issues of the body. There are times that I have needed God to intervene with a miracle of healing.

The good news is this: The Holy Spirit resides in us. We are His temple, and as we diligently care for ourselves, we give honor to Him. In doing so, God blesses our effort.

The fact is, to do God's will may require a strong body, or a healthy heart, or some other strength of the body. What practices of good health, whether physical, mental, emotional or spiritual, do you need help with? Do you need a miracle? Do you need to develop a plan of improvement? With God in the core of your heart as you place Him in the highest authority, honor and importance, you can do so much for the kingdom of God.

_____
_____
_____

# January 9

> In You our ancestors put their trust; they trusted and You delivered them. To You they cried out and were saved; in You they trusted and were not put to shame.
> —Psalm 22:4–5 (NIV)

> The earth is the Lord's, and everything in it, the world, and all who live in it; for He founded it on the seas and established it on the waters.
> —Psalm 24:1–2 (NIV)

You belong to God, God is with you, and God is for you. This is the gospel—the good news!

One day you're strolling along a nice path—on a beautiful, peaceful day—and then a pot-hole you didn't see in your way sends you tumbling down, leaving you with broken bones. This is how it seems to go many times with tragedies unexpected, leaving you broken. Unexpected loss of lives, broken marriages, lost homes and jobs, and runaway prodigals, leave you wondering what to do next. With lives and dreams shattered into millions of pieces that we cannot put back together again, our only hope is in God.

God is for you even when you don't understand—no matter what you go through, no matter what happens, no matter what your emotions are, or the pain you go through. When you are in the darkest moment of your journey, this one thing will keep you at peace: knowing that God is with you, He is in control, and that you are His child.

> The Lord controls the flood. The Lord will be King forever. The Lord gives strength to His people; the Lord blesses His people with peace
> —Psalm 29:10–11 (NCV)

# January 10

> Yes, my soul, find rest in God; my hope comes from Him. Truly He is my rock and my salvation; He is my fortress, I will not be shaken. My salvation and my honor depend on God; He is my mighty rock, my refuge. Trust in Him at all times, you people; pour out your hearts to Him, for God is our refuge.
> —Psalm 62:5–8 (NIV)

Are you tired? Overwhelmed? With life, comes financial struggles, marital discord, heath issues, many losses, and problems of every-day life. Sometimes, you feel weighed down and trapped by your circumstances. In times like these, we are reminded just how much we need God. When trouble comes, we need God to unlock the chains of anxiety and set us free.

There was a time when I cried out to everyone, but God. I cried out to Mama. I complained to my family and friends. I looked within myself to find ways to resolve the issues. Then, I would cry because I couldn't find a way to fix the problem. One day, when I was at my lowest point, I realized—I needed to stop crying out to the wrong people, and stop trying to fix things myself without first going to God for His direction. Our Father knows our limits—we can't hide our innermost thoughts. Refusing to tell Him does not hide it from Him. Go to Him with honest confession, and an open heart to receive what He has for you.

As you begin to trust God at *all* times, you will find that pouring your heart out to Him will bring rest. What is it that you need rest from? What might be holding you back from your rest in God? As the psalmist said, "My salvation and my honor depend on God."

_____

_____

_____

_____

# January 11

This is the verdict: Light has come into the world, but people loved darkness instead of light because their deeds were evil. Everyone who does evil hates the light, and will not come into the light for fear that their deeds will be exposed. But whoever lives by the truth comes into the light, so that it may be seen plainly that what they have done has been done in the sight of God.
—John 3:19–21 (NIV)

Are you on the cusp of making a big decision? Before you decide what you're going to do, take it to the Lord today. Apply the light of His Word. Making a decision on your own without God's direction would be like driving your car on an unlit country road without the headlights on, yet expecting to stay on the road. You're headed for a catastrophe—if not immediately, at some point in a turn of the road.

The same is true for living a godly life. Your plans, your desires, and your way of thinking will either give glory to God, or will lead to sin and dishonor Him. Just as Adam and Eve hid from God in the Garden of Eden, we seem to think hiding in the darkness is the answer to deal with our sinful ways. Though it may be difficult to give up some of these hidden things in your life, it will bring you incredible peace if you do. As we submit our ways to God, He will direct us in the path that is right—we will do what we do, go where we go, and be who we are in character, based on the truths God has provided in His Word. Of course, we will all fall short of His righteousness; and that's why it is not by our righteousness, but by the righteousness of Jesus that we are saved. But, we *can* save ourselves from a lot of trouble, and live unashamed as we allow the Holy Spirit to work in us as we walk in the light of His way.

# January 12

> Follow God's example, therefore, as dearly loved children and walk in the way of love, just as Christ loved us and gave Himself up for us as a fragrant offering and sacrifice to God.
>
> —Ephesians 5:1–2 (NIV)

You are loved. You are God's child. Mirror the heart of God. The next opportunity you have, when dealing with others, whether the relationship is in conflict or is at peace, offer a sacrifice of love. Expect nothing in return—rather, let it be unconditional. Your reward may not come from that person, but your Father will take notice and your reward from Him will far outweigh any reward you may receive from a man or woman.

_____
_____
_____
_____

# January 13

> For I know the plans I have for you," declares the Lord, "Plans to prosper you and not to harm you, plans to give you hope and a future."
> —Jeremiah 29:11 (NIV)

God's plan for one person might be a difficult plan; and for another person, His plan may be easier. But each is used to work for our good, and so that we can glorify God. God will equip you with all that you need to move forward in His plan—and thus reveal His glory. You may feel anxious that you are not doing what you should be doing. You may feel like you should be more successful in life than where you are right now. Trust God to search your heart and lead you in the direction you should go. Then, take one step. Be brave and courageous.

> All Scripture is God-breathed and is useful for teaching, rebuking, correcting and training in righteousness, so that the servant of God may be thoroughly equipped for every good work.
> —2 Timothy 3:16–17 (NIV)

> Search me [thoroughly], O God, and know my heart; test me and know my anxious thoughts; and see if there is any wicked *or* hurtful way in me, and lead me in the everlasting way.
> —Psalm 139:23–24 (AMP)

_____
_____
_____

# January 14

So that we are no longer children [spiritually immature], tossed back and forth [like ships on a stormy sea] and carried about by every wind of [shifting] doctrine, by the cunning *and* trickery of [unscrupulous] men, by the deceitful scheming of people ready to do anything [for personal profit]. But speaking the truth in love [in all things—both our speech and our lives expressing His truth], let us grow up in all *things* into Him [following His example] who is the Head—Christ.
—Ephesians 4:14-15 (AMP)

A "little white lie" is still a lie. Misleading someone to believe something that isn't true is dishonest. A mature Christian knows that, even if the truth is going to hurt, they need to speak the truth anyway.

I remember one day, I was asked to lie to cover up a mistake. When faced with this difficult situation, I had to make a decision. I had to choose to lie and avoid confrontation with the one asking me to lie, or stand up for what's right and tell the truth. I took a deep breath and, willing to face the consequences of the confrontation, I refused to lie.

That's not easy to do. We face issues, and challenges, and even bullies who will cause anxiety, and bring temptation to waiver in our walk with the Lord. In real terms, truth is the self-expression of God. That is the biblical *meaning* of truth. Because the definition of truth flows from God, truth is theological. Jesus came from the Father into our world and became flesh, and He is full of grace and truth (John 1:14). To say we have Jesus living within our hearts, is to say that we have Truth living in us. Our lives should express the Truth (that is the gospel and person of Christ) by what we do, and what we say every day.

Are you ready to take on that responsibility? Ask Jesus for courage to carry out your responsibilities. Jesus said His yoke is easy and His burden is light (Matthew 11:30). Allow Him to carry your burden and live the life of truth you were intended to live.

_____
_____
_____
_____

# January 15

> Do not be deceived: God cannot be mocked. A man reaps what he sows. Whoever sows to please their flesh, from the flesh will reap destruction; whoever sows to please the Spirit, from the Spirit will reap eternal life. Let us not become weary in doing good, for at the proper time we will reap a harvest if we do not give up.
> —Galatians 6:7–9 (NIV)

Keep doing right. The world tells us, "Nice guys finish last." That may be true; but remember what Jesus said about the one who is last: "The last will be first and the first will be last." (Matthew 20:16 and Matthew 19:30). Giving up the fight to be first is an excellent example of one's dedication to live a life of sacrifice to serve in the Lord's Kingdom.

Don't give up on doing what is right.

I cannot say that I have always been nice. I've certainly acted out to please my flesh—I've wanted my way, how I wanted, and when I wanted. I've thrown my childish fits—yes, even fits with God, and especially when I'm exhausted. But, as a child of God, the Holy Spirit living in me reminds that I must strive to do what is right, and by doing so, I will please the Spirit. The fight between flesh and Spirit will rage on until we enter into heaven and the war will be over.

My daughter, Rebecca, in my opinion, is the nicest person I know. I've never seen her treat someone cruel. That doesn't mean she has never dealt with conflict, because I know she has. But, how she deals with conflict is never with a mean spirit. What an amazing world we would live in if we would all—or even simply those who call themselves Christians—act nobly and do right, treating everyone with kindness; realizing, too, that kindness should not be mistaken for weakness. You will have difficult confrontations and conversations. And when you do, you will need the Spirit to be strong within you for you to be able to act with a noble character. Even tough love is still based on "love". I think we often tend to forget the "love" and focus on "tough".

In trying times, don't quit trying. Don't give up. When you're tired, and your heart is heavy, and you feel like you won't make it, keep pressing forward.

# January 16

> Brothers and sisters, if someone is caught in a sin, you who live by the Spirit should restore that person gently. But watch yourselves, or you also may be tempted. If anyone thinks they are something when they are not, they deceive themselves. Each one should test their own actions. Then they can take pride in themselves alone, without comparing themselves to someone else, for each one should carry their own load.
> —Galatians 6:1–5 (NIV)

Has someone you know been overtaken by sin? You, who are led by the Holy Spirit should reinstate him/her gently, without any portrayal of condescension. Be careful not to be caught up in the sin, by going to the person, and in turn take part in their sin. Be prepared, taking on the full armor of God—truth, righteousness, preparation of the gospel of peace, faith, salvation and the Word of God. And pray, pray and pray again.

You may have been wronged by someone who fell into sin, and who has ultimately sinned against you. Remember that the person has sinned against God as well; you're not alone. Even in these difficult times, when you feel offended and mistreated, when you approach the person, you will need to remember to go with the intention to restore and not to tear down. And just the same, be cautious. Your emotions may get in the way of the mission to resolve the issue. Many times it comes too easy for one to lash out and fight back, rather than act with humility, and let their strength show in their self-control. Prepare yourself and keep the armor of God in mind when you address the issue with them. If you're not ready, then don't go!

## The Armor of God

> Finally, be strong in the Lord and in His mighty power. Put on the full armor of God, so that you can take your stand against the devil's schemes. For our struggle is not against flesh and blood, but against the rulers,

against the authorities, against the powers of this dark world and against the spiritual forces of evil in the heavenly realms. Therefore put on the full armor of God, so that when the day of evil comes, you may be able to stand your ground, and after you have done everything, to stand. Stand firm then, with the belt of truth buckled around your waist, with the breastplate of righteousness in place, and with your feet fitted with the readiness that comes from the gospel of peace. In addition to all this, take up the shield of faith, with which you can extinguish all the flaming arrows of the evil one. Take the helmet of salvation and the sword of the Spirit, which is the word of God.

And pray in the Spirit on all occasions with all kinds of prayers and requests. With this in mind, be alert and always keep on praying for all the Lord's people.
—Ephesians 6:10–18 (NIV)

# January 17

> People will come from east and west and north and south, and will take their places at the feast in the kingdom of God. Indeed there are those who are last who will be first, and first who will be last."
>
> —Luke 13:29–30 (NIV)

When we decide to follow Jesus' example, we have chosen to walk in the Spirit. We will not think so highly of ourselves; rather we will be willing to serve others no matter who they are or what their background. This way of thinking is opposite of how the world behaves. People led by greed will try and succeed at the expense of others. It happens when the taxpayer is dishonest. It happens when the co-worker takes credit for the work of someone else. It happens when a person receives something they weren't supposed to receive, yet they keep it for themselves. It happens more often than we realize. With a sense of entitlement, they shout out, "The world owes me!" This misconception is epidemic in the work world, because people believe that they have earned what they have worked so hard for, and they feel that they deserve what they have coming to them. And it is contrary to biblical teaching. When we are honest with ourselves, we will realize what *we have coming to us* is not good, but punishment of our sin. However, Jesus took the punishment so that we no longer receive *what's coming to us,* but have everlasting life.

Ask yourself, "What am I striving for? What are my goals? Do I have goals to help others or only myself? Am I setting goals only in the material sense? Am I setting goals spiritually as well?" Answer these questions and begin your mission to become a servant to those around you. It's okay to start small. Simply start somewhere.

_____

_____

_____

_____

# January 18

> Jesus answered, "I am the way and the truth and the life. No one comes to the Father except through Me. If you really know Me, you will know my Father as well. From now on, you do know Him and have seen Him."
> —John 14:6–7 (NIV)

Jesus told the people on several occasions that He and the Father were one. He performed miracles and offered eternal life to those who would follow Him. He predicted His betrayal and Peter's denial. And the time was quickly approaching when Jesus would be betrayed and led to the cross to be crucified. Before this happens, Jesus began speaking to the disciples, comforting them, and encouraging them so that they would believe and have peace. He told them that He was the *only* way; that He is the truth and the life.

The Way—When I have lost my way, I am found in Jesus.

The Truth—The whole world may eventually be a lie, but Jesus remains true.

The Life—There is no other way of life that can satisfy my soul, but the life I have in Jesus.

Many will say, "This way", and, "That." But the way to the Father is only through Jesus—by believing He is the Son of God and was sent so that we can have everlasting life. Believe that, and you will have the peace that Jesus spoke about.

# January 19

"If you love me, keep My commands. And I will ask the Father, and He will give you another advocate to help you and be with you forever—the Spirit of truth. The world cannot accept Him, because it neither sees Him nor knows Him. But you know Him, for He lives with you and will be in you. I will not leave you as orphans; I will come to you. Before long, the world will not see Me anymore, but you will see Me. Because I live, you also will live. On that day you will realize that I am in My Father, and you are in Me, and I am in you. Whoever has My commands and keeps them is the one who loves Me. The one who loves Me will be loved by My Father, and I too will love them and show Myself to them. But the Advocate, the Holy Spirit, whom the Father will send in My name, will teach you all things and will remind you of everything I have said to you."
—John 14:15–21, 26 (NIV)

The Holy Spirit living in you, will be your advocate and help you do as the Lord commands. Whoever keeps His commands, show their love for Him. The Holy Spirit will teach and remind you of everything Jesus has said and will point you in the direction which you should go.

Search your own heart. Do you need help? Do you need direction? Seek the guidance of the Holy Spirit so that your life reflects the love of Christ.

_____
_____
_____
_____

# January 20

> Peace I leave with you; My peace I give you. I do not give to you as the world gives. Do not let your hearts be troubled and do not be afraid.
> —John 14:27 (NIV)

There is nothing to fear; not your past; not your future. Though things may seem bleak, that doesn't mean God doesn't have a plan for tomorrow. Allow the peace of God rest on your heart today. Let that peace, that only comes from Jesus, calm your restless spirit and ease your cluttered mind. Do not leave this moment until you break through to the place of peace. Quiet your mind. Rest. Be still. Listen.

_____
_____
_____
_____

# January 21

Guide me in Your truth and teach me, for You are God my Savior, and my hope is in You all day long.
—Psalm 25:5 (NIV)

May the Lord direct your steps today—that you will follow and have hope in Him.

### Confident Trust

So, do not throw away your confidence; it will be richly rewarded. You need to persevere so that when you have done the will of God, you will receive what He has promised.

For, "In just a little while, He who is coming will come and will not delay."

And, "But My righteous one will live by faith. And I take no pleasure in the one who shrinks back."

But we do not belong to those who shrink back and are destroyed, but to those who have faith and are saved.
—Hebrews 10:35–39 (NIV)

_____
_____
_____
_____

# January 22

Those who know Your name trust in You, for You, Lord, have never forsaken those who seek You.
—Psalm 9:10 (NIV)

For You have been my hope, Sovereign Lord, my confidence since my youth.
—Psalm 71:5 (NIV)

Trust God. In all things, believe He is able; He will not forsake you; He will deliver you. He is your protector. Hope in the Lord God.

Jesus has kept me brave through so many difficult days. Even as a young girl, I knew He was the only one who could help me be brave. I was afraid of the dark—He gave me courage. I was afraid of strange sounds outside my window—He sat at the foot of my bed until I fell asleep. I was afraid of losing my family—He taught me how to trust only in Him. Do I still face fear today? Absolutely. But when I do, I remember who I am and who I can run to—Jesus!

Run to Him. Trust Him. Allow Jesus to teach you to trust Him and be brave.

# January 23

> You will keep in perfect peace those whose minds are steadfast, because they trust in You.
> —Isaiah 26:3 (NIV)

A deep breath, in perfect peace, is refreshing to the soul. With your thoughts kept on God, and His power, and His love, you can have that perfect peace.

I know what it feels like to be anxious about the future. I understand the pain of abandonment and feeling worthless. When I came to the crossroads of change, I realized I wasn't in control—and found that it was okay that I wasn't. When I finally realized that God was in control, no matter the circumstances, I could take a deep breath, smile, and though my world had completely changed, declare, "You are God. Thank you for my life."

_____

_____

_____

_____

# January 24

Some trust in chariots and some in horses, but we trust in the name of the LORD our God.
—Psalm 20:7 (NIV)

Many are the woes of the wicked, but the LORD's unfailing love surrounds the one who trusts in Him.
—Psalm 32:10 (NIV)

Nothing on earth can compare to God. No peace is perfect without Him. The peace that this world provides is fallible. It will waver based on circumstances. But, not so with the peace of God that lives strong within us.

Are you hurting? Look to God and He will surround you with His mercy.

What is it that you need to trust God for? What are you holding on to that needs to be released into the hand of the Lord? Give that to Him today so that all that you have is in His control. Stop fighting for control and let God lead you. When you do, you will find peace like no other.

---
---
---
---

# January 25

> Unless the LORD builds the house, the builders labor in vain. Unless the LORD watches over the city, the guards stand watch in vain.
>
> —Psalm 127:1 (NIV)

As a little girl, I enjoyed going on our family camping trips. I played by the lake's edge, building my tower out of pebbles that I had found along the shore. I would build and build until, eventually, a large enough wave from the wake of the boats passing by, would come and knock it all down. That didn't bother me; I simply began again, singing my little song, "Gonna build a tower, in another hour. In another hour, gonna build a tower." On and on it went, building and crashing; singing and building again.

When I was older, my brother shared how he would cringe at how I would continue to relentlessly build the tower of rocks right by the water, knowing it would only be torn down by the waves. He grew annoyed by the vain venture and the tune that was repetitious and constant.

But at that young age, of about four years old, the joy of building was all I needed. I wasn't trying to build the highest tower, or the strongest. I just built.

Life, as I grew older, became so much different than a little girl at play. The demands for the strongest, and the competition to be the best, drives us to build something great that cannot fall. The conquest for success—not failure—can become overwhelming.

But, friends, if the Lord didn't build it, the endeavor is futile and the outcome will be just the same as my tower at the lake. It will fall, so you labor in vain. You cannot build it to withstand all that the world may hurl at you. And you cannot protect all that you own, no matter how hard you try. God is the only one who can build something of your life and protect what He builds no matter the circumstance.

# January 26

Two Rules
By Lanette Godsey
Pastor's wife ~ Remnant Church Imperial Valley

Some of us may have lives that haven't turned out the way we expected—a son is in jail; or a sixteen-year-old daughter is pregnant; or you are someone whose husband has left you; or you are dealing with a difficult marriage, or you have no marriage; no children, or difficult children; health problems; loss of faith. And this is all in addition to the everyday problems like getting the bills paid and the laundry done. Maybe you feel like you're just barely hanging on. The bad news is that you're not perfect, and you never will be. But the good news is that you *can* actually become the woman that God wants you to be and do it even while you're still not perfect!

I lived many years trying to live the way everybody told me that I should live; doing the things that everybody said I ought to do, and what I thought I should do by reading the Bible to find out how I should live. I was tearing myself apart. And all the while never found my way until I realized something. You can't become the woman God wants you to be by living that way—believing I could be made *right* by following the rules.

God does not want you to think of the Bible as a list of rules and regulations.

Believe it or not, there are only two rules you need to follow, and as we follow those two rules everything else will fall into place.

Sounds good, doesn't it? Two rules! We make it so difficult. But God didn't intend it to be so complicated.

When we think of a list of rules that might be in the Bible, the first that comes to our mind are the Ten Commandments.

Jesus was asked which of the commandments is the most important.

The Greatest Commandment

Hearing that Jesus had silenced the Sadducees, the Pharisees got together. One of them, an expert in the law, tested Him with this question: "Teacher, which is the greatest commandment in the Law?"

Jesus replied: "'Love the Lord your God with all your heart and with all your soul and with all your mind.' This is the first and greatest commandment. And the second is like it: 'Love your neighbor as yourself.' All the Law and the Prophets hang on these two commandments."

—Matthew 22:37–40 (NIV)

Follow those two rules and you will automatically follow all the others. If you're familiar with the Ten Commandments, you may or may not have noticed that the first four are about God—have no other gods, don't make idols, don't take God's name in vain, remember the Sabbath day; and the last six are regarding others/your neighbor— honor your parents, do not murder, don't commit adultery, don't steal, don't lie about your neighbor, don't covet.

The first greatest commandment—"Love the Lord with all your heart, soul and mind", and the second—"Love your neighbor as yourself," together cover all ten of the original commandments.

~

These two rules will set the foundation for God to form us how He sees fit. Imperfect, yet perfect—through God's grace and Christ's sacrifice, we become who God wants us to be in the very moment when we accept His Son and become a part of God's family—we become a child of God, purified, sanctified and made whole. Our lives, then, are dedicated to the love we have for God, and for others.

_____
_____
_____
_____

# January 27

For we are God's fellow workers. You are God's field, God's building.

—1 Corinthians 3:9 (ESV)

Stone by stone, brick by brick, moment by moment, God builds you into what He wants you to be. Trust that His plan is good. His masterpiece is you; the blueprint is His making.

# January 28

> For every house is built by someone, but the builder of all things is God.
>
> —Hebrews 3:4 (ESV)

You may *think* that you are successful in "this" or "that" by your own ability and creativity—a career, raising children, owning a large house on the beach, education, accomplishments. But in reality, everything you have achieved in this life, God has given you the ability to do—the tools and the know-how to accomplish it. He made you, and created everything that you used to achieve all that you have.

Thank Him today for your accomplishments, for your success, for all that He's provided for you to be able to do the things you do.

# January 29

> Be strong and courageous. Do not be afraid or terrified because of them, for the LORD your God goes with you; He will never leave you nor forsake you.
> —Deuteronomy 31:6 (NIV)

Strong. Brave. Courageous. You may be faced with something that, by all means, you have reason to fear. Yet, when you realize you're not alone, you become brave—like the little bear cub standing up against the cougar, as she stood on her little hind legs and let out the loudest roar she could muster, and the cougar runs away in fear; but it is only because mama bear was standing right behind her, tall and strong, and with a loud roar that put fear in the enemy predator.

God is with you. Whatever the circumstances today, He is with you. He is stronger; He is louder.

# January 30

> The Lord is my strength and my shield; my heart trusts in Him, and He helps me. My heart leaps for joy, and with my song I praise Him.
> —Psalm 28:7 (NIV)

Praise Him—even if it is in the middle of the storm. Seriously. I mean it. Go spend time and praise the God who is your strength, and your help in time of trouble; the one who gives you joy and a reason to sing.

# January 31

Railroad crossings can stop us in our busy tracks when we pull up to the crossings and the lights begin to flash and the safety bars slowly drop down, blocking our path.ABetraC Trains are fascinating to me, but at times have become a huge obstacle in the way.

Life sometimes can take an abrupt turn and catch us by surprise—when tragedy hits. We find ourselves unsure of what lies on the other side of the tracks and fear what we might find. We certainly don't want to stay in the moment of tragedy. It may change everything; and it hurts.

Though life carries on as if your pain is unnoticed by others, you feel stuck, unable to move. Though tempted, don't turn to a different path that the world provides. If you must wait, then wait. God will be your comfort, and He will be your deliverer.

> The LORD is good, a refuge in times of trouble. He cares for those who trust in Him.
> —Nahum 1:7 (NIV)

> In you, LORD my God, I put my trust. I trust in You; do not let me be put to shame, nor let my enemies triumph over me.
> —Psalm 25:1–2 (NIV)

# February

Since, then, we do not have the excuse of ignorance, everything—and I do mean everything—connected with that old way of life has to go. It's rotten through and through. Get rid of it! And then take on an entirely new way of life—a God-fashioned life, a life renewed from the inside and working itself into your conduct as God accurately reproduces His character in you.

—Ephesians 4:22–24 (MSG)

# Be Renewed

# February 1

> Finally, brothers and sisters, whatever is true, whatever is noble, whatever is right, whatever is pure, whatever is lovely, whatever is admirable—if anything is excellent or praiseworthy—think about such things. Whatever you have learned or received or heard from me, or seen in me—put it into practice. And the God of peace will be with you.
> —Philippians 4:8–9 (NIV)

So, you have determined that you will forget the past and press on toward the future that God has purposed for you. Now, begin to think how God would have you to think. When your thoughts are getting carried away to the "old ways", stop. Rethink it—think about these things that Paul taught the Philippians.

# February 2

"Listen! A farmer went out to sow his seed. As he was scattering the seed, some fell along the path, and the birds came and ate it up. Some fell on rocky places, where it did not have much soil. It sprang up quickly, because the soil was shallow. But when the sun came up, the plants were scorched, and they withered because they had no root. Other seed fell among thorns, which grew up and choked the plants, so that they did not bear grain. Still other seed fell on good soil. It came up, grew and produced a crop, some multiplying thirty, some sixty, some a hundred times."

The farmer sows the word. Some people are like seed along the path, where the word is sown. As soon as they hear it, Satan comes and takes away the word that was sown in them. Others, like seed sown on rocky places, hear the word and at once receive it with joy. But since they have no root, they last only a short time. When trouble or persecution comes because of the word, they quickly fall away. Still others, like seed sown among thorns, hear the word; but the worries of this life, the deceitfulness of wealth and the desires for other things come in and choke the word, making it unfruitful. Others, like seed sown on good soil, hear the word, accept it, and produce a crop—some thirty, some sixty, some a hundred times what was sown."

—Mark 4:3–8, 14–20 (NIV)

Don't let your heart become hardened and allow the worries of this life, and the deceitfulness of desired wealth and "things" keep you from believing God's Word. Trust His Word to be true. His Word is faithful; His Word is sufficient.

It becomes more difficult to maintain a joyful attitude because of the hardness of the world. That is why we need our joy to come from within and not from the exterior things.

# February 3

He went to Nazareth, where He had been brought up, and on the Sabbath day He went into the synagogue, as was His custom. He stood up to read, and the scroll of the prophet Isaiah was handed to Him. Unrolling it, He found the place where it is written:
"The Spirit of the Lord is on Me, because He has anointed Me to proclaim good news to the poor. He has sent Me to proclaim freedom for the prisoners and recovery of sight for the blind, to set the oppressed free, to proclaim the year of the Lord's favor."
Then He rolled up the scroll, gave it back to the attendant and sat down. The eyes of everyone in the synagogue were fastened on Him. He began by saying to them, "Today this scripture is fulfilled in your hearing."

—Luke 4:16–21 (NIV)

The Spirit of the Sovereign Lord is on Me, because the Lord has anointed Me to proclaim good news to the poor. He has sent Me to bind up the brokenhearted, to proclaim freedom for the captives and release from darkness for the prisoners, to proclaim the year of the Lord's favor and the day of vengeance of our God, to comfort all who mourn, and provide for those who grieve in Zion—to bestow on them a crown of beauty instead of ashes, the oil of joy instead of mourning, and a garment of praise instead of a spirit of despair. They will be called oaks of righteousness, a planting of the Lord for the display of His splendor.

—Isaiah 61:1–3 (NIV)

Imagine Jesus reading the scriptures for you. What an incredible moment that would be! I pray the Word of the Lord will come alive in your life today.

Jesus brings good news!

Look into the heart of God and see what Jesus proclaimed that day, as He read from the scroll of the prophet Isaiah.

He is for the poor and the brokenhearted.

He proclaims freedom for the prisoners—the bondage of sin is broken!

He is for the blind—those living in a spiritual darkness will be able to see the truth and live!

He is for the oppressed—He will set you free and comfort those who have been hurt by Satan and by sin.

May the Lord turn your ashes into beauty, and your mourning into joy, and despair into a garment of praise.

_____
_____
_____
_____

# February 4

> Yet You, Lord, are our Father. We are the clay, You are the potter; we are all the work of Your hand.
> —Isaiah 64:8 (NIV)

He is the potter; we are the clay.

He is the Father, and He forms us exactly how He desires.

The potter takes the huge slab of clay and places it on the turning wheel. He removes all of the clay inside the now-forming pottery. We can't see what the potter sees as he continues to form and mold. The potter doesn't mind getting clay all over his hands and clothes, and even cheek, as the clay presses upon his face; all the while in control of the massive piece of art in the making. Only he knows what needs to be done. The potter cares about the details, as he puts the final touches on the pottery, with beautiful designs and shapes woven into the clay. And then, into the kiln the pottery goes—the fire perfecting the clay in its final stages, no longer soft and weak, but strong and beautiful—now able to be used for its purpose that the potter intended.

What does the Potter need to remove or refine in you? Are you willing to allow God to remove what does not belong, so you will be enabled to fulfill His purpose for you?

_____

_____

_____

_____

# February 5

Praise be to the God and Father of our Lord Jesus Christ! In His great mercy He has given us new birth into a living hope through the resurrection of Jesus Christ from the dead, and into an inheritance that can never perish, spoil or fade. This inheritance is kept in heaven for you, who through faith are shielded by God's power until the coming of the salvation that is ready to be revealed in the last time. In all this you greatly rejoice, though now for a little while you may have had to suffer grief in all kinds of trials. These have come so that the proven genuineness of your faith—of greater worth than gold, which perishes even though refined by fire—may result in praise, glory and honor when Jesus Christ is revealed. Though you have not seen Him, you love Him; and even though you do not see Him now, you believe in Him and are filled with an inexpressible and glorious joy, for you are receiving the end result of your faith, the salvation of your souls.
—1 Peter 1:3–9 (NIV)

Just as the pottery goes through the fire, you also will go through trials in this life. And just as the pottery is made strong and ready to be used, these trials have come so that your faith is proven genuine and may result in praise, glory and honor when Jesus is revealed. So, be strong through the fire—you are being refined—renewed.

# February 6

> But also for this very reason, giving all diligence, add to your faith virtue, to virtue knowledge, to knowledge self-control, to self-control perseverance, to perseverance godliness, to godliness brotherly kindness, and to brotherly kindness love. For if these things are yours and abound, *you* will be neither barren nor unfruitful in the knowledge of our Lord Jesus Christ. For he who lacks these things is shortsighted, even to blindness, and has forgotten that he was cleansed from his old sins.
>
> —2 Peter 1:5–9 (NKJV)

It all starts with faith. Without faith, nothing can be added to it. You must believe. Without faith, goodness is flawed, knowledge is lacking, and self-control is limited by our selfish flesh. Why would we persist, if not for our faith in God? And no godliness can be found in a faithless heart. What kind of brotherly kindness or love would we experience, if not all of the prior were added first? Life would be barren and unfulfilling. But with the knowledge of our Lord Jesus Christ, all of this has meaning and purpose.

---
---
---
---

# February 7

### Thankful and Happy

"Blessed are the poor in spirit, for theirs is the kingdom of heaven." (Matthew 5:3 NIV)

Jesus began speaking to the people in this sermon the Bible calls, "The Sermon on the Mount". In this sermon, Jesus teaches the ethical guidelines for life in His kingdom; and the guidelines point to the quality of righteousness and characterizes life in the kingdom, now in part and then fully in the future. Jesus began with the word "Happy" (Blessed). He continued to explain that following these guidelines, happiness is the result. The "Kingdom" only has room for the humble. There's a logical sequence to *"The Beatitudes"*. It's not by chance that Jesus began his sermon by saying that those who recognize their own spiritual bankruptcy will be blessed. We must first and foremost become humble in the Kingdom of God. We must first become poor in our own spirit by removing ourselves from the equation and allowing the kingdom of heaven to reside in our innermost being. We need to die to our own desires and allow Jesus to fill us with His desires—His heart.

"Blessed are those who mourn, for they will be comforted." (Matthew 5:4 NIV)

The scripture here is not saying that you are happy because you mourn; but instead that you are happy because you will be comforted. And to keep the meaning in context here, the mourning here is speaking of a spiritually mourning.

Spiritual mourning is when we have a deep sorrow that causes our soul to ache until we repent. With deep regret and remorse comes repentance. It is a mourning for the sinfulness that causes the suffering and sadness in life.

This spiritual death may cause you pain and grief, but Jesus won't leave you in your emptiness; for when you mourn, you will be comforted.

> Blessed are the meek, for they will inherit the earth. (Matthew 5:5 NIV)

We become meek—submissive—to the Lord's will and ready to be filled with His righteousness and mercy. Meekness is when someone has the power or opportunity to take what they want, but instead shows self-control.

> Blessed are those who hunger and thirst for righteousness, for they will be filled. (Matthew 5:6 NIV)

God has placed a longing / emptiness in our hearts that can only be filled by Him. This beatitude is not simply describing those who are righteous, or who try to do good things. It is describing passion in life—those who hunger and thirst for it—desperate for it. It begins with the submission of our own will to the desires of God's will. The Holy Spirit will lead the believer into righteousness. Being righteous is to live in line with the truth of God and live under the covering of Jesus—His righteousness.

> Blessed are the merciful, for they will be shown mercy. (Matthew 5:7 NIV)

Mercy is compassion or forgiveness shown toward someone, whom it is within one's power to punish or harm. Mercy requires action. God has the power to destroy, but instead shows mercy.

> Blessed are the pure in heart, for they will see God. (Matthew 5:8 NIV)

We then are purified and know God. We see what He is doing in our own lives and those around us. We see the spiritual world that seemed not to exist. Pure means that it is not mixed with any other; set apart and holy, consecrated by God. With our devotion to God, we will not place anything above Him.

> Blessed are the peacemakers, for they will be called children of God. (Matthew 5:9 NIV)

We receive peace from God through the promise of hope. No longer at war because of disobedience, we become His child living the life in the way He intended. We will do what Jesus would do, hear what Jesus tells us to do, and go where Jesus would go.

This may have changed all of your plans—the transformation that has taken place will change your perspective. But the road the Lord chooses for you, as you yield to His leading, will be one with happiness and reward, and you will rejoice knowing you are in His will and His perfect plan.

_____
_____
_____
_____

# February 8

### Thankful and Happy

> Blessed are those who are persecuted because of righteousness, for theirs is the kingdom of heaven. (Matthew 5:10 NIV)

You would think that Jesus would end this opening message with an upbeat statement, like, "Blessed are they that live a life of righteousness, for they will receive a bigger house. Blessed are those who live this new way of life, for they will have a bigger bank account." But that is not how He finished this opening statement.

Jesus opened His sermon by saying, "Blessed are the poor in spirit for theirs is the kingdom of heaven." He spoke of inheritance of the earth, which is a part of inheritance in the kingdom when we are humble and give control over to Him. And again Jesus speaks of the kingdom of heaven. Is it any question that Jesus wants us to be heavenly minded? When trouble comes, look up. And believe me when I say, "There will be trouble."

Jesus made it personal, "Blessed are *you*." "Rejoice and be glad," He said. You will be persecuted, you will lose, but rejoice!

Living a life of righteousness means knowing Christ and being found in Him. True life will come through death of self—by placing others before self; God's way, not your own way.

> This third I will bring into the fire; I will refine them like silver and test them like gold. They will call on My name and I will answer them; I will say, "They are my people," and they will say, "The Lord is our God."
> —Zechariah 13:9 (NIV)

_____
_____
_____

# February 9

### Jesus Heals a Blind Beggar

As Jesus approached Jericho, a blind beggar was sitting beside the road. When he heard the noise of a crowd going past, he asked what was happening. They told him that Jesus the Nazarene was going by. So he began shouting, "Jesus, Son of David, have mercy on me!"

"Be quiet!" the people in front yelled at him.

But he only shouted louder, "Son of David, have mercy on me!"

When Jesus heard him, He stopped and ordered that the man be brought to Him. As the man came near, Jesus asked him, "What do you want Me to do for you?"

"Lord," he said, "I want to see!"

And Jesus said, "All right, receive your sight! Your faith has healed you." Instantly the man could see, and he followed Jesus, praising God. And all who saw it praised God, too.

—Luke 18:35–42 (NLT)

The noise and criticism of the enemy may distract you—what you do about it is the key. Will you trust Jesus and believe He has the answer? Or will you allow the voices of doubt overtake you, causing you to be afraid and cower down into despair and lose hope? Will you believe Jesus has the answer for your problem, as the blind man did and would not allow others to discourage him? He called out to Jesus for healing. His faith brought healing. Believe Jesus for your answers.

# February 10

> Husbands, love your wives, just as Christ loved the church and gave Himself up for her to make her holy, cleansing her by the washing with water through the word, and to present her to Himself as a radiant church, without stain or wrinkle or any other blemish, but holy and blameless.
>
> —Ephesians 5:25–27 (NIV)

What an amazing example of love. Oh, what a glorious day that will be when we—the bride of Christ—will stand before Jesus, radiant, without stain, or any blemish. We will be holy and blameless—all made possible because of His love, and that He gave His life up for us.

I've heard many sermons on these verses, teaching men how to love their wives. Jesus is the perfect example of how to love—relentlessly and unconditionally. What Jesus has done and will do for us is beyond imagination.

# February 11

> Have I not commanded you? Be strong and courageous. Do not be afraid; do not be discouraged, for the LORD your God will be with you wherever you go.
> —Joshua 1:9 (NIV)

Even in our unlovable state, God is there.

Even when we make mistakes, God is there.

When you are alone, abandoned and brokenhearted, God is there.

Don't let this place of darkness create *in you* something that is dark. Don't let it bring fear and anxiety. Instead, take courage, be strong and call out His Name. God is there.

# February 12

> But the seed on good soil stands for those with a noble and good heart, who hear the word, retain it, and by persevering produce a crop.
> —Luke 8:15 (NIV)

This is what our heart should look like:

A noble heart—one with high moral principles—honorable. A good heart, full of goodness and love, acting in that love.

This is the heart that will hear what the Word says, remember it, memorize it, believe it, and live it.

And we, then, will see life-changing results. Out of the abundance of the heart, the mouth speaks. So, what do you proclaim today? Are your words good or evil? Sour or sweet? A heart that is not noble and not good cannot hear what the Word says, and therefore, when words come out of their mouth, they pull from a well that is sour. The heart is full of evil, and the only way to create a new heart within you, is to give your heart to God and allow Him to fill your heart with nobility and good that flows from the Holy Spirit.

> But the things that come out of a person's mouth come from the heart, and these defile them. For out of the heart come evil thoughts—murder, adultery, sexual immorality, theft, false testimony, slander.
> —Matthew 15:18–19 (NIV)

> A good man brings good things out of the good stored up in his heart, and an evil man brings evil things out of the evil stored up in his heart. For the mouth speaks what the heart is full of.
> —Luke 6:45 (NIV)

# February 13

> For I consider [from the standpoint of faith] that the sufferings of the present life are not worthy to be compared with the glory that is about to be revealed to us *and* in us!
> —Romans 8:18 (AMP)

The splendor of God's love and presence is freely shared with you *today*. Begin looking forward to the great things God will reveal to you, His children. Open your eyes, and see. In prayer, stop to listen. Let the scriptures speak to your heart; let nature declare His glory; and may your heart respond with honor, praise and thanksgiving to Him.

# February 14

> Love never fails [it never fades nor ends].
> —1 Corinthians 13:8a (AMP)

Friends may fail you. Your health may fail. Your finances may diminish. Your family may abandon you. Your career may end abruptly. But love… Love will never fail you. God's love will never leave you and it will never come to an end. Place your hope and faith in His love.

# February 15

Suffering for Being a Christian

Dear friends, do not be surprised at the fiery ordeal that has come on you to test you, as though something strange were happening to you. But rejoice inasmuch as you participate in the sufferings of Christ, so that you may be overjoyed when His glory is revealed. If you are insulted because of the name of Christ, you are blessed, for the Spirit of glory and of God rests on you. If you suffer, it should not be as a murderer or thief or any other kind of criminal, or even as a meddler. However, if you suffer as a Christian, do not be ashamed, but praise God that you bear that name. For it is time for judgment to begin with God's household; and if it begins with us, what will the outcome be for those who do not obey the gospel of God?

And, "If it is hard for the righteous to be saved, what will become of the ungodly and the sinner?"

So then, those who suffer according to God's will should commit themselves to their faithful Creator and continue to do good.

—1 Peter 4:12–19 (NIV)

The process of refining metals is often used in the Bible as a metaphor of spiritual purification. Refining is a process by which all of the dross is removed and only the pure metal remains.

God's desire for us is that we be holy as He is holy. That means there are things that need to be removed from our lives. God, the master of refining fire, will not destroy us in the process. He will make us better—pure.

Allow His hand to form you—He will not allow anything more than you can handle that will result in the loss of your soul. The good news is this: As we trust God to work in us, we are changed—purified. It is not because of who we are but because of who has touched us. His holiness becomes ours.

> It is because of Him that you are in Christ Jesus, who has become for us wisdom from God—that is, our righteousness, holiness and redemption. Therefore, as it is written: "Let the one who boasts boast in the Lord.
> —1 Corinthians 1:30–31 (NIV)

_____

_____

_____

_____

# February 16

> Through Jesus, therefore, let us continually offer to God a sacrifice of praise—the fruit of lips that openly profess His name. And do not forget to do good and to share with others, for with such sacrifices God is pleased.
>
> —Hebrews 13:15–16 (NIV)

God smiles when we acknowledge Him and praise His Name. He is pleased when we give to the needy. When I am pleased, I smile. So, why is it so difficult to picture God smiling? Why do we tend to think He is so serious all of the time? Relax and realize God is a God who is pleased and takes joy in His children when they call out His Name and when they do good things for others. Take a moment to picture God smiling.

# February 17

> My command is this: Love each other as I have loved you. Greater love has no one than this: to lay down one's life for one's friends. You are My friends if you do what I command. I no longer call you servants, because a servant does not know his master's business. Instead, I have called you friends, for everything that I learned from My Father I have made known to you. You did not choose Me, but I chose you and appointed you so that you might go and bear fruit—fruit that will last—and so that whatever you ask in My name the Father will give you. This is My command: Love each other.
> —John 15:12–17 (NIV)

Do you have a friend who knows just about everything there is to know about you and still loves you? Do you keep some things to yourself, for fear you might lose that friendship? You can be transparent with Jesus. You don't have to be popular to be accepted into His arena of friends. You don't have to keep secrets from Him for fear of rejection. You don't have to be rich. You don't have to be perfect. He knows you, and He loves you anyway.

Jesus considers us His friends, if we do what He commands. There is no greater love than what we have in Jesus. There is no greater friend than Jesus. He is always ready to help, and ready to listen. He chose us and appointed us. Yes, it is good to serve, but remember that our friendship is the reason we serve. The title we are given is "friend".

# February 18

> Therefore, I urge you, brothers and sisters, in view of God's mercy, to offer your bodies as a living sacrifice, holy and pleasing to God—this is your true and proper worship.
>
> —Romans 12:1 (NIV)

What can we offer God as a proper sacrifice when Jesus has given His very life? Ourselves—holy, devoted, consecrated, and well pleasing to God. In all we do (raising a family, going to work, and your every-day life), realizing God's mercy, embrace what God has for you.

# February 19

> Therefore, since we are surrounded by such a great cloud of witnesses, let us throw off everything that hinders and the sin that so easily entangles. And let us run with perseverance the race marked out for us, fixing our eyes on Jesus, the pioneer and perfecter of faith. For the joy set before Him He endured the cross, scorning its shame, and sat down at the right hand of the throne of God.
> —Hebrews 12:1–2 (NIV)

Ask yourself this question: If anything, what, or who is the one thing in your way? Do you say to God, "Do what you will with anything else, but please don't touch 'this'"? Or, "Send me anywhere, God, except 'there'."? If you can fill in the blank with anything at all, then that one thing has become an idol, and has been placed above God. I've caught myself thinking this way. I was placing limits on my devotion to God. Although it was difficult to say, and though I was tempted to take it back the instant I said it, I told God I would accept whatever He had.

It's not easy to open up all of the areas in your life and offer it to Him. But give whatever that is to the Lord, so you will not be entangled by sin. Trust God with whatever it is.

# February 20

> He is the atoning sacrifice for our sins, and not only for ours but also for the sins of the whole world.
> —John 2:2 (NIV)

The blood of Jesus was enough. Jesus is the atoning sacrifice for all the world. There is no need to carry the guilt of past sin. Accept this gift. The debt is paid in full.

Have you ever had someone forgive a debt or pay for a huge debt on your behalf? Though you might feel you owe them, they say, "No, you don't have to pay me back!" That's what happened with Jesus—and the debt He paid was one that we would have never been able to pay!

_____

_____

_____

_____

# February 21

> What shall we say, then? Shall we go on sinning so that grace may increase? By no means! We are those who have died to sin; how can we live in it any longer? Or don't you know that all of us who were baptized into Christ Jesus were baptized into His death? We were therefore buried with Him through baptism into death in order that, just as Christ was raised from the dead through the glory of the Father, we too may live a new life.
>
> —Romans 6:1–4 (NIV)

This debt was paid on our behalf and given out of God's mercy and favor. If someone paid a debt you owed, do you go right back out and get yourself into debt? Certainly not! That would be a dishonor to the one who helped you finally get out of debt.

God's gift is much more valuable—He brings salvation, and a new life made possible by His glorious power. Why would we want to demean the gift by going out and sinning again as if it is not a big deal?

A new life—today, we can proclaim yet again, our New Year's Day. Every day we can wake up and start over again.

Every day I strive to do God's will, because I have died to sin. But if I fail, Jesus has paid the price for sin for all time, and for eternity until we share in the resurrection of life everlasting. What a day that will be! So, every day I am new—forgiven, because of Jesus.

_____

_____

_____

_____

# February 22

### My Way *or* the Highway

We like to do things our own way. I know I do. We get an idea, then we plan, and then need everyone to work together to accomplish it. But teamwork takes flexibility. You may have a great idea, but others may have an idea just as well. Communication and collaboration goes much further. It will take a little bit of sacrifice and a lot of love.

### "My Way *is* the High Way"

When it comes to the best way to do anything, we need to submit to God's way, just as you would work on a project with a friend or co-worker. God wants this collaboration to be a labor of love as well. God wants a healthy, authentic relationship with you, rather than watch you complete your "To Do List" for Him. He knows the best way, so take the higher road.

> "For My thoughts are not your thoughts, neither are your ways My ways," declares the LORD. "As the heavens are higher than the earth, so are My ways higher than your ways and My thoughts than your thoughts."
> —Isaiah 55:8–9 (NIV)

# February 23

> Therefore, if you are offering your gift at the altar and there remember that your brother or sister has something against you, leave your gift there in front of the altar. First go and be reconciled to them; then come and offer your gift.
> —Matthew 5:23-24 (NIV)

Note here that you are the one who has offended someone. You know of it, and know you haven't apologized. Please, don't let conflicts with others destroy your offering to the Lord. Go and make things right.

There are godly ways to deal with someone who is sinning against you or others, but what the Bible is speaking of here is the need to make right what you have done to someone else. With humility, go and ask forgiveness.

I remember a situation where I needed to go and apologize to someone else. It wasn't easy. But, once I did, I had peace.

Sometimes you may feel the other person is in the wrong, but if you have a tug on your heart to apologize for how you reacted, then that is exactly what you need to do.

_____
_____
_____
_____

# February 24

> Therefore I tell you, do not worry about your life, what you will eat or drink; or about your body, what you will wear. Is not life more than food, and the body more than clothes?
> —Matthew 6:25 (NIV)

Your life and all you need in this life is in God's hands. Worrying does not help—in fact it makes it worse. By worrying, you add stress, and lose sleep, and could develop stress-related health issues. By trusting and resting in God's presence, there is peace. You'll wake up with peace, instead of waking with stress already on your heart.

# February 25

> Show me your ways, Lord, teach me Your paths.
> He guides the humble in what is right and teaches them His way.
> —Psalm 25:4, 9 (NIV)

Each morning, and until you lay your head down to rest after the day is done, hope in God. The sorrows of this life will come. But the joys will soon follow. Let God be your guide, directing your steps in His way. Learn from God and His scriptures. Listen to His voice when He gives direction. As you do, trust. Even though it may not make any sense at the time, believe. Wait. See the hand of the Lord work on your behalf.

_____

_____

_____

_____

# February 26

> Lord, You have been our dwelling place throughout all generations. Before the mountains were born or You brought forth the whole world, from everlasting to everlasting You are God.
> —Psalm 90:1–2 (NIV)

Our human minds cannot grasp the thought that God has no beginning. God was there before creation, and before that, and before that, and His existence goes backward for eternity just as it goes forward in eternity. That blows my mind. I can imagine no ending, but the thought of no beginning is absolutely astounding.

Everything we see with our eyes has a beginning and will have an end. But the spirit is eternal.

When we realize He is a huge God and our understanding can't handle all that He is, we realize He is God. Why believe in a god that has limitations? That kind of god is comprehendible, because we have limitations. But one who has no limits, even time itself is a mighty God.

> Whoever dwells in the shelter of the Most High will rest in the shadow of the Almighty. I will say of the Lord, "He is my refuge and my fortress, my God, in whom I trust."
> —Psalm 91:1–2 (NIV)

# February 27

> But the fruit of the Spirit is love, joy, peace, forbearance, kindness, goodness, faithfulness, gentleness and self-control. Against such things there is no law. Those who belong to Christ Jesus have crucified the flesh with its passions and desires. Since we live by the Spirit, let us keep in step with the Spirit.
> —Galatians 5:22–25 (NIV)

When I look at a tree and see apples in the branches, I know it is an apple tree. If I see lemons on the tree, I know it is a lemon tree. So, when people look at you, what do they see? Are you presenting the fruits you were meant to bear—love, self-control, joy? Let's make sure we tend to the tree and bear good fruit.

The next time you interact with someone, ask yourself what they might be seeing in you. It is not to boast in what you do or who you are, but to self-evaluate how you are presenting Jesus who lives in you.

_____
_____
_____
_____

# February 28

The great conductor of our lives speaks hope into our hearts. Just as the conductor of a great locomotive is in charge of the cargo and passengers on his train, our God is in charge of us on our journey here on earth, and on into eternity. Remember He is all you really need to survive the ride.

> For what You have done I will always praise You in the presence of Your faithful people. And I will hope in Your Name, for Your Name is good.
> —Psalm 52:9 (NIV)

# March

He says, "Be still, and know that I am God; I will be exalted among the nations, I will be exalted in the earth."

—Psalm 46:10 (NIV)

Be Still Know I Am God

# March 1

The Lord will guide you always; He will satisfy your needs in a sun-scorched land and will strengthen your frame. You will be like a well-watered garden, like a spring whose waters never fail.

—Isaiah 58:11 (NIV)

Have you ever felt worn? Like a desert land, we too can feel scorched when we come to a place in our lives that has exhausted all of our strength. Though it may be difficult in the moment, wait on God to show you the next move. He will always guide you. If you are in a place or time where you feel empty and lost, and unsure of what to do or where to go, allow the Lord to give you rest, and all that you need, to sustain you, and to restore your strength. Rest in the moment and draw from the waters of life that only God can provide.

# March 2

> Do you not know? Have you not heard? The LORD is the everlasting God, the Creator of the ends of the earth. He will not grow tired or weary, and His understanding no one can fathom. He gives strength to the weary and increases the power of the weak. Even youths grow tired and weary, and young men stumble and fall; but those who hope in the LORD will renew their strength. They will soar on wings like eagles; they will run and not grow weary, they will walk and not be faint.
> —Isaiah 40:28–31 (NIV)

When we are faced with conflict, and are afraid, there is a human tendency to turn our thoughts to the fear we are facing, rather than the powerful God we serve. Our thoughts and emotions become based on that fear, such as the fear of failure, abandonment, betrayal, or rejection. And when our thoughts are meditating on what we fear, we act out on those negative emotions, such as anger, denial, defensiveness, bitterness or hate. Wouldn't you prefer to respond in a positive way to break that cycle? A negative thought will bring negative emotions, which, in turn, create negative responses. And as the response is negative, it creates further issues, and the merry-go-round of fear starts all over again.

Instead, when faced with conflict and chaos, or sins of another, think on the truths of God's Word. "I will wait on the Lord. He is my help." Break that chain and find peace.

> Surely God is my help; the Lord is the one who sustains me.
> —Psalm 54:4 (NIV)

> The LORD is my rock, my fortress and my deliverer; my God is my rock, in whom I take refuge, my shield and the horn of my salvation, my stronghold.
> —Psalm 18:2 (NIV)

# March 3

> Above all else, guard your heart, for everything you do flows from it.
> —Proverbs 4:23 (NIV)

We are very capable of building walls around our hearts to protect ourselves from being hurt. But building our own walls, based on our own emotions developed in pain, can only cause more pain, thus leading to depression and callousness. Rather than build up walls of bitterness and anger, allow God to build the walls of protection around your heart and mind as you present your brokenness to God. He will bring peace in such a supernatural way, you will know it is not anything of your own that brought peace, but from God alone.

The inner core of a person—the thoughts, feelings, desires, will, and choices—make that person who he/she is. We guard our hearts when we determine to choose thoughts, feelings, desires, and determination after what God desires.

# March 4

> On the last and greatest day of the festival, Jesus stood and said in a loud voice, "Let anyone who is thirsty come to me and drink. Whoever believes in Me, as Scripture has said, rivers of living water will flow from within them." By this He meant the Spirit, whom those who believed in Him were later to receive. Up to that time the Spirit had not been given, since Jesus had not yet been glorified.
> —John 7:37–39 (NIV)

Believe in Jesus, and rivers of living waters will flow from you. Rivers of living water—what a refreshing way to describe the Holy Spirit.

Our family has made many vacation trips to the river. On a hot day, jumping in that cool river was the best! The Holy Spirit pours over you in those heated moments, providing a covering and refreshment so that you can handle the heat. The heat doesn't go away just because you are in the water, just as the difficulties may not go away. However, the Holy Spirit will be your help.

"Living waters" tells me that this refreshing river will be active, not stagnant. It will move. It will have purpose. Just as a river can take you down stream, this river of life from the Spirit, if we allow it, will take us where He has charted. He is alive and working in you as you give in to His will for you.

_____
_____
_____
_____

# March 5

> Cast your cares on the LORD and He will sustain you;
> He will never let the righteous be shaken.
> —Psalm 55:22 (NIV)

You may feel shaken by circumstances, but not overwhelmed. He will help you withstand the storm. When I look at the word "sustain", I think of the musical term. When the sustain pedal on a piano is held down with your foot, it will hold the music you've played on the keyboard, and continue to play that note or chord when you lift your hands from the keyboard, and until it fades. It can hold that note and blend into the next when you play the different note. The word "sustain" can be relative in your waiting between *what was* and *what will be*. While you have played a note before, you are waiting for the next note to be played. The Lord is with you and will help you through that period, between the past and the future. Without the Lord's sustaining grace, the emptiness between what was and what will be is too overwhelming. Instead, let His sustaining presence bring music to your heart as you wait on the Lord.

# March 6

> I will remember the deeds of the LORD; yes, I will remember Your miracles of long ago. I will consider all Your works and meditate on all Your mighty deeds."
> Your ways, God, are holy. What god is as great as our God? You are the God who performs miracles; You display Your power among the peoples. With Your mighty arm You redeemed Your people, the descendants of Jacob and Joseph.
> The waters saw You, God, the waters saw You and writhed; the very depths were convulsed. The clouds poured down water, the heavens resounded with thunder; Your arrows flashed back and forth. Your thunder was heard in the whirlwind, Your lightning lit up the world; the earth trembled and quaked. Your path led through the sea, Your way through the mighty waters, though Your footprints were not seen.
> —Psalm 77:11–19 (NIV)

When the children of Israel came to the Red Sea, the waters seemed impassable. Yet God led them through the sea.

As you dedicate your life to the obedience of faith, God will lead you. Sometimes your journey will take you to places which appear to be hopeless. You may question God's plan, and wonder how you can go on, unsure of what lies just up ahead. But God has not abandoned you. He will continue to lead you even when there seems to be no way. I have faced situations that seemed hopeless, and I was insecure, but God reminded me that He would not leave me. His Word assures us that He is with us wherever we go, and there is nothing to fear.

Some days you will not see His hand or footsteps; but know that He is there and always at work for you! Remember the good things God has done for you. And know that He did not lead you to the place you are today only to leave you alone and abandoned. He will continue to lead you and, if needed, will perform miracles on your behalf, just as He did for the children of Israel when He parted the Red Sea.

# March 7

> For I am convinced that neither death nor life, neither angels nor demons, neither the present nor the future, nor any powers, neither height nor depth, nor anything else in all creation, will be able to separate us from the love of God that is in Christ Jesus our Lord.
> —Romans 8:38–39 (NIV)

It doesn't say, "Except" anywhere in this scripture. Remember there is *nothing* that can separate us from the love of God. It doesn't say, "except our unworthiness", "except our sin", "except our weaknesses", "except the circumstances". It says, "Nothing". His love is not conditional; it is not based on what we have done, or what we have become, or what we haven't done. It is based on God's heart—God's unconditional, loving, gracious, merciful, forgiving heart!

    I remember one day when I questioned His love. It was in a moment of despair. I was overwhelmed and cried out. The circumstances I was facing began to weigh heavily on me. *No, I screamed out, No! I cannot handle this. I've lost so much. I can't take anymore loss. I can't hear You. I can't see You. Why are You so quiet? Why don't You speak to me?* I began to wonder what I kept doing wrong. *Where are You God? How can any of this be true? Nothing makes sense. Nothing even matters anymore. How can You be in this? This is nothing but pain and hate. This is not love.* And just at that moment I heard a slight whisper in my heart saying, "Wasn't My love displayed enough on the cross for you? Wasn't My dying proof enough of My love?" *Aah, but God! There is nothing good about this!* Again my thoughts were interrupted, "All things work together for good, for them that love the Lord." *I don't see You, God. Where are You?* "Lo, I am with you even to the ends of the earth". Then I was quiet. I said nothing. I just experienced the love of a Father that cannot be moved—not even by a temper-tantrum.

    He will not stop loving you no matter what. Even when it doesn't make sense; even when you don't understand why things are happening the way they are; even if you think you can't go another step; even if it feels like the world is full of hate, God still loves you.

# March 8

> I sought the Lord, and He answered me; He delivered me from all my fears. This poor man called, and the Lord heard him; He saved him out of all his troubles. The angel of the Lord encamps around those who fear Him, and He delivers them.
> —Psalm 34:4, 6–7 (NIV)

When we seek the Lord, He will deliver us from all our fears. The righteous cry out, and the Lord hears them. He is close. He will deliver us. Hide under His wing.

In a world full of tragedies, it seems as if the Lord does not deliver us from our troubles. We ask, "Why? Where were You, God?" But, the fact is, He does deliver us and He never leaves us. This world suffers from the sting of sin and death, and has been decaying ever since the first sin of Adam and Eve in the Garden of Eden. Its sin will take its course until, finally, it is destroyed. Until then, we will be touched by disasters, evil, and corruption. Sometimes He removes us *from* the circumstances, and sometimes He stays with us *through* the circumstances. God has the power to remove the circumstances, but sometimes He removes the fear of it.

I remember a moment when I did not escape a place where I desperately needed help. I was trapped. As I called out to God beneath my breath, I saw Him take me away from that place and whisper to me, "He may take your body, but he cannot take your soul." It was the first and only time I had ever been removed mentally from an experience so that I could survive it physically. The pain of the experience may linger, but the memory is full of God's rescue in a time when I needed Him most.

Loss can leave us broken, but God can repair and restore. Life can throw mountains at us, but God can move mountains. Circumstances may seem unbearable, but God can deliver us.

# March 9

> Now a man named Lazarus was sick. He was from Bethany, the village of Mary and her sister Martha. So the sisters sent word to Jesus, "Lord, the one You love is sick."
>
> When He heard this, Jesus said, "This sickness will not end in death. No, it is for God's glory so that God's Son may be glorified through it."
>
> —John 11:1, 3–4 (NIV)

In this story of Lazarus, the family sent for Jesus when Lazarus was very sick. They knew Jesus loved him, because they said, "The one You love is sick". The story goes on to say that Lazarus died. It appeared as if Jesus was too late—that it was over! But it wasn't.

> "Lord," Martha said to Jesus, "if You had been here, my brother would not have died. But I know that even now God will give you whatever you ask." Jesus said to her, "Your brother will rise again."
>
> So they took away the stone. Then Jesus looked up and said, "Father, I thank You that You have heard Me. I knew that You always hear Me, but I said this for the benefit of the people standing here, that they may believe that You sent Me."
>
> When He had said this, Jesus called in a loud voice, "Lazarus, come out!" The dead man came out, his hands and feet wrapped with strips of linen, and a cloth around his face. Jesus said to them, "Take off the grave clothes and let him go."
>
> —John 11:21–23, 41–44 (NIV)

Jesus loves you. Just as Mary and Martha knew He loved their brother, you can know that He loves you. When you call on Him, He will answer you. He can step in and bring back to life what was once dead. Anything that binds you, He will strip from you and you will be free. Jesus spoke out so that the people standing around could hear Him and believe. He moves on your behalf so that you, and anyone standing around watching, will know and believe that He is God.

---
---
---
---

# March 10

> Brothers and sisters, as an example of patience in the face of suffering, take the prophets who spoke in the name of the Lord. As you know, we count as blessed those who have persevered. You have heard of Job's perseverance and have seen what the Lord finally brought about. The Lord is full of compassion and mercy.
> —James 5:10–11 (NIV)

Patience. You've heard it before, I'm sure, that if you pray for patience you better get ready, because you will only receive it by suffering and perseverance. That may be true, but when you are in the midst of your suffering, James reminds us to be patient and persevere through it. Remain faithful, and you will be blessed. No, you are not blessed because you are suffering. But, you *are* blessed because you persevered.

# March 11

> In your struggle against sin, you have not yet resisted to the point of shedding your blood. And have you completely forgotten this word of encouragement that addresses you as a father addresses his son? It says, "My son, do not make light of the Lord's discipline, and do not lose heart when He rebukes you, because the Lord disciplines the one He loves, and He chastens everyone He accepts as His son." Endure hardship as discipline; God is treating you as His children. For what children are not disciplined by their father?
> —Hebrews 12:4–7 (NIV)

Think about that for a moment. Children will do whatever it is to be noticed. If bad behavior is what will get your attention, then that is what they will do. An involved parent will show the child that they are present and care about their good behavior, just as much as their bad behavior. Parents who are involved and care about their children will make sure they watch what they are doing. If a child is misbehaving, the child is disciplined. If a child has done well, they are rewarded. And if a child is running toward a busy street, obviously the parent will stop them and teach them the dangers of running into the street.

If a child is out of control, the future of that child is going to be just as difficult, if not worse. According to child psychologist, Jacob Azerrad, Ph.D., and Paul Chance, Ph.D.,[1] "Such disgraceful behavior in young children predicts serious problems later in life. As adolescents, they are more likely to drop out of school, use drugs, engage in delinquency and be clinically depressed. And when I read newspaper articles about road rage, commuter rage and office rage it seems to me that many out-of-control children are growing up to be out-of-control adults."

Our heavenly Father is a perfect Father. He watches us day and night. He cares about us and is very involved. Remember, He lives within us! He is fair and just. And as we submit to the Father's discipline, we receive life—and life abundantly. God will discipline us for our good, in order that we may share in His holiness and have a good future. Discipline may be unpleasant at the moment, but in due time, it will produce good character—one that desires righteousness. His children will have an eternal home in Heaven. Now *that's* a good future.

# March 12

> For God, who said, "Let there be light in the darkness," has made this light shine in our hearts so we could know the glory of God that is seen in the face of Jesus Christ.
>
> We now have this light shining in our hearts, but we ourselves are like fragile clay jars containing this great treasure. This makes it clear that our great power is from God, not from ourselves.
>
> We are pressed on every side by troubles, but we are not crushed. We are perplexed, but not driven to despair. We are hunted down, but never abandoned by God. We get knocked down, but we are not destroyed.
>
> That is why we never give up. Though our bodies are dying, our spirits are being renewed every day. For our present troubles are small and won't last very long. Yet they produce for us a glory that vastly outweighs them and will last forever! So we don't look at the troubles we can see now; rather, we fix our gaze on things that cannot be seen. For the things we see now will soon be gone, but the things we cannot see will last forever.
> —2 Corinthians 4:6–9, 16–18 (NLT)

Only a short time, and we will see the glory of God. Hold on! It won't last forever!

> By faith—by believing God—we know that the world and the stars—in fact, all things—were made at God's command; and that they were all made from things that can't be seen. (Hebrews 11:3 TLB)

Pottery that falls to the tile floor will shatter. That is how we are—breakable. Without God's power in us, we would crumble beneath life's pressure. But we are not. We are not destroyed because He renews us every day. God, who made something out of nothing, can restore you even when you have nothing to pull from.

Have you ever arisen in the middle of the night and walked around in the dark? If so, you know what it's like as you feel around for the closest light source, taking baby steps in hopes that you don't stub your toe. Then suddenly you find the light and switch it on, and relief comes over your body. When it comes to finding our way in life, God promises to be our light in the darkness. The Bible says His Word is a lamp for our feet. We can trust God when the path is uncertain and have peace even in our darkest days.

_____
_____
_____
_____

# March 13

"Write it on your heart that every day is the best day in the year.

He is rich who owns the day, and no one owns the day who allows it to be invaded with fret and anxiety.

Finish every day and be done with it. You have done what you could. Some blunders and absurdities, no doubt crept in. Forget them as soon as you can, tomorrow is a new day; begin it well and serenely, with too high a spirit to be cumbered with your old nonsense.

This new day is too dear, with its hopes and invitations, to waste a moment on the yesterdays."

—Ralph Waldo Emerson

Paul said it this way, in a letter to the Philippians:

Brothers and sisters, I do not consider myself yet to have taken hold of it. But one thing I do: Forgetting what is behind and straining toward what is ahead, I press on toward the goal to win the prize for which God has called me heavenward in Christ Jesus.

—Philippians 3:13–14 (NIV)

Your past does not have to define you or determine your future. If your past has created chaos in your present life's situation, God can meet you there. Maybe your past is the only way you know to live, and now the identity you had worked so hard for is gone. God can meet you there just the same, and give you a new identity and a new future.

It's not over yet. The journey may seem long at times, but keep trusting God. You will find that the closer you are to God, and the more time you spend in His presence, the more you will long to see Him face-to-face. You will continue to press toward heaven, and you will be able to forget the past. You don't have to live as if your past successes are all that mattered in your life and that you have nothing to offer today. Nor are you identified by your past failures that may tempt you to give up. No matter where you've been, or where you are today, press on! Keep moving forward to heaven. What is done for His kingdom and His glory is what matters—not the things that we did or didn't do for our own glory. Our future is promised and is ready for us because Jesus made it possible—not anything we've done will either secure our future or take it away. We need only to believe and trust Him.

# March 14

> Do you not know that your bodies are temples of the Holy Spirit, who is in you, whom you have received from God? You are not your own; you were bought at a price. Therefore honor God with your bodies.
> —1 Corinthians 6:19–20 (NIV)

### Body

I'd like to take the next few days and focus on becoming healthy in all areas of our lives. Today we start with the body.

Physical health is the developing and strengthening of our bodies (our whole bodies). Our beliefs call us to offer ourselves (our whole self) to God as a living sacrifice—holy and acceptable to Him, which becomes our spiritual worship.

I'm sure you've heard this scripture before, and know how important it is to have a healthy body. And it's important to take a moment to consider whether you are honoring God with your body or giving into worldly desires. We should take note that the scripture leading up to this statement was speaking of sexual immorality. Everywhere we turn, the mind can be tempted in the area of sexual sin. Commercials, social media, and even walking down the street in the summertime, we are faced with so much sexual temptation. Advertisements use sexual attraction to try and get our attention so that the consumer will want what they have to sell. However, the temptation is not the sin. What we do with the temptation is key to honoring God.

When we consider our bodies as being owned by God, we care for ourselves, choosing the best for our bodies. In turn, we offer ourselves in service to Him, which gives honor to Him. It comes down to choices—choosing to refrain from the enticement which the world works so hard to ensnare us.

What choices are you making to ensure your body is treated like the temple of the Holy Spirit? Men, do you gawk at the woman walking by in her bikini? And women, do you stare at a man's body on the beach? Or do you turn away so as not to fall into temptation? Are you married and flirt with the opposite sex? Do you open yourself up to vulnerable situations?

Placing too many tasks on yourself can be overwhelming and cause defeat and depression. The wrong diet can cause lethargy, poor sleeping habits, and poor health, including diseases. We need to look to God to show us what we should remove from our busy schedules or anything that may be causing anxiety or physical illness. Do you eat the right foods and make sure you rest when you need to? Do you get enough exercise? I can admit that I fail miserably in the area of fitness and getting enough rest and eating the right foods. And the fact that we are living in a human body makes certain that we will fail in one or more of these areas. And, I know that America has a lot of "junk food" and foods that are filled with unhealthy fats, sugars and ingredients; so, it makes it hard to keep in shape. But, again, the key is how you respond to the diet available. Do you give any consideration to health? If so, don't beat yourself up, just stay on course every new day. If you've failed in the past, forget the past. Look forward and do the best you can with what you've been given. If we are the best we can be, we will be able to do much more for the kingdom. If you are only seeking to fulfill your own desires or if you are tired and weak, I'm sure you've come to the realization that this way of living is not giving your best to the Lord. Keep marching forward friends. With the help of the Holy Spirit living within us, we can make the right choices, whether related to sexual sins or bodily health.

---
---
---
---

# March 15

> Do not conform to the pattern of this world, but be transformed by the renewing of your mind. Then you will be able to test and approve what God's will is—His good, pleasing and perfect will.
>
> —Romans 12:2 (NIV)

## Mind

Thinking is a part of our soul. Our sub-conscious mind holds our belief system. Therefore, what we believe is based on how we think.

The patterns of this world look to so many self-help remedies to better oneself. The world will tell you that no one matters but "you"; that success is the key to happiness; and to look out for number "one". The Word cautions us not to conform to these patterns of the world; but instead to be transformed—changed completely by, first, renewing your mind to think like Christ. If you are looking to better yourself, get on board with God's plan—His good plan. If you want to know His pleasing and perfect will, allow God to transform you, by setting your mind on His Word, no longer thinking the way the world thinks and doing what the world does by looking to wealth, or even drugs, alcohol, or any other substance to find peace.

There will be days that you will respond to conflict or temptation with the ways that society would respond. When you do, stop. Stop the train of thought and replace it with God's Word. Are you frustrated that things aren't going the way you've planned? Stop, and remember what His Word says, "For I know the plans I have for you," declares the Lord, "Plans to prosper you and not to harm you, plans to give you hope and a future." (Jeremiah 29:11) This is the true character of God—He has good plans for His children today just as He did in the days of Jeremiah. When you remind yourself of the promises of God, you will be able to rest, knowing God has a better plan. Chaos and trials will come, but if you have followed the Lord's direction and you are where He has led you, then rest assured that He will see you through whatever it is you are facing today.

We don't have to worry about making sure we get what we think we deserve. That is the way the world thinks. We can give to others and love others, expecting nothing in return, and we will be at peace.

---
---
---
---

# March 16

> Yet to all who did receive Him, to those who believed in His Name, He gave the right to become children of God—children born not of natural descent, nor of human decision or a husband's will, but born of God.
> —John 1:12–13 (NIV)

### Spirit

Meditate on this awe-inspiring truth—you are a child of God. The spirit within you has no end, but will live forever. Living with the knowledge that you are a child of the King of all the universe is empowering. Be strong. Stand firm for what you believe—God's Word is true and nothing can take that away.

Spiritual health brings meaning and purpose to life. Our relationship with God becomes an intricate part of developing our personality and beliefs. Staying in communion with God will play an important role on all other aspects of our life (our thinking, actions, and interaction with others). When we accept the invitation to become a child of God and are committed to do what He asks of us, we are answering *yes* to God—that we are ready to do what God asks of us no matter how hard it might be to do.

_____
_____
_____
_____

# March 17

> So do not worry, saying, 'What shall we eat?' or 'What shall we drink?' or 'What shall we wear?' For the pagans run after all these things, and your heavenly Father knows that you need them. But seek first His kingdom and His righteousness, and all these things will be given to you as well.
> —Matthew 6:31–33 (NIV)

### Finances

We've discussed our mental health which is the way we think—training and transforming of the mind to think how God thinks, and not how the world thinks. By training our mind to keep our minds set on things that are above and not earthly things, we do not become weary, anxious and overwhelmed. Instead we have peace, hope and joy. We determine to make decisions that are sound and led by the Lord and His Word. We ask for God's guidance to make good choices in every area. This includes our Finances.

The scripture does not say, "Seek first my 401K", or "Seek first my needs", or "Seek first *getting* anything here on earth." The Word says to seek God's kingdom and righteousness first. We are not to worry, because all of these earthly needs will be taken care of by God. They will be *given* to you. God is the gift-giver and He knows what we need before we even ask. Don't worry that you might miss out on something you feel you should have. God wants what is best for you and He has all of the resources in heaven and under heaven to provide it for you.

If your retirement plan is not going the way you expected, don't worry. If you don't have the big home you've always dreamed of, don't worry. If you look at your bank account and the budget you planned is not sufficient to meet your needs, stop looking at your bank account to supply all of your needs. Remember, He will meet all of your needs *according to His riches*, not yours.

The focus must be on what we need in order to fulfill God's purpose. What is it that will best serve the purpose of God's kingdom?

We don't give up when things don't seem to be developing how we envisioned or as fast as we would like them to go. We don't give up when we don't know what the future holds. We trust God and His plan.

---

---

---

---

# March 18

Most important of all, continue to show deep love for each other, for love covers a multitude of sins. Cheerfully share your home with those who need a meal or a place to stay.

God has given each of you a gift from His great variety of spiritual gifts. Use them well to serve one another. Do you have the gift of speaking? Then speak as though God Himself were speaking through you. Do you have the gift of helping others? Do it with all the strength and energy that God supplies. Then everything you do will bring glory to God through Jesus Christ. All glory and power to Him forever and ever! Amen.

—1 Peter 4:8–11 (NLT)

Social ~ Relationships

Social health can make a difference by offering generosity to others, by encouraging and uplifting them, and providing for a need they may have.

Our personality will determine how we will interact with others, socially developing relationships, and how we treat others. Remember, our relationship with God will develop our personality and belief system that will be the foundation for all you do when it relates to others.

To be able to make an impact on the people around us, we will need to make sure our body, soul and spirit are all in good health. Without a sound basis of who you are, you can fall into trouble. Too often, we like to jump right into relationships too soon.

Is your daily schedule keeping you so busy that you find no time to pay attention to those around you? I remember when I was a young mom, how simply getting through the tasks of the day were enough to wear me down. I also remember some days when my son or daughter would ask me a question and I would answer quickly, without even looking at them, in hopes that my short answer would be sufficient and end the questioning. We can get so caught up in the busy-ness of our day that we miss the importance of showing love to those around us.

Are you showing love and affection to those who are brokenhearted? In what ways can your relationship with others (socially interacting with others) be a part of living the life God calls you to live? Do you take the time to listen to the person in church who is ignored by others? Are you ready spiritually (have you prayed, and read the Word to prepare yourself) to start a serious relationship that may lead to marriage?

> Don't be fooled by those who say such things, for "bad company corrupts good character."
> —1 Corinthians 15:33 (NLT)

Let's slow down. Notice those around you—even the little children. Souls will last forever; the material things around you will not. Invest in people, and you will be investing in the kingdom.

---
---
---
---

# March 19

> Yes, my soul, find rest in God; my hope comes from Him.
>
> —Psalm 62:5 (NIV)

### Emotional

Hope expects with confidence. And the lack of hope crushes the heart. No hope brings a person to despair. Our soul—the very heart of our emotions—can find peace and rest in God. He brings hope; He restores every broken heart. When He does, your darkness is lifted, and your anxious heart miraculously finds peace.

We cannot let our emotions lead our actions. Our faith must be our motivator in all that we do. Despite how we feel, we must move forward in faith.

One day, when I was becoming distraught with emotions running wild because of a situation I was facing, I started to pray as I always had before—for strength, for an answer to my need, for God's will. Then, I realized that the one thing I needed most was peace. The truth of the matter was that I could handle what I was facing if I only had peace. I remembered the scriptures—that God would supply all of my needs; that God is for me and not against me; that His plans are good; that the Lord is my rock and my fortress and my deliverer. There was no reason to be anxious. What was I worried about that God couldn't handle? So, my prayer changed. And His peace rested on me incredibly and so abruptly that it astounded me.

Peace is an amazing thing. It removes fear. It removes worry and anxious thoughts. I had peace in a moment that usually would call for panic, and I didn't understand how I could have peace in such a moment. Still, it was there, and I was able to receive peace because it came from Jesus, and not from the world.

# March 20

> The earth is the Lord's, and everything in it, the world, and all who live in it.
>
> —Psalm 24:1 (NIV)

### Home ~ Planet

God owns the earth. God owns the sky, galaxy and all that is in the world. God owns everything created; and that includes you. Keeping the perspective that God owns it all, causes me to be conscious of the fact that I should care about it.

Although we don't place our trust in our earthly treasures, we still are called to manage what God has given us.

I should care about pollution, and do my part to improve it. I should care about the planet and do my part to preserve it. I should care about the animals, the plant-life and all that lives. You may think that your commitment will not make a difference in the greater scheme of things, but your part is the only part that you are expected to tend to. God cares about your heart and your character. You can, at a minimum, care for your own home and make the home a good environment who live there and enter it. It is, in a sense, your own little world.

_____
_____
_____
_____

# March 21

Be still before the LORD and wait patiently for Him; do not fret when people succeed in their ways, when they carry out their wicked schemes.
—Psalm 37:7 (NIV)

Is there someone in your life making you miserable? You watch them in their deceit, succeeding as they lie, cheat and steal. Their dishonesty appears to be working, since they are the ones who are getting the promotions and recognition. Stand strong. Their evildoing will someday come back to bite them. They will be found out. Remain faithful in doing right and wait for the Lord to move on your behalf.

# March 22

> Do not say, "I'll pay you back for this wrong!" Wait for the Lord, and He will avenge you.
> —Proverbs 20:22 (NIV)

The book of Proverbs is a compilation of tidbits of wisdom. The advice given in the Proverbs is sound.

When you have been wronged, or cheated by someone, the pain can turn to anger, and then to bitterness, and could even result in revenge. It can be a minor offense, such as dishonesty, or major offense, such as betrayal. In either circumstance, it is human nature to want to pay back evil for evil. But, wait. Anything you can do in vengeance cannot compare to the vengeance of the Lord. If you try to pay back the pain poured out on you, this will only cause more anxiety within you, and add more strife to the situation.

When I watch children take things into their own hands and hurt another child as a payback, I find it hard to discipline the child who initiated it when he/she is already hurt by the one who took vengeance; like children on a playground returning harsh words for harsh words; or a child saying, "He hit me first." We grow up and continue the behavior as adults. But as an adult our paybacks are on a higher level of vengeance—cheating the cheater, stealing from the thief, lying to the dishonest, destroying and taking things from the vulnerable, belittling and blaming. When we become children of God, we no longer need to feel that we have to defend ourselves. We have a Father who can defend us. So, instead of paying back your offender, wait upon the Lord, and draw close to Him.

# March 23

### Ask, Seek, Knock

"Ask and it will be given to you; seek and you will find; knock and the door will be opened to you. For everyone who asks receives; the one who seeks finds; and to the one who knocks, the door will be opened.

"Which of you, if your son asks for bread, will give him a stone? Or if he asks for a fish, will give him a snake? If you, then, though you are evil, know how to give good gifts to your children, how much more will your Father in heaven give good gifts to those who ask Him! So in everything, do to others what you would have them do to you, for this sums up the Law and the Prophets.
—Matthew 7:7–12 (NIV)

When Jesus told them to ask, seek and knock, He followed up by saying we need to treat everyone the way we would want to be treated. I can understand why He said it that way. Sometimes we need kindness and help, but don't deserve it. We may have made a wrong choice and it landed us in a situation where we need desperate help. Though undeserved, we would want someone to help us. So, when you see someone in need, even if you feel they don't deserve it, help them anyway. Even when someone does not deserve your kindness, even if they have hurt you, treat them with respect, kindness and love—just how you want to be treated. The Father will answer when we ask for help; and we are called to mirror the heart of God and show lovingkindness.

If you are being mistreated, if you are lacking any thing, ask the Lord for help and He will answer. We don't need to worry about the wicked succeeding. We don't need to repay those who've wronged us. And we can treat others how we would want them to treat us.

# March 24

> Trust GOD from the bottom of your heart; don't try to figure out everything on your own.
> Listen for GOD's voice in everything you do, everywhere you go; He's the one who will keep you on track.
> —Proverbs 3:5–6 (MSG)

Waiting is never easy; and as we look to God for direction, trusting Him for His wisdom, we sometimes struggle with disappointment and fear.

When you are anticipating something hoped for, and it hasn't yet come, don't try to figure out everything on your own. Listen for GOD's voice in everything you do, everywhere you go; He's the one who will keep you on track. As you continue to trust Him with all your heart, your answer will finally come. The darkness of the path will be illuminated and you will be able to see which way to go.

The AMP version of the Bible says it this way:

> Trust in *and* rely confidently on the LORD with all your heart. And do not rely on your own insight *or* understanding.
> —Proverbs 3:5 (AMP)

Are you putting your confidence and faith in the things around you? Do you become anxious when the possessions you have are threatened to be taken or lost? Some people seem to be able to trust God with their eternal salvation, but have trouble trusting Him for their every-day life. Take comfort from these words in scripture. Know that He will direct you and provide all that you need. Realize there is so much more to this life than meets the eyes.

# March 25

What if God, although willing to show His [terrible] wrath and to make His power known, has tolerated with great patience the objects of His wrath [which are] prepared for destruction? And what if He has done so to make known the riches of His glory to the objects of His mercy, which He has prepared beforehand for glory, *including* us, whom He also called, not only from among the Jews, but also from among the Gentiles? Just as He says in [the writings of the prophet] Hosea:

"I WILL CALL THOSE WHO WERE NOT MY PEOPLE, 'MY PEOPLE,' AND [I will call] HER WHO WAS NOT BELOVED, 'BELOVED.'"
—Romans 9:22–25 (AMP)

The outcome of God's plan is eternal life for people who did not deserve it—us. He is going to show us the riches of His glory!

God knows the secret plans for you and they are good! The anticipation of what God will do is exhilarating. Like a race-horse restless to be released from the starting gate; like a child on Christmas Eve who can't fall asleep and gets up in the middle of the night to ask if it's time to get up yet; we too have wonderful things in store for us! We know that the Promised Land is just up ahead!

God has wonderful plans to prepare you for your ultimate home in Glory. So, let's get ready!

# March 26

Remember Who Jesus Is

For a child is born to us, a son is given to us. The government will rest on His shoulders. And He will be called: Wonderful Counselor, Mighty God, Everlasting Father, Prince of Peace. His government and its peace will never end. He will rule with fairness and justice from the throne of His ancestor David for all eternity. The passionate commitment of the Lord of Heaven's Armies will make this happen!
—Isaiah 9:6 (NLT)

# March 27

> Therefore humble yourselves under the mighty hand of God [set aside self-righteous pride], so that He may exalt you [to a place of honor in His service] at the appropriate time, casting all your cares [all your anxieties, all your worries, and all your concerns, once and for all] on Him, for He cares about you [with deepest affection, and watches over you very carefully].
> —1 Peter 5:6–7 (AMP)

God's timing is perfect. It may seem as though God is not coming to your rescue, but He is. He will come because He loves you. And at the perfect time, He will lift you up. Therefore, when you are weary reach up to God. He will save you. Set aside your pride, and ask for help.

# March 28

> What do workers gain from their toil? I have seen the burden God has laid on the human race. He has made everything beautiful in its time. He has also set eternity in the human heart; yet no one can fathom what God has done from beginning to end.
> —Ecclesiastes 3:9–11 (NIV)

Our minds cannot grasp the fullness of who God is and what He does. There is so much more to the kingdom of God than the things we touch and see. In fact, the spiritual world is more the reality than the physical world. The spiritual world is much bigger, much deeper, and will last forever. This earth is a tiny speck in correlation to God's world. And, God takes our everyday busy lives and makes it beautiful in its time, even if we can't see it. He takes something tiny and makes it magnificent.

# March 29

Has God forgotten to be merciful? Has He in anger withheld His compassion?"

Then I thought, "To this I will appeal: the years when the Most High stretched out His right hand. I will remember the deeds of the Lord; yes, I will remember Your miracles of long ago. I will consider all Your works and meditate on all Your mighty deeds."

—Psalm 77:9–12 (NIV)

Are you wondering where God is? Do you sometimes feel like He has forgotten you? A look at your past can remind you of His great hand of deliverance. Look back and remember the wonderful things He has done for you.

If you were to look back on those moments in life that seemed to come only to destroy you, what would you see? What would you remember?

Life—in all its agony and brokenness as well as all its glorious moments is where I live. And it's where you live today, whether you are aware of it or not. But I remember—I remember where it all started; that day when my life changed and I realized this life's struggle is only temporary. When all of the tragedy, and the pain that is so great is filtered through the cross, through the holiness of God, the difficulties of this life are meaningless. The more I see God, the smaller this world becomes.

# March 30

> I cry to you, LORD; I say, "You are my refuge, my portion in the land of the living."
> —Psalm 142:5 (NIV)

I understand the cries of a child that touch the heart of a mother. When my son, Israel, was born, I couldn't believe the love I had for such a tiny little baby. His cry in the middle of the night woke me up from a deep sleep.

With each passing year his cry would change a little bit, from a baby's cry to a toddler's cry and then to a young boy's cry. I would hear a call out, "Mama!", and I knew it was Israel. I knew his voice in a crowded playground and even from a distance.

Later years, a call can come and I hear my son or daughter on the phone ask for advice—just as I call my mama for her wisdom or her prayers in times of need. No matter how old they are, I will always be their mom.

This is who we have in our God. He is our Father, and we can call out to Him in our time of need. It can be a cry with no words. We can call out one Name, "Father." He knows our voice, and He hears us and will answer our call.

_____

_____

_____

_____

# March 31

Waiting… Have you ever found yourself sitting at railroad crossings becoming agitated as you wait? I once was waiting for a train to pass by when, for some unknown reason, the train began to slow and ultimately came to a full stop. That's when the stress began to build. I had reluctantly accepted the idea that I would need to wait, but on my terms. I didn't agree to wait while the train quit moving at all!

Things in life can cause us to wait. When that happens, take a deep breath and spend a moment in prayer. The Lord will see you through it and He will set your life back into motion again. Don't try to figure out how long you will need to wait—your ideas may be shattered when circumstances change yet again (like the train completely stopping in front of me). Until it's time to move again, wait upon the Lord and see the beauty around you as you settle in this place of stillness.

# April

My beloved spoke and said to me, "Arise, my darling, my beautiful one, come with me.
—Song of Songs 2:10 (NIV)

# You're Beautiful Treasured One

# April 1

My beloved has gone down to his garden, to the beds of spices, to browse in the gardens and to gather lilies. I am my beloved's and my beloved is mine; he browses among the lilies.

You are as beautiful as Tirzah, my darling, as lovely as Jerusalem, as majestic as troops with banners.

—Song of Songs 6:2–3 (NIV)

The love story between us and Jesus is more precious than any other. Imagine Jesus picking the lilies one-by-one; and, there you are among the lilies. Jesus gathers those He loves—the bride of Christ.

There may be days when the only thing you hear is that you're not worth anything. Left wondering if you ever could be loved, here He comes, strolling in the garden. He tells you how beautiful you are and that you belong to Him.

You are treasured; you are sacred; you are His. You are beautiful.

# April 2

> The voice of the LORD *is* over the waters;
> The God of glory thunders;
> The LORD *is* over many waters.
>
> The voice of the LORD *is* powerful;
> The voice of the LORD *is* full of majesty. The voice of
> the LORD breaks the cedars,
> Yes, the LORD splinters the cedars of Lebanon.
> He makes them also skip like a calf,
> Lebanon and Sirion like a young wild ox.
> The voice of the LORD divides the flames of fire.
>
> The voice of the LORD shakes the wilderness;
> The LORD shakes the Wilderness of Kadesh.
> The voice of the LORD makes the deer give birth,
> And strips the forests bare;
> And in His temple everyone says, "Glory!"
>
> —Psalm 29:3–9 (NKJV)

When God speaks, all of creation respond and trembles. His Word is powerful. It is the foundation for everything that exists. Listen to His voice—don't be afraid when His voice shakes you. Embrace the message He has for you. He is creating a life for you that is better than you could have imagined.

---------

---------

---------

---------

# April 3

> "Come to me, all you who are weary and burdened, and I will give you rest. Take My yoke upon you and learn from Me, for I am gentle and humble in heart, and you will find rest for your souls. For My yoke is easy and My burden is light."
> —Matthew 11:28–30 (NIV)

Jesus invites us to come to Him. "Come to Me," He calls. And He will provide rest for your soul. In the days when Jesus walked the earth, the crops were plowed by animals. Oxen or cattle would pull the plow behind them as they were yoked together by wooden beams. The yoke would represent hard work, even servitude and bondage in the ancient days.

So one would wonder how rest can be found in the yoke.

"Learn from Me. My yoke is easy and My burden light." This is what Jesus says about the yoke between us and Him.

First of all, we need to understand what this yoke is all about. First, there is a teamster—the one directing the team that is in charge. And as long as the team of oxen acknowledge who is in charge, they will react to the teamster's leading. I see the Father as the teamster. He directs our every step, as we acknowledge Him. The teamster must be firm, consistent and patient. And isn't that our God?

Then there is the yoke of oxen or cattle. The pairing of the oxen requires the teamster to understand the uniqueness of each animal. Each animal responds differently to commands, to handling, and to the various tasks offered to them. God speaks to us individually and knows us intimately.

When you work with Jesus at your side, He takes the heavy load. As He leads, follow; as He nudges this way or that, submit to Him, and you will find peace.

The placement of the team of oxen is a critical part of pairing. The two must be paired and matched that work best together. There is the nigh side which is on the left where the teamster will need to guide the animal more closely. The one placed on the nigh side is usually the harder to control, or slower, smaller or less powerful. The one on the off side is usually the larger, more powerful ox. Placing the larger ox in the furrow when plowing levels the yoke. Also, the teamster can see the larger ox on the right by looking over the smaller ox on the left. Can you see that? God sees Jesus. He sees the one who bears the weight. He sees clean; He sees perfect; spotless; He sees His Son, Jesus. Begin to see yourselves as perfect just as He is perfect. Not in anything that we are, or appear to be, to others, but inwardly and by God's own design. God sees us as perfect children. He looks at us and sees His perfect Son.

_____
_____
_____
_____

# April 4

Then I heard again what sounded like the shout of a vast crowd or the roar of mighty ocean waves or the crash of loud thunder:

"Praise the LORD! For the Lord our God, the Almighty, reigns.

Let us be glad and rejoice, and let us give honor to Him.

For the time has come for the wedding feast of the Lamb, and His bride has prepared herself. She has been given the finest of pure white linen to wear." For the fine linen represents the good deeds of God's holy people.

And the angel said to me, "Write this: Blessed are those who are invited to the wedding feast of the Lamb." And he added, "These are true words that come from God."

—Revelation 19:6–9 (NLT)

Every person will have a wedding day. It's all planned out. If you are single today, you represent the bride-to-be who is faithful to her groom as she waits for her wedding day. If you are married today, you represent what a marriage should look like—husbands loving their wives as Christ loves us; and wives submitting to their husbands as unto the Lord. No matter your roll, you can show the commitment, love and faithfulness between Jesus and His bride, the church.

# April 5

### Empowered for Good

> May our Lord Jesus Christ Himself and God our Father, who loved us and by His grace gave us eternal encouragement and good hope, encourage your hearts and strengthen you in every good deed and word.
> —2 Thessalonians 2:16–17 (NIV)

God, the Father, and Jesus Christ loves you.

That should encourage you—to know that you are loved. His love gives hope—hope for a life under the protection of His grace.

Wild animals have learned to hide under the brush, under rocks and underground and even in my boots, where they know that the covering will protect them—from the sun, the predators and the rough environment. They have learned how important it is to stay covered. We can learn from them. Knowing of the covering we have in God, then wouldn't we be careless to step outside of that covering and live unprotected outside of it? His covering—His righteousness provides shelter and safety. Outside of that realm leaves us vulnerable to the enemy's enticement and weapons he uses to destroy us.

Jesus came to earth to bring us an abundant life under His covering. He is here to encourage you, make you strong, and provide everything you need.

# April 6

> If you remain in Me and My words remain in you, ask whatever you wish, and it will be done for you.
> —John 15:7 (NIV)

I have found that, when I daily spend time with the Lord, and seek His will for my life, sometimes the desires I once had are replaced with new desires—a better plan than I had dreamed of. Sometimes, desires can be from an evil heart. This is why it is so important to remain in Him and keep His words in our hearts.

*As water reflects the face, so one's life reflects the heart* (Proverbs 27:19 NIV). You can see what you look like, as you see your face in the reflection of water, or a mirror. And what your heart desires is shown as a reflection of your life.

Out of the abundance of the heart, the mouth speaks, the feet go, the hands do—your actions will be based on what you have in your heart.

Fill your heart with His words; remain in His presence; *then,* you will receive what your heart desires.

# April 7

> In the last days, God says, I will pour out My Spirit on all people. Your sons and daughters will prophesy, your young men will see visions, your old men will dream dreams. Even on my servants, both men and women, I will pour out my Spirit in those days, and they will prophesy.
> —Acts 2:17–18 (NIV)

Do you have a dream? Has God poured out His Spirit upon you and has revealed a promise to you? Believe. If God has spoken to your heart, and the dream is in agreement with His Word, pray and ask God to reveal the details of His plan for your life, so that you can achieve that dream He has given. First and foremost, God's plan is salvation and eternal life. Additionally, because of His gifts of grace, and mercy, and salvation, God will show you what you can do in the newfound supernatural life to bring glory to Him. Let your eternal spirit begin living abundantly today.

_____

_____

_____

_____

# April 8

> Beloved, do not believe every spirit, but test the spirits to see whether they are from God, for many false prophets have gone out into the world.
> —1 John 4:1 (ESV)

We hear the phrase, "God told me" many times in our Christian lives. Some have heard it said lightly and some use the phrase to approve their sacrilegious acts, and selfish motivation. There are some people who claim to be spiritual, but give no mention of God. Some will say that they believe there is a god, but will not admit that God is the *only* God. Let's not be misled. How do we ascertain what is of God or not of God? Let all things point to the magnitude of God—not man, not angels, not any action or deed, but only God. Let your dream, your hopes, your vision for a future have reason and purpose to benefit the kingdom of God and not your own pride or selfish desires. Easy to do? No. Being *self-seeking* is easy. We act on our feelings. We love, if we are loved. We do, if it is done for us. We go, if we know we'll see benefit in going. It's very natural to look out for "number one". And that's why we need to look to the Holy Spirit for strength to do what is unnatural—to love, and give without expectations or ulterior motives.

---
---
---
---

# April 9

> For God speaks in one way, and in two, though man does not perceive it. In a dream, in a vision of the night, when deep sleep falls on men, while they slumber on their beds, then He opens the ears of men and terrifies them with warnings, that He may turn man aside from his deed and conceal pride from a man; He keeps back his soul from the pit, his life from perishing by the sword.
>
> —Job 33:14–18 (ESV)

Many times throughout my prayer life, the Lord has shown me visions and dreams as I drew close to Him. He showed up in time of despair; He spoke to my broken heart to bring hope. In every case, it has pointed to God and His great power and love in my life or the lives of those around me, so that I would believe and so that those around me would see God and believe.

Please understand that I am not boasting of this for my own glory; I am an ordinary person. But when I have faced troubles, God has reached out and made it clear that He was there assuring me that He was not going to leave me alone. This blessed assurance can be yours just the same.

# April 10

"Knowing His Secrets"

The secret counsel of the LORD is for those who fear Him, and He reveals His covenant to them.
—Psalm 25:14 (HCSB)

A strange and wonderful thing happens when you spend time with God—circumstances begin to reveal God's promises; the happenstances begin to make sense to you that never had before. Your spirit becomes sensitive to the important details of life, and you are able to discern how various situations will turn out. This is not merely about supernatural premonitions; rather, your heightened perception has to do with understanding God's will for you, and seeing His activity in your life with spiritual eyes.

# April 11

> Is not this the kind of fasting I have chosen: to loose the chains of injustice and untie the cords of the yoke, to set the oppressed free and break every yoke? Is it not to share your food with the hungry and to provide the poor wanderer with shelter—when you see the naked, to clothe them, and not to turn away from your own flesh and blood? Then your light will break forth like the dawn, and your healing will quickly appear; then your righteousness will go before you, and the glory of the LORD will be your rear guard. Then you will call, and the LORD will answer; you will cry for help, and He will say: Here am I.
>
> —Isaiah 58:6–9 (NIV)

When you begin praying the heart of God and fasting for the desires of God's heart, you will see results. Our heavy burdens will be lifted. When was the last time you set aside some time to pray—and fast—so that your spirit would be made stronger? God looks for a kind of fasting that will make a difference in the kingdom, and to empower His people to meet the needs of others.

Before Jesus began His ministry on earth, He fasted. "After His baptism, as Jesus came up out of the water, the heavens were opened and He saw the Spirit of God descending like a dove and settling on Him. And a voice from heaven said, "This is my dearly loved Son, who brings Me great joy." Then Jesus was led by the Spirit into the wilderness to be tempted there by the devil. For forty days and forty nights He fasted and became very hungry." (Matthew 3:1–4:2 NLT).

What an incredible scene. They saw the Spirit of God descend from heaven. They heard God's voice. What better time to begin a public ministry than when God Himself publicly proclaims His pleasure in you and approves who you are! But instead of capitalizing on the situation, Jesus went into total isolation for 40 days, eating nothing and being tempted by the devil. Jesus fasted in the desert before He preached one sermon, before He healed anyone, and before He called any disciples.

When Jesus finally completed His fast, He was prepared for the spiritual battles ahead as He stepped out to begin fulfilling His purpose on earth.

What spiritual battles are you experiencing in your life? Do you need breakthroughs in your personal life, your family, your finances, your church or your community? Do you want to see things begin to happen for God's glory? Follow Jesus' example. Pray and fast for a release of God's power to overcome and be victorious. God will prepare you to fulfill the purpose He has planned for you.

_____
_____
_____
_____

# April 12

> Jesus straightened up and asked her, "Woman, where are they? Has no one condemned you?" "No one, sir," she said. "Then neither do I condemn you," Jesus declared. "Go now and leave your life of sin."
> —John 8:10–11 (NIV)

The heart of God is to forgive and show mercy; so that you may go in peace and sin no more. You are now free—changed—transformed! Just as the adulterous woman was not condemned that day, neither are you. The people wanted to stone the woman, but Jesus showed up. People may mistreat you; they may disown you. But your life will change when Jesus shows up. Whatever has happened in your past is forgiven. You are freed from guilt and shame the moment you accept God's gift of forgiveness. Your past is the past. Don't live in it today. Look back only to see how God delivered you. Look back and see His love and acceptance. Don't look back with regret and self-condemnation. Then you will be able to look forward to the life that God has for you.

# April 13

> You were taught, with regard to your former way of life, to put off your old self, which is being corrupted by its deceitful desires; to be made new in the attitude of your minds; and to put on the new self, created to be like God in true righteousness and holiness.
>
> —Ephesians 4:22–24 (NIV)

As we draw close to God and listen to His voice, by prayer, fasting and reading the Word of God, as well as sitting quietly in His presence while we wait for Him, we begin to change our way of thinking. The things that were once important are no longer so important. Our dreams, our hopes, and our goals are no longer only earthly desires and limitations, but riches only God can give. We begin to think about others and how we can help them. Husbands and wives share the same dreams and have goals that will meet the needs of their children.

Go ahead and be faithful with what God has given you—plan and work hard. God expects you to manage business well. And as you begin to spend more time with God, you will find that the things that are treasures in heaven is where your true heart lies.

Enjoy the blessings God gives you today—but hold them loosely so that, if He sees fit, you are able to release them back into His hands.

# April 14

> Paul and Barnabas appointed elders for them in each church and, with prayer and fasting, committed them to the Lord, in whom they had put their trust.
>
> —Acts 14:23 (NIV)

In reading the book of Acts, you will hear of the miracles and mighty move of the Holy Spirit that was poured out as the disciples went about preaching the gospel.

Paul and Barnabas understood where to place their trust and knew the importance of prayer and fasting.

Prayer and fasting will enable us to conquer the flesh and the desires of this world, and to walk in the Spirit of God. Prayer feeds the spirit, while fasting puts the flesh in the "back seat" for a while. In doing so, the spirit is made strong which makes us sensitive to hear the voice of God so that He can give us direction; and opens up the supernatural, giving us the power and the anointing to do the works of God. As Paul committed the elders to the Lord, they did so as God led them.

Keep in mind, when you fast you do not fast only to get something for yourself—for selfish gain—but rather to hear what the Lord wants for you and to obtain courage and strength to accomplish the commission.

I remember a moment when God showed me some things as a caution to prepare for what was about to come. He called me to pray and fast, for I would need strong faith to battle what was about to be revealed. Is God showing you things you need to see?

# April 15

Luke 10:38–42 tells of the story of two sisters, Mary and Martha. Martha was working diligently in the kitchen while Mary wanted to sit at Jesus' feet and worship Him. Martha was bothered by this as she was left to do all of the work without Mary's help. So, she complained to Jesus. Jesus reminded Martha, "You are worried and upset about many things, but few things are needed—or indeed only one. Mary has chosen what is better, and it will not be taken away from her."

We need to do this one thing that is needful: sit at His feet and listen to His Word, and worship Him. All of what Martha was doing was good. She was showing hospitality, preparing for the Lord and serving Him. But don't let these busy things become more important than worshipping Jesus. Remember the reason you are doing all that you do.

# April 16

The thief comes only to steal and kill and destroy; I have come that they may have life, and have it to the full.

—John 10:10 (NIV)

Jesus brings abundant life; fullness of life. This "happily ever after" that Jesus brings is so much greater and more exhilarating than any fairy tale that claims living "happily ever after". The fairy tale dream is about an earthly prince and princess finding happiness in each other and their own story. Jesus is the true Prince, and we are His princesses. His story is about happiness found in being in His story, as children of the King of Kings, living forever with Him—abundant life in its abounding fullness of joy and strength of mind, body and soul! It is not about earthly wealth, achievements or status. No. It's all about Jesus.

# April 17

> Since, then, you have been raised with Christ, set your hearts on things above, where Christ is, seated at the right hand of God. Set your minds on things above, not on earthly things. For you died, and your life is now hidden with Christ in God. When Christ, who is your life, appears, then you also will appear with Him in glory.
> —Colossians 3:1–4 (NIV)

The things of this earth, including suffering, will not last. But the glory of the Lord living within you, and the magnificent plan He has for you, is eternal. Hold on, dear friends; He will bring you back to a firm foundation—strong and with purpose in your heart. The enemy will not devour you, so do not fear his roar. Have you lost something you cherished greatly? It's okay to mourn the loss of something or someone you held so dearly. At times it seems impossible to sense anything but dread. Especially when you're afraid of losing so much. But look up. The things He has for you is much more valuable than anything you have received as a gift here on earth. And, with the new eternal perspective, the old ways and old desires will fade away. It may take time for the pain to subside. Some of the pain may never leave you. But you will know in your heart that there's a better day ahead.

Begin to live like you will live forever. Place value on what really matters—the things of God, which will never pass away—your soul and the souls of others, love, compassion, kindness, humility, gentleness and patience. The character you are becoming is the one you will take into eternity. Through the losses of this life, cling to Him ever more so tightly.

# April 18

> I remain confident of this: I will see the goodness of the LORD in the land of the living. Wait for the LORD; be strong and take heart and wait for the LORD
> —Psalm 27:13–14 (NIV)

Let your heart take courage. It takes courage to go through some difficult trials. Being brave means you are willing to go through it even though you are afraid. And God, in His goodness and grace, will remove fears that hold you captive, and will help you see Him through the rain and hear His voice in the crackling of the thunder. You will know He is near. Courage will rise up.

I remember when my brother was diagnosed with cancer, and were told that his days with us would be short. I remember the fear of losing him and not being able to call him up or see him—not until we would see each other again in heaven. I remember telling him that I would try to be brave and strong, even though I was afraid. I knew I would need to lean on God heavily to survive such loss. And God was there ready to lift the burden. Cry? Yes, I did. Even sobbed. And God's comfort settled in my heart through it all.

_____
_____
_____
_____

# April 19

Invitation to the Lord's Salvation

> Is anyone thirsty? Come and drink—even if you have no money! Come, take your choice of wine or milk—it's all free! Why spend your money on food that does not give you strength? Why pay for food that does you no good? Listen to Me, and you will eat what is good. You will enjoy the finest food.
> Come to Me with your ears wide open. Listen, and you will find life. I will make an everlasting covenant with you. I will give you all the unfailing love I promised to David.
> —Isaiah 55:1–3 (NLT)

The invitation the Lord provided to the peoples of Jerusalem is one for us still today. He calls to you, "Come." He beckons you, "Listen." He promises His unfailing love, abundant life, mercy and forgiveness. You may be tired, overwhelmed to exhaustion; you may wonder if there's any hope of rest. There is. The Lord will come as you draw near to Him, and He will surely restore you. Waste no more time on anxious thoughts. No effort, no cost, no requirements—His forgiveness, salvation and restoration is free.

Maybe you need fearless faith; fearless faith in who God is, and says He is, in your life; fearless, expectant faith that He will heal, redeem, and restore you.

# April 20

> Our soul waits for the LORD; He is our help and our shield. For our heart is glad in Him, because we trust in His holy name. Let your steadfast love, O LORD, be upon us, even as we hope in You.
> —Psalm 33:20–22 (ESV)

The writer of this Psalm gives every reason why we should praise God—for His general character, His faithfulness, and His desire for righteousness, justice and love (Psalm 33:4–5); the fact that He made the universe; and the awe of His wisdom and power displayed by Him in creation (Psalm 33:6–9); the stability of His counsel and plans (Psalm 33:10–11); and the blessings which He bestows upon those who acknowledge Him to be their God and place their hope in Him—blessings of care, protection, and deliverance in danger (Psalm 33:12–19). In conclusion of all this, the purpose of the writer, and of those who were associated with him, is clear. We are to praise God.

The psalm is one that is appropriate to all people of all times. We all praise Him as we become more acquainted with the character of God and who He is.

At one point, we will meet calamity. And when we do, we will need to persevere with our hope in Him—the one who can help us. Even as we are waiting for rescue, we have that blessed hope that only comes when we trust the Lord. We believe in His great love for us; we believe He is the master of our lives and that He will protect us in the middle of the battle.

# April 21

I wait for the LORD, my whole being waits, and in His word I put my hope. I wait for the Lord more than watchmen wait for the morning, more than watchmen wait for the morning.
—Psalm 130:5–6 (NIV)

In the darkest hour, the watchmen waits for the morning. And in your darkest hour, your soul waits for the Lord. As night guards look anxiously for the break of day that they may be relieved, you long for your night to be over. The night seems long; you are weary, and want repose; all around is cheerless, gloomy, and still; and you long for the first signs that light will again visit your world.

In affliction—the long, dark, dreary, gloomy night of sorrow—the sufferer looks for the first indication, the first faint ray of comfort to the soul; a small glimmer of light to show the night is soon over.

To the one who has fallen under deep conviction for sin, and deep apprehension of the wrath of God—that night, dark, dreary, gloomy, often long—the soul looks for some ray of comfort, that God will be merciful, and will speak peace and pardon.

This is who our God is. He delivers. He brings light. Let the scriptures—God's Word—give you hope. Your morning will come. Look for that glimmer of hope. It will only come from God.

_____
_____
_____
_____

# April 22

> Hope in the LORD and keep His way. He will exalt you to inherit the land; when the wicked are destroyed, you will see it.
>
> —Psalm 37:34 (NIV)

The wicked may have success in life, but their riches will not secure their place with God. Don't stray from the path. Do not allow any temptation, or any opposition, to cause you to swerve from that path. The promise of a future eternally in the presence of God brings peace to the soul and hope for the heart.

_____
_____
_____
_____

# April 23

> I waited patiently for the LORD to help me, and He turned to me and heard my cry. He lifted me out of the pit of despair, out of the mud and the mire. He set my feet on solid ground and steadied me as I walked along. He has given me a new song to sing, a hymn of praise to our God. Many will see what He has done and be amazed. They will put their trust in the LORD.
> —Psalm 40:1–3 (NLT)

I have been in the lowest places of the pit; my heart was broken and life, as I knew it, was shattered. It was a dark night; and when the morning would finally come, the hours and details of that night played over and over in my mind, tormenting me, haunting me, taunting me. I had no words, no strength. I pulled back into a shell I had created in a dark place of nothingness so to hide myself from the world. I didn't want to come back. Then without an outward cry, a tear fell from my face. I saw Jesus enter my room and sit down by my side. He took me and held me close. It seemed to be hours that passed and then He took me to a spiritual place. He stood me up. I felt as if I would fall, but He kept me standing. He helped me take one step. Again my legs were as if I had been paralyzed in a terrible accident. Slowly I took each step until I was rehabilitated in the heart. I then opened my eyes, and stood up.

I had just experienced the saving grace of our Lord as He repaired my broken spirit and set my feet on solid ground. I realized He had steadied my way.

Any loss you might be facing today, remember His salvation. May the Lord remind you of the days He has done amazing things on the behalf of His children. Your challenges may be greater than I have experienced. There is no way to place our sorrows on a scale and determine if one causes greater pain than the other. To even think that someone's pain can be measured is unthinkable. No pain is insignificant. My circumstances may seem minor. Nevertheless, God cares about our hurts whether great or minor in our own measurements. He is there when we are heartbroken.

He'll be with you, and you will see that His presence is all that matters.

# April 24

> Therefore do not worry about tomorrow, for tomorrow will worry about itself. Each day has enough trouble of its own.
> —Matthew 6:34 (NIV)

Our plans for the future may be destroyed, when unforeseen happenstances fall to our path; but God's plan will not be shaken. His kingdom cannot be moved. When our plans fail, we can trust God for our future, when we realize this incredible truth—His plans cannot fail. We will have trouble. This is a promise—one that we don't like to hear. However, there is no need to worry when we know the God who is in control of our tomorrow.

# April 25

> Shout for joy to the LORD, all the earth. Worship the LORD with gladness; come before Him with joyful songs. Know that the LORD is God. It is He who made us, and we are His; we are His people, the sheep of His pasture. Enter His gates with thanksgiving and His courts with praise; give thanks to Him and praise His name. For the LORD is good and His love endures forever; His faithfulness continues through all generations.
> —Psalm 100:2–5 (NIV)

Know this:

The Lord is God.
God made you.
You belong to God.
We are a part of God's family
You are dear to Him and valuable—like sheep are to the shepherd.
You are free to enter into the place where God is!
God loves you—and His love will last forever.
God is faithful—even to the end of this life!

---
---
---
---

# April 26

> Now I want you to know, brothers and sisters, that what has happened to me has actually served to advance the gospel. As a result, it has become clear throughout the whole palace guard and to everyone else that I am in chains for Christ. And because of my chains, most of the brothers and sisters have become confident in the Lord and dare all the more to proclaim the gospel without fear.
> —Philippians 1:12–14 (NIV)

Paul's captivity was used to advance the gospel. The Lord promises to use all things to bring something good out of it—even the ugly things. Our greatest ministry may come from our greatest pain. Our courage can spark the same bravery in others, so that they can share God's love.

Believe today that your life can be used for God's glory. Even when things seem to be going all wrong, those things and the way you respond can be a testimony of God's grace and the tenacity to persevere.

> We can be so sure that every detail in our lives of love for God is worked into something good.
> —Romans 8:28 (MSG)

# April 27

> I look to you, heaven-dwelling God, look up to You for help. Like servants, alert to their master's commands, like a maiden attending her lady, we're watching and waiting, holding our breath, awaiting Your word of mercy. Mercy, GOD, mercy! We've been kicked around long enough, kicked in the teeth by complacent rich men, kicked when we're down by arrogant brutes.
> —Psalm 123:1–4 (MSG)

How long? How much further? Are we there yet? Do you remember the long road trips, and the child wanted to know how long until you would arrive? The answer, "Until we get there," wasn't enough to stop the questions and the restlessness of the child in the back seat. No answer would appease the anticipation.

Our cries for mercy are much deeper than that of a child inquiring when the end a long road trip will come. Our cries long for the end of the pain we endure through the trials of life. The psalmist looked to God for help, awaiting His mercy; with undivided attention for God to move. A servant is always attentive to the master's commands. The maiden doesn't stop attending her lady. The wait was demanding and long.

Sometimes we don't mind the waiting as long as we can grumble along the way. We wait in lines of all kinds. We wait in the grocery line. We wait in traffic. We wait in line at Disneyland or Disney World. We wait and wait. But often, our waiting comes with complaining. But God wants you to wait patiently. We, like the psalmist, can look to heaven and cry out to God for help. In the waiting, again like the psalmist, we can keep coming back to God to see if He is going to answer.

Like little children, we can get impatient while we're waiting for God to answer a prayer. We get nervous and restless. A child would not be wise to ask his parents to move aside so he can drive. We, too, need to leave it in God's hands; not to blame God for the wait; and not to complain that He hasn't answered yet. That's not easy to do. But, if we wait with sincere anticipation of God's move, we will not become anxious. We can trust that He will act.

As a child's heart filled with anticipation, keep your eyes toward the one who can make a difference, *until you get there.* Stay alert and keep your attention on Him. God's mercy *will* come.

# April 28

> Whenever I pray, I make my requests for all of you with joy, for you have been my partners in spreading the Good News about Christ from the time you first heard it until now. And I am certain that God, who began the good work within you, will continue His work until it is finally finished on the day when Christ Jesus returns.
> —Philippians 1:4–6 (NLT)

In us, God's work began. It continues to be worked, and will continue until it is finished in completeness on that day we see Jesus Christ face to face in all of His glory—when all is done.

You and I share in the call to spread the word that God brings good news. The partnership is between all brothers and sisters all across the world. Keep sharing your story within God's story. God is still working.

_____

_____

_____

_____

# April 29

> For to me, to live is Christ and to die is gain. If I am to go on living in the body, this will mean fruitful labor for me. Yet what shall I choose? I do not know! I am torn between the two: I desire to depart and be with Christ, which is better by far; but it is more necessary for you that I remain in the body.
> —Philippians 1:21–24 (NIV)

Paul made it obvious that he would rather leave the sinful world and accompany Jesus in heaven. He realized necessity outweighed his desire. There was a point in my life I would have rather died. For me, death was the better option than to live. It was because of my pain, that I wanted to leave. Paul felt the same when he was in prison. But he also knew that it was necessary for him to stay alive for the sake of the Philippians—for the progress and joy in their faith. The desire to depart this world may have been due to the fact that he felt he was a spiritual being trapped in the world of flesh. He was challenged, threatened, beaten, and imprisoned because of the opposition from those who refused to believe. We are essentially cursed here on Earth until that glorious day when we are freed from our earthly shells.

Whatever the reason he was torn, he was, in fact, torn between wanting to stay and wanting to go—whether it was because of his captivity in the prison or in his physical body and the pain that comes with it.

For the same reasons, it was true for me as well. My time here on earth is not yet done, though my spiritual body wants to go home.

You have work to do. God has a purpose for you. Live being Christ's messenger, just as Paul said, "To live is Christ."

# April 30

> You, LORD, hear the desire of the afflicted; You encourage them, and You listen to their cry, defending the fatherless and the oppressed, so that mere earthly mortals will never again strike terror.
> —Psalm 10:17–18 (NIV)

On one dark day, she pulls up to the railroad crossing. The light is just ahead, with no rail guards to separate her car from the tracks. She pulls forward just enough to straddle the track inviting death in hopes to end the madness of pain. Then God shows up. His words quietly spoken over her soul pierced to the core, revealing His good plans, His love for her—bringing her hope. She is in awe. When she leaves that place, she will never be the same.

When you cross over the tracks from this side of tragedy to the other side of restoration, you will be able to leave that place of brokenness and find comfort. Nothing else matters much than to simply live in His covering.

# May

However, as it is written:

What no eye has seen, what no ear has heard, and what no human mind has conceived—the things God has prepared for those who love Him—these are the things God has revealed to us by His Spirit.
—1 Corinthians 2:9 (NIV)

# Holy Spirit Rain Down

The Spirit you received does not make you slaves, so that you live in fear again; rather, the Spirit you received brought about your adoption to sonship. And by Him we cry, *"Abba,* Father." The Spirit Himself testifies with our spirit that we are God's children. Now if we are children, then we are heirs—heirs of God and co-heirs with Christ, if indeed we share in His sufferings in order that we may also share in His glory.

—Romans 8:15–17 (NIV)

# May 1

> Nevertheless I tell you the truth. It is to your advantage that I go away; for if I do not go away, the Helper will not come to you; but if I depart, I will send Him to you. And when He has come, He will convict the world of sin, and of righteousness, and of judgment: of sin, because they do not believe in Me; of righteousness, because I go to My Father and you see Me no more; of judgment, because the ruler of this world is judged.
> —John 16:7–11 (NKJV)

The Holy Spirit will convict us of sin. We can't run from the conviction, if we have accepted Jesus as our savior, and are now a child of God. Jesus said, "It is to your advantage that I go away," so that the Holy Spirit can be our comfort and guide. Letting go of what is hurting you, and accepting the Holy Spirit, will bring you peace.

I was out pulling weeds the other day, and it brought back a memory of when my gramma showed me how to pull weeds. She told me, "You need to pull them from the roots, or else they will grow back again." I had to work my little hands down to the dirt and pull it out by the roots.

Sin is like that. We need to get to the root of the problem and remove it. There are things that may grow from the root, but the actual root is the thing that needs to be removed. Alcoholism causes overwhelming consequences; but alcoholism is a result of an underlying issue. It could be insecurity, or pain, or anger issues. The evil desires of the heart will breed sin, and the actions of the sin will have repercussions. Greed and selfishness will breed anger, and bitterness—if not dealt with, it can sprout abuse, adultery, and thievery. By accepting the Holy Spirit's conviction and taking on the righteousness of Jesus, we remove the sinful issue, and the result will give glory to God.

Is it time for you to pull weeds? Have you checked your garden lately?

# May 2

> I still have many things to say to you, but you cannot bear *them* now. However, when He, the Spirit of truth, has come, He will guide you into all truth; for He will not speak on His own *authority,* but whatever He hears He will speak; and He will tell you things to come.
> —John 16:12-13 (NKJV)

The Holy Spirit will shed light to righteousness, showing us what is right to do. Sometimes we are unsure of what is right to do and need the Holy Spirit to give insight. Ask the Holy Spirit to guide you—He will reveal to you good judgment.

You will know your destiny by choosing the path He provides toward righteousness. He will remind you that the prince of this world now stands condemned. He has no power over you and your future. God does.

Jesus said it was better that He left this world and returned to heaven, because the Holy Spirit could come and be our comfort. (John 16:7 NIV) Why is it better? Because Jesus lived as a human while here on earth. His Spirit can be everywhere, and also live in you and help you live the life the way you should live it.

How does the Holy Spirit guide your life? When you choose to become a Christian, you will begin to recognize the voice of the Holy Spirit. And the more you walk with Him, the more you will recognize Him. You will know what you need to know at the very moment you need it. It may be a scripture from the Bible that comes to remembrance when it applies to the situation. It may be a Christian song that gives you hope in a moment when you needed it the most. It may be a message you heard in church that speaks to you in a personal way.

Are you spending time reading the Bible, listening to Christian songs, and sermons?

# May 3

> He will glorify Me, for He will take of what is Mine and declare *it* to you. All things that the Father has are Mine. Therefore I said that He will take of Mine and declare *it* to you.
>
> —John 16:14–15 (NKJV)

The Holy Spirit will glorify Jesus in all that He does. He will let us know that Jesus is the Truth; Jesus is the Life; Jesus is the only way to the Father—to salvation.

Our world needs followers of Jesus to take on the personality of the Holy Spirit, striving to point people in the direction of Jesus; therein glorifying Him in all we do. I would like to encourage you to pray and ask the Holy Spirit to convict, shed light, comfort and reveal the things of the Father to you; and be a witness to anyone you may be in conflict with, so that the Holy Spirit will move and orchestrate His incredible plan.

Many times, the Bible tells of examples where the Holy Spirit speaks and directs personally. One example in Acts 8:29, an angel of the Lord told Philip, "Go south to the road—the desert road—that goes down from Jerusalem to Gaza." That's very specific. The instructions were detailed and required perfect timing. God had a specific reason for Philip to go that direction at that very moment. On his way, Philip met an Ethiopian eunuch, an important official. The man had gone to Jerusalem to worship, and on his way home was sitting in his chariot reading the Book of Isaiah the prophet. He was reading the passage of scripture about Jesus, the Messiah. Acts 8:29 says, "The Spirit told Philip, 'Go to that chariot and stay near it.'" Philip ran up to the chariot and heard the man reading Isaiah the prophet. Philip began speaking with the man. The man asked for help understanding what the scripture was about. Philip began with that very passage of Scripture and told him the good news about Jesus. The eunuch asked if he could be baptized. So he was. He went on his way rejoicing.

As you listen to the Holy Spirit, you will be able to know what you need to know, go where you need to go, and say what you need to say. The more you listen, the more you will understand and know the voice of God. Has God told you to go? Has He told you to wait? Do you want to know what the Holy Spirit has for you? Are you ready to fill your mind and heart with the Word of God, praying for Him to reveal the meaning of what He has said, and His purpose in your life? Find a quiet place and listen. It's important to quiet your mind. You are most likely to hear the Holy Spirit when you are relaxed. If you are tense, nervous, upset, angry or fearful, the voices you hear in your mind in fear, or anger can be misconstrued, and not from the Holy Spirit. Read the scriptures and believe what He says, and allow Him to reveal the Truth, and remind you when you need to remember what He said. The more you read, the more the Holy Spirit will remind you of what you read.

_____

_____

_____

_____

# May 4

> On the last day, that great *day* of the feast, Jesus stood and cried out, saying, "If anyone thirsts, let him come to Me and drink. He who believes in Me, as the Scripture has said, out of his heart will flow rivers of living water." But this He spoke concerning the Spirit, whom those believing in Him would receive; for the Holy Spirit was not yet *given,* because Jesus was not yet glorified.
> —John 7:37–39 (NKJV)

You may have thought that the Holy Spirit is not for you. But as you can see here in scripture, Jesus said that those who believe in Jesus would receive the Holy Spirit. The Holy Spirit still works conviction in the hearts of those who accept Jesus; He still reveals truth and judgment; He still comforts you; He still glorifies Jesus; He still sheds light on the things of God. Just as the physical sun brings warmth and light to the earth, the Holy Spirit sheds the light of the gospel (the good news of forgiveness of sins) abroad in our hearts.

If we begin saying the Holy Spirit is not for today, we will then easily say that salvation through Jesus is not for today, and that our convictions are not of the Spirit, but of our own heart's ideas—which is full of evil—and ultimately become corrupt. Does that sound like the world you see around you? People make up their own rules based on their feelings, their own goodness, and agendas. They believe their way is actually good. Our righteousness is but only filthy rags compared to God's righteousness. The world's view of what is right is skewed by their own desires. Be reminded that we live in the days that Jesus spoke of, where the Holy Spirit was poured out. And He is very much alive and working in us today. Galatians 5:16 says, "So I say, walk by the Spirit, and you will not gratify the desires of the flesh." The Holy Spirit will give you the power to say *no* to sinful desires. Are you struggling with desires that are sinful? We will certainly struggle with unacceptable desires. But the key is that He will give us the power to refuse to *gratify* the desires. We have the power within us that gives us the strength to do what's right. As we choose to listen to the Holy Spirit and allow the power to work within us, we won't act them out—we will stop. Each time you obey His instruction, by doing what the Holy Spirit says to do, or refraining from doing something the Holy Spirit tells you not to do, you increase the ability to hear His voice, and obey Him further. Be led by the Holy Spirit.

# May 5

> Therefore, brothers and sisters, we have an obligation—but it is not to the flesh, to live according to it. For if you live according to the flesh, you will die; but if by the Spirit you put to death the misdeeds of the body, you will live.
> For those who are led by the Spirit of God are the children of God.
> —Romans 8:12–14 (NIV)

Have you accepted Jesus as your savior? Do you believe He is the Son of God? If so, then you are a child of God! That means you are blessed with every spiritual blessing; you are chosen; you are holy and without blame before God through His Son Jesus Christ. You are predestined to be adopted by and accepted by God; you are redeemed through Christ's blood; you are forgiven and will live forever in eternity with Him! Praise His Holy Name!

Rely on His power, not your own willpower. Start a new journey with Him as your guide and comforter.

My first instinct when I see a spider is to, first scream, and then stomp to kill it. Yes, to all those who believe that killing a bug is cruel, that is what I do. Why? The answer is fear. I am afraid of a tiny little spider. I'm afraid it might bite me. And when I had young children in the home, it was a protective mechanism built within a mother that impelled me to kill it. Okay, sometimes I would try and catch a bug and set it back outside out of empathy. But, most cases, it was stomped. When it comes to killing the misdeeds of the body, it calls for the same actions. First, acknowledging what it can do; and then getting rid of it. Kill it. Cut it off. The misdeeds of the body are a result of our acting out the sinful desires of the heart. Recognize that the sinful desires can lead to sin, and living according to what you feel is right by your own desires will lead to death. Whatever is causing you to think about sinful things needs to be killed. Know that the misdeeds can be as tiny as a spider. They creep in—cheating on your taxes, because you feel you shouldn't have to pay so much to the government; lying to a friend or spouse, because you are afraid of confrontation; keeping that extra item in your shopping bag that the cashier missed and didn't charge, because you feel you paid enough for what you got. No matter how small, no matter how immense, the misdeeds will lead to death. The answer to this dilemma of death? Be led by the Spirit. As a child of God, we have the Holy Spirit as a guide to reveal sin. And it is by His might that we can resist sinful desires.

# May 6

> And hope does not put us to shame, because God's love has been poured out into our hearts through the Holy Spirit, who has been given to us.
> —Romans 5:5 (NIV)

God poured out His love into our hearts by the Holy Spirit. With God's love in our hearts, we will be able to see how great His love truly is, and we will in turn be able to love others in this same unconditional way. The Holy Spirit keeps us moving forward with hope, believing for the good to come. The greatest hope is that we will spend eternity in heaven with Him. Sometimes, hopes on this earth are dashed. The hope of a marriage, hopes for children, or our dream-career, may not come into fruition. But the hope He gives will not disappoint us. *This* hope is in God. Plans and dreams will fall apart at times, but the hope that will last is built within us. God's love will not perish, and with His love, we have hope. Allow His hope to settle in your heart and say, "His hope is all I need."

# May 7

> You see, at just the right time, when we were still powerless, Christ died for the ungodly. Very rarely will anyone die for a righteous person, though for a good person someone might possibly dare to die. But God demonstrates His own love for us in this: While we were still sinners, Christ died for us.
> Since we have now been justified by His blood, how much more shall we be saved from God's wrath through Him! For if, while we were God's enemies, we were reconciled to Him through the death of His Son, how much more, having been reconciled, shall we be saved through His life! Not only is this so, but we also boast in God through our Lord Jesus Christ, through whom we have now received reconciliation.
> —Romans 5:6–11 (NIV)

It's easy to admire beauty. Not so easy to admire ugly. We look at a sweet little girl and think, "She deserves all the good things in this life." Sadly, when some people look at a troublesome child, they think they deserve what they get when they fail or fall.

Here's a story of two boys who were on the playground, both playing on a slide. The older boy was climbing up the slide and the younger boy slid down and hit the other boy, knocking him off. The younger boy apologized and hugged the older boy. Later, the rolls reversed. The younger boy started up the slide and the older boy was sliding down and hit the younger boy, knocking him off. The older boy said, "That's what he deserves." He deserved the pain? He fell just the same as the older boy did prior; it was still an accident; yet, one seemed justified. Haven't you heard that kind of story before? "He hit me first." "He's mean, so I don't feel sorry for him." "He isn't nice, so I don't want to share with him."

Even children have an instinct to love the lovable and repel the ugly. Justice. What's fair is fair. But that's not how God is. His love is unconditional. And His actions back up His love. The truth is, justice for us means punishment. We were ugly with sin. We deserved rejection, because we rejected Him first. We were all born with the sting of death that began in the Garden of Eden. But we escaped punishment when Jesus stood in the gap and took on our punishment. You may think you're not worthy of love. You will have days when you feel inadequate, insufficient, and even ugly when you look at yourself. But believe me when I say this, *God loves you anyway*! The Bible says when we were still sinners, Christ died for us. God demonstrated His own love for us when we were still ungodly—ugly. And now in this incredible exchange, you have received life in Jesus, and you are beautiful.

# May 8

> Therefore, since we have been justified through faith, we have peace with God through our Lord Jesus Christ, through whom we have gained access by faith into this grace in which we now stand. And we boast in the hope of the glory of God. Not only so, but we also glory in our sufferings, because we know that suffering produces perseverance; perseverance, character; and character, hope.
> —Romans 5:1–4 (NIV)

How are we justified? How do we come to that place of forgiveness, being made pure as though we had no sin? How can we be at peace, made right with God? Faith! By believing and trusting the Lord Jesus Christ with all of your heart. And by this faith we have access to God's grace—undeserved privilege.

Through our suffering, we do not give up, but instead persevere. And through perseverance, we build character—refined by the fire, generating hope. We can stand with confidence and joy as we look forward to sharing God's glory. His glorious love poured out on us gives hope that sustains us in our suffering. It can be taken by nothing, or anyone! Keep alert and watch what God will do next. Expect God's glory to shine, even in moments seemingly impossible to give Him glory. There may be times when you can't think of any path that could lead to good; and that no matter which way you go, it will only lead to pain. Persevere. Remain faithful. And your hope *will* be renewed.

# May 9

> Now there was a man in Jerusalem called Simeon, who was righteous and devout. He was waiting for the consolation of Israel, and the Holy Spirit was on him. It had been revealed to him by the Holy Spirit that he would not die before he had seen the Lord's Messiah. Moved by the Spirit, he went into the temple courts. When the parents brought in the child Jesus to do for him what the custom of the Law required, Simeon took him in his arms and praised God, saying:
>
> "Sovereign Lord, as You have promised, You may now dismiss Your servant in peace. For my eyes have seen Your salvation, which You have prepared in the sight of all nations: a light for revelation to the Gentiles, and the glory of Your people Israel."
>
> The child's father and mother marveled at what was said about Him. Then Simeon blessed them and said to Mary, His mother: "This child is destined to cause the falling and rising of many in Israel, and to be a sign that will be spoken against, so that the thoughts of many hearts will be revealed. And a sword will pierce your own soul too."
>
> —Luke 2:25–35 (NIV)

The Holy Spirit prompted Simeon to go to the temple. Because Simeon listened, he witnessed, and even took part in, the revelation of Jesus as being the Messiah—the most incredible moment in all history. Simeon was dedicated, and consecrated to the Lord. He listened, he heard, and he was moved. What if Simeon would have made excuses? Imagine if he ignored the nudge of the Holy Spirit and didn't go to the temple. If Simeon had not followed the moving of the Holy Spirit, and go to the temple at the very moment, he would have missed what he had been waiting for his entire life.

We, too, can see the hand of God work in our lives as we listen and submit to the Holy Spirit's direction. If you chose to ignore His prompting, chances are you are going to miss out on something big. Even if it does not make sense, if we obey His instruction, we will see the result of our obedience, just as it was for Peter and the others when Jesus told them to cast their nets on the other side. Simon Peter answered Jesus, "Master, we've worked hard all night and haven't caught anything. But because You say so, I will let down the nets." They were tired. They had already tried to catch fish. They had every reason to doubt Jesus. But, when they pulled in the nets from the other side, they had caught such a large number of fish that their nets began to break. (Luke 5:4–7)

You may be tired; you may have a good reason of your own not to do what is being asked of you, but listen and do it anyway and watch how God comes through for you. Be moved. Be ready for the Holy Spirit to reveal the promises of God for you and the wondrous plans for your life.

_____

_____

_____

_____

# May 10

> Jesus, full of the Holy Spirit, left the Jordan and was led by the Spirit into the wilderness, where for forty days He was tempted by the devil. He ate nothing during those days, and at the end of them He was hungry. Jesus returned to Galilee in the power of the Spirit, and news about Him spread through the whole countryside.
> —Luke 4:1–2, 14 (NIV)

Jesus was human. He was full of the Holy Spirit. And He was led by the Holy Spirit. Jesus was tempted by Satan for forty days! Jesus was led by the Spirit to go into the desert; He was full of the Holy Spirit and combatted the temptations with scripture. He returned still in the power of the Spirit.

You will have your wilderness experiences. You might be doing exactly what you are supposed to be doing. You may be fasting; you might be serving in ministry. No matter where you are or what you do, you *will* face temptation. You can hide yourself away where no one follows, where you can't see anything that is unholy, and surround yourself with all good things, but you will still have your mind to content with. Satan may even use what appears to be right and good, but twist it to trip you up. When those thoughts are placed in your mind, reject them and replace those thoughts with truths from the scripture. Say it out loud if you need to. Acknowledge that the Word *is* Jesus. He is the one who will destroy the wicked ways of the enemy. The Holy Spirit, which lives within you, can help bring to memory the Word to overpower the temptations. And then, when you walk out of that desert place, you will be able to rejoice that you, too, remain in the power of the Spirit, and not the power of sin.

# May 11

> On one occasion, while He was eating with them, He gave them this command: "Do not leave Jerusalem, but wait for the gift My Father promised, which you have heard Me speak about. For John baptized with water, but in a few days you will be baptized with the Holy Spirit."
>
> Then they gathered around Him and asked Him, "Lord, are You at this time going to restore the kingdom to Israel?"
>
> He said to them: "It is not for you to know the times or dates the Father has set by His own authority. But you will receive power when the Holy Spirit comes on you; and you will be My witnesses in Jerusalem, and in all Judea and Samaria, and to the ends of the earth." After He said this, He was taken up before their very eyes, and a cloud hid Him from their sight.
>
> —Acts 1:4–9 (NIV)

What a sight to see! Jesus being taken up into heaven right before them! With such an incredible display of His glory, their faith must have increased immensely that day. Then, they waited.

Wait. Wait for the Holy Spirit and be patient—then you will receive power; you will be Jesus' witnesses. When trouble comes, wait and watch for the Holy Spirit to lead you. Too many times, we act before we should. Excitement can do that, and so can the need to be in control. When I hear of a great plan, I become excited and want to start on the plan immediately. I begin by planning the details, thinking it through, and then placing it into action. I also like to be in control. That way I know things will be done the way I want them to be done. However, I realize when someone else can do a better job than I can, it's wise to submit to their way of doing it—allowing them to be in control. Easy? Not at all. But, wise, nonetheless. God knows the best way of doing things, so it is wise to submit to Him in all things. When you wait on the Holy Spirit, the power you need to overcome a situation will far outdo what you could have done on your own. And when you allow the Holy Spirit to work, Jesus will receive the glory. You will be able to share a testimony of how God moved in a situation you needed Him most. You will be able to tell others of miracles, or of His grace. So, wait. Listen to the plan. Then, go.

_____

_____

_____

_____

# May 12

> Then Peter stood up with the Eleven, raised his voice and addressed the crowd: "Fellow Jews and all of you who live in Jerusalem, let me explain this to you; listen carefully to what I say. These people are not drunk, as you suppose. It's only nine in the morning! No, this is what was spoken by the prophet Joel:
> 'In the last days, God says, I will pour out My Spirit on all people. Your sons and daughters will prophesy, your young men will see visions, your old men will dream dreams. Even on My servants, both men and women, I will pour out My Spirit in those days, and they will prophesy. I will show wonders in the heavens above and signs on the earth below, blood and fire and billows of smoke. The sun will be turned to darkness and the moon to blood before the coming of the great and glorious day of the Lord. And everyone who calls on the name of the Lord will be saved.'"
> —Acts 2:14–21 (NIV)

The book of Acts is full of stories of how the Holy Spirit was poured out. This was the first moment that the Holy Spirit was poured out on the apostles. Peter addressed the crowd—he was bold and told the people that the outpouring of God's Spirit that was once prophesied, was now coming true. Remember Peter? He's notorious for denying Jesus in the last days of Jesus' life here on earth. He was eager to follow Jesus from the beginning. Peter met Jesus while was fishing at Lake Galilee. Jesus called them to follow Him. Peter and his brother didn't ask questions, but simply dropped their nets and followed. (Matthew 14:18) Peter later answered the question as to who Jesus was, saying, "You're the Christ, the Messiah, the Son of the living God." Jesus commended Peter, saying, "You didn't get that answer out of books or from teachers. My Father in heaven, God Himself, let you in on this secret of who I really am. And now I'm going to tell you who you are, *really* are. You are Peter, a rock. This is the rock on which I will put together My church, a church so expansive with energy that not even the gates of hell will be able to keep it out." (Matthew 16:16-18 MSG) Yet, only a few days later and Peter messed up again. Peter protested to the plan that Jesus would suffer and be killed. So, Jesus told him, "Get away from me, Satan! You are a dangerous trap to me. You are seeing things merely from a human point of view, not from God's." (Matthew 16:23 NLT) Peter's faith was strong—He knew who Jesus truly was. He even walked on water when Jesus called him out of the boat! But again, Peter did sink in the water when he took his eyes off Jesus and onto the storm around him. He was the one who drew a sword against the mob when Jesus was about to be taken away by soldiers—he cut off the ear of the high priest's servant—then, Jesus told him to put away his sword.

Peter eagerly followed Jesus. He listened to God and was told who Jesus really was. He walked on water. He defended Jesus with his sword. But, like us all, he failed many times. His excitement caused him to act too quickly. His own pride got in the way of God's plan. His fear caused him to sink and ultimately deny knowing Jesus. It seemed over. Jesus was dead. Peter must have felt a failure and unworthy to be the one Jesus would build His church upon.

But then, one day—Jesus, resurrected from the dead, was walking on the beach by the Sea of Galilee. Yes, right back where Jesus found Peter the day they met. Peter was with the other disciples, back to the old fisherman life he once knew, forgetting the commission that he was called to. When the disciples recognized that it was Jesus, Peter jumped out of the boat and swam to Jesus. Jesus had a personal conversation with Peter and made sure Peter knew what he was called to do. "Feed my sheep." "Follow Me.". (John 21) Redeemed. Peter was reinstated.

Now, we see Peter is the first to proclaim the Gospel on the day of Pentecost. Peter was also the first to take the Gospel to the Gentiles (Acts 10:1-48). In a sense, Peter was the rock "foundation" of the church. Peter was called "rock" because God the Father gave Peter the knowledge of whom Jesus was. Jesus knew that it would be one of the twelve that would lead His church and it was revealed to Jesus by His heavenly Father that it would be Peter.

We live in that era today. I hope that excites you as much as it does me. We are part of an amazing prophesy—God's plan in action. Let God be present in your life and heart as He pours out His Spirit upon you. But, remember, you're not in the driver's seat. God decides what will happen, even when it may be a way you don't agree with. Trust Him. Feed His sheep. Follow Him.

# May 13

> Now Stephen, a man full of God's grace and power, performed great wonders and signs among the people. Opposition arose, however, from members of the Synagogue of the Freedmen (as it was called)—Jews of Cyrene and Alexandria as well as the provinces of Cilicia and Asia—who began to argue with Stephen. But they could not stand up against the wisdom the Spirit gave him as he spoke.
>
> —Acts 6:8–10 (NIV)

Don't be afraid when you face opposition. Speak as the Holy Spirit gives you the words to say. It may seem that Stephen failed in his argument as he was ultimately stoned to death by the council members (Acts 7:59). But even death has no stand against God's power. Stephen knew that, even though he was going to die, he was about to see God face to face. He called out, "Lord Jesus, please welcome me!" Times may be difficult, but you are not failing. "Greater is He that is in you, than he that is in the world." (1 John 4:4) The world cannot stand up against the Spirit and win. On that final day, we will have won, because Jesus already conquered the enemy.

_____
_____
_____
_____

# May 14

> Meanwhile, Saul was still breathing out murderous threats against the Lord's disciples. He went to the high priest and asked him for letters to the synagogues in Damascus, so that if he found any there who belonged to the Way, whether men or women, he might take them as prisoners to Jerusalem. As he neared Damascus on his journey, suddenly a light from heaven flashed around him. He fell to the ground and heard a voice say to him, "Saul, Saul, why do you persecute Me?"
> "Who are You, Lord?" Saul asked.
> "I am Jesus, whom you are persecuting," He replied. "Now get up and go into the city, and you will be told what you must do."
> —Acts 9:1–6 (NIV)

Paul planned to kill Christians. He was a man who persecuted, imprisoned and condoned the killing of Christians. Then he encountered Jesus. He recognized the voice to be the Lord. He addressed Him as "Lord". But he didn't realize he was speaking to Jesus. The men traveling with Saul were speechless. They heard the Lord's voice, but didn't see anything. For three days Paul was blind, and did not eat or drink anything. Ananias met him in Damascus and placed his hands on Saul. He said, "Brother Saul, the Lord—Jesus, who appeared to you on the road as you were coming here—has sent me so that you may see again and be filled with the Holy Spirit." (Acts 9:17) Immediately, Saul could see again. He got up and was baptized.

Saul was changed that day. His entire belief system changed. Everything Paul stood for, he now realized was wrong! He had to start all over again—this time, filled with the Holy Spirit, healed, baptized, he would be God's instrument to spread the gospel.

God can transform your life, and this very day can be your New Year's Day—a brand new "you" with a new outlook on life. Your view will change; and you may experience a spiritual blindness to all you once knew to be a reality. Your eyes will be open by God to a new mission and purpose. Transformation may be painful—you may go through a period of time when you are being reformed, like pottery in the fire. But, if you allow this transformation to take place, God can make a difference in you, and in the world around you.

# May 15

> May the God of hope fill you with all joy and peace as you trust in Him, so that you may overflow with hope by the power of the Holy Spirit.
> —Romans 15:13 (NIV)

Live. Really live! There is hope; there is joy and peace, when you trust in Him. The power so great, that it raised Jesus from the dead, is the same powerful Spirit living in you! Incredible, right? No matter the circumstances you may experience, His power can bring you hope.

# May 16

> Then Peter said, "Surely no one can stand in the way of their being baptized with water. They have received the Holy Spirit just as we have." So he ordered that they be baptized in the name of Jesus Christ. Then they asked Peter to stay with them for a few days.
> —Acts 10:47–48 (NIV)

Peter was speaking to the crowds and as he was still speaking, the Holy Spirit came on all who were hearing the message. Many of the believers who had come with Peter were astonished that the gift of the Holy Spirit had been poured out even on Gentiles. If you are not Jewish, then you are Gentile. I once wondered if any of the promises were really for me, because I'm not Jewish. I read so much of the old stories about the children of Israel and the promises of God. But I finally came to realize that all the promises that were once only for the children of Israel, were now made to the rest of the world. It happened when God adopted us into His family. This scripture is an example of one of God's promises being for all who believe. No matter who you are, if you believe in Jesus, His Holy Spirit is a gift for you. All that God offers can be poured out to you because you belong to Him. No one can deny you the gift of life that God has promised you.

# May 17

> Jesus replied, "Anyone who loves Me will obey My teaching. My Father will love them, and We will come to them and make Our home with them. Anyone who does not love Me will not obey My teaching. These words you hear are not My own; they belong to the Father who sent Me.
>
> All this I have spoken while still with you. But the Advocate, the Holy Spirit, whom the Father will send in My Name, will teach you all things and will remind you of everything I have said to you. Peace I leave with you; My peace I give you. I do not give to you as the world gives. Do not let your hearts be troubled and do not be afraid.
>
> —John 14:23–27 (NIV)

Imagine the scene. Jesus has just informed the disciples that He was going to die soon, and He spent the time to comfort them, encourage them, and give them hope and peace. He told them about the Father's house with many rooms; and that He was going to prepare a place for them also. He promised to return and take them back to be with Him.

My brother Gary was diagnosed with lung cancer just before Christmas. He knew this would be terrible news to us, his family who loved him. So he waited to tell the family until after the New Year.

In the last five months of his life he took the time to comfort his family. His life was in a storm, but he took the time to help calm *our* hearts. He spoke of the Lord and how he was going to be better off than any of us who would still be here so there was no reason to cry. He did not ask for anything from us. His last wishes were all based on how it would help us after he was gone. The promises he asked of us were to remember to take care of his wife, Ruthie, and our mom, and to remember how to survive and pull together when times would be hard.

Saying good-bye felt unbearable, and it became obvious that the loss of my brother was to be a burden each of us would bear no matter how much we didn't want to accept it.

God was with Gary to the very last breath. God was with each one of us through each month, each day, and each hour and down to the last minute. God is with you through your tragedies of life and will stand by you just the same.

Our Father has the power to control the sun and the moon. He is able to save you through the fire with the power of His hand and with just one word. Your hope is in Him alone. He has prepared a place for each of us in heaven. As Jesus promised, He and the Father will love you, and come and live with you. Whatever you face in your life, remember these Words that Jesus has spoken to encourage you.

# May 18

> Yet I have written you quite boldly on some points to remind you of them again, because of the grace God gave me to be a minister of Christ Jesus to the Gentiles. He gave me the priestly duty of proclaiming the gospel of God, so that the Gentiles might become an offering acceptable to God, sanctified by the Holy Spirit.
> Therefore I glory in Christ Jesus in my service to God. I will not venture to speak of anything except what Christ has accomplished through me in leading the Gentiles to obey God by what I have said and done—by the power of signs and wonders, through the power of the Spirit of God. So from Jerusalem all the way around to Illyricum, I have fully proclaimed the gospel of Christ.
> —Romans 15:15–19 (NIV)

Paul made it a point to speak of the things Christ accomplished through him. He understood God's grace; he realized his past was not something to boast about—whether good or bad; and he kept looking forward to the things God had prepared for him in glory.

How about you? Do you have an honorable past? Or do you have a past that you would rather not speak of? Once you have spoken honestly with the Lord about the past failures, you can leave it in the past. Rejoice in the new future that can be full of God's plan. You are forgiven. And no matter how much of a mess you may feel you have made of your life, God can use it for good. He can take broken, and make it beautiful.

And then there are those who may feel as if the best of life is behind you, and that you could never match what you've accomplished in the past. Let Christ accomplish things through you as you allow Him to work in you and lead you to new ventures. Press forward with perseverance and determination. Share your story of how God has made a difference in your life. Tell someone what He has done for you. Use those experiences as encouragement and faith to move forward, knowing that if He did it then, He will do it again. You can remember those experiences to draw faith from as well. You can make a difference in someone else's life by sharing what you have experienced yourself.

---
---
---
---

# May 19

> So I say, walk by the Spirit, and you will not gratify the desires of the flesh. For the flesh desires what is contrary to the Spirit, and the Spirit what is contrary to the flesh. They are in conflict with each other, so that you are not to do whatever you want. But if you are led by the Spirit, you are not under the law.
>
> But the fruit of the Spirit is love, joy, peace, forbearance, kindness, goodness, faithfulness, gentleness and self-control. Against such things there is no law. Those who belong to Christ Jesus have crucified the flesh with its passions and desires. Since we live by the Spirit, let us keep in step with the Spirit.
> —Galatians 5:16–18 and 22–25 (NIV)

When you take a walk, do you notice your surroundings? Do you notice the smell of fresh flowers in someone's garden or fruit trees, maybe pine or oak? Maybe you hear the birds or the neighbor's dog barking as you pass by. Your senses are alert, aren't they? The same is true when you walk in the Spirit. If you allow your senses to be alert to the spiritual things of God, your desires will mirror that of God's desires. You will be able to see with eyes of love, joy, peace—as you see someone in need, you will care, rather than turn the other way. You will sense gentleness and self-control when faced with difficult situations and decisions. Ask the Lord today to strengthen your walk with Him, to show you the desires of His heart.

As you walk with the Lord, moved and motivated by His Spirit, you will escape the sting of death and will be given a full, satisfying life from the Spirit.

Too many people think that a satisfying life comes from having stuff. Having more things is the desire of the flesh. Not that having things is wrong, but the lie that the things will bring happiness, and satisfaction, is the downfall. Compulsions of selfishness will destroy your contentment. Living in the Spirit needs to be a permanent, consistent determination in your own heart. You cannot live at times one way and at times another way according to how you feel on any given day.

We will need to apply the ways of the Spirit in every detail of our lives. That means we will not compare ourselves with each other as if one of us were better and another worse. When we live by the Spirit, we find peace within ourselves and with others.

# May 20

> Do not quench the Spirit.
> —1 Thessalonians 5:19 (NIV)

To quench something is to extinguish or snuff out. Imagine a fire in a camping site, and someone comes along and snuffs it out. The fire was intended for your light so that you could see at night, and for warmth, and protection from the wild animals. This uncaring person has taken that away from you.

I don't like to admit that I am unable to do something. I don't like to admit I'm wrong. I begin to make excuses. But the fact is, I'm guilty and I need help. I need the fire. Jesus knew we would need the Holy Spirit. Let the Holy Spirit work in you, and for the glory of Jesus; let's not prevent the development and workings of the Holy Spirit. We need Him.

# May 21

> I pray that out of His glorious riches He may strengthen you with power through His Spirit in your inner being, so that Christ may dwell in your hearts through faith. And I pray that you, being rooted and established in love, may have power, together with all the Lord's holy people, to grasp how wide and long and high and deep is the love of Christ, and to know this love that surpasses knowledge—that you may be filled to the measure of all the fullness of God.
> —Ephesians 3:16–19 (NIV)

By the Spirit, your inner self is strengthened. In the very heart of your soul, resides our Lord. In moments of peace, let your heart be strengthened, so that when times of trouble come, you will be able to dig deep within your soul and find God. It is not of yourself and not of your own strength, but from the glories of heaven, which is implanted by the incredible, unexplainable love of God.

# May 22

> And pray in the Spirit on all occasions with all kinds of prayers and requests. With this in mind, be alert and always keep on praying for all the Lord's people.
> —Ephesians 6:18 (NIV)

This is one area of multi-tasking that I highly recommend. In all you do, let your spirit continue to pray and stay in touch with the Spirit of God. Have you ever been passionate about something? I'm sure you have. Maybe a new way of healthy eating, or maybe you have been blessed with a new grandchild. Throughout the day, you are reminded of this new *something*. Whatever the subject, you can associate it with your passion. This is how passion works with the Spirit. Each moment, and each conversation, always considering what that means to your spiritual walk, and so praying accordingly.

# May 23

> For who knows a person's thoughts except their own spirit within them? In the same way no one knows the thoughts of God except the Spirit of God. What we have received is not the spirit of the world, but the Spirit who is from God, so that we may understand what God has freely given us. This is what we speak, not in words taught us by human wisdom but in words taught by the Spirit, explaining spiritual realities with Spirit-taught words. The person without the Spirit does not accept the things that come from the Spirit of God but considers them foolishness, and cannot understand them because they are discerned only through the Spirit. The person with the Spirit makes judgments about all things, but such a person is not subject to merely human judgments, for, "Who has known the mind of the Lord so as to instruct him?" But we have the mind of Christ.
>
> —1 Corinthians 2:11–16 (NIV)

Without the Spirit, you will be confused, and not able to understand the things of the Spirit. When God shows you something, you are never going to be confused. He speaks so that you will be able to understand. He is a loving God, and can cause you to understand His instruction. God's wisdom is revealed by the Spirit. The deep things of God is known by the Spirit of God and we have received His Spirit to understand what God has given and is doing. We speak what we learn from God's Spirit; God opens up the doors to communication and His plan of salvation and life—we can communicate with God spirit to Spirit!

Isaiah asked the question, "Who has known the mind of the Lord so as to instruct Him?" (Isaiah 40:13) We can't possibly instruct God as to how He should do things. His ideas are high above our own. And we have the Spirit living in us—the one who knows the deepest thoughts of God. I think it wise to simply trust that He knows.

# May 24

> When you send Your Spirit, they are created, and You renew the face of the ground.
> —Psalm 104:30 (NIV)

The Sprit (the breath of God) brings life to all creation. With one breath, everything can change. With one breath, He can destroy the enemy. Another breath, He can give the first breath to a newborn baby. His breath can whisper peace in your heart; His breath can move mountains! When God's Spirit is present in our circumstances, what once had no life, springs to life; what once was desolate is now blooming. A dry and thirsty land is quenched. Are you empty? Do you need life to be restored? Call out to God and His Spirit upon you will change everything. Don't be mistaken by that statement. Your circumstances may or may not change; but, your spirit certainly will! His breath can calm you in any storm. Some things will need to be destroyed—the enemy. Some things may need to be removed—like the mountains. Some things may need to be revived—like a new life. Believe He has the power to do all that needs to be done in your life.

# May 25

> Therefore put on the full armor of God, so that when the day of evil comes, you may be able to stand your ground, and after you have done everything, to stand.
> —Ephesians 6:13 (NIV)

There was a time that I felt I couldn't even stand. I had given up the will to fight. I couldn't bear to think of putting on any armor and pressing on. That was when this scripture rang loud in my heart. I had put on the armor, I thought. And I fought hard. "I can do this," I told myself. I had done everything I could; and I was spent. I had nothing left to fight with. I felt defeated. Then, a friend and sister in the Lord handed a note with this verse from Ephesians and a note saying, "the battle is not our own, but the Lord's" That is how the Holy Spirit works. That was my reminder. It was Jesus and His power that I was to put on. In every part of the armor, it speaks to Jesus. He is the armor! The battle was not mine. I could stand and let the Lord fight this battle for me!

That is why you need to put on God's full armor. You will be able to stand strong. Remember every battle we win is a result of God's hand. It is not of our own strength, nor our ability, but the armor itself, being God and all that He brings to the battlefield. So, stand behind that great and strong shield that He holds up for you, and let Him fight for you. Stand bold. Stand brave. Don't give up!

_____
_____
_____
_____

# May 26

> Do not let your hearts be troubled. You believe in God; believe also in Me. My Father's house has many rooms; if that were not so, would I have told you that I am going there to prepare a place for you?
> —John 14:1–2 (NIV)

Jesus keeps His word. If He told us there will be a place for us, then believe it. Jesus wants you to know that He has prepared a place for you.

I have often thought of what my custom-built home would look like and even jot down some thoughts, specs, plans, dreams. Jesus has created the perfect custom-built home in heaven. Jesus is able to build a home far more elaborate than I can ever dream of. How amazing do you think that home will be? Now, I know we are not to place our materialistic ideas on the reality or dreams of what heaven will look like. That's not what I'm trying to point out here. What I do say is this: No matter how much you build or dream or plan here on earth, His Spirit working in us can do so much more than we can ask for; and heaven will be far better than we can imagine!

> With God's power working in us, God can do much, much more than anything we can ask or imagine. To Him be glory in the church and in Christ Jesus for all time, forever and ever. Amen.
> —Ephesians 3:20–21 (NCV)

# May 27

> If the world hates you, keep in mind that it hated Me first. If you belonged to the world, it would love you as its own. As it is, you do not belong to the world, but I have chosen you out of the world. That is why the world hates you.
>
> —John 15:18–19 (NIV)

You will come to know that, as you make choices to do right by God's standards, others may oppose you. Even those closest to you, if they don't believe and follow the Lord, may turn their back on you—because of their own guilt, or shame, or for selfish reasons. Stay strong. Jesus knows and He understands what you're going through. He endured the same hateful treatment.

_____
_____
_____
_____

# May 28

> After Jesus said this, He looked toward heaven and prayed:
>
> "Father, the hour has come. Glorify Your Son, that Your Son may glorify You. For You granted Him authority over all people that He might give eternal life to all those You have given Him. Now this is eternal life: that they know You, the only true God, and Jesus Christ, whom You have sent. I have brought You glory on earth by finishing the work You gave Me to do. And now, Father, glorify Me in Your presence with the glory I had with You before the world began."
> —John 17:1–5 (NIV)

There they were—God, the Trinity—the Father, the Son and the Holy Spirit, before the world began. Knowing the sacrifice it would mean, they created us, "Let Us make man in Our own image," Jesus knew He would need to leave the glory He had with the Father in heaven and come to earth to die a human death, and conquer sin and death so that He could give us eternal life. They knew man would sin. They knew there would be sacrifice.

Jesus, in His prayer, reminds us that eternal life is to know the Father, who is the only true God, and Jesus Christ. He spoke of Himself in third person. I think He may have been showing us a picture of what once was, and what was about to happen; that Jesus being the Son of God, and who was once in heaven with the Father; and becoming human, was sent to earth to save man; and now was taking that step from humanity back into glory. He was in glory; He became human; He was ready to return to the Father. It all came down to that moment—when everything was about to change.

He finished the Work—now we can live!

# May 29

> "I have revealed You to those whom You gave me out of the world. They were Yours; You gave them to Me and they have obeyed Your word. Now they know that everything You have given Me comes from You. For I gave them the words You gave Me and they accepted them. They knew with certainty that I came from You, and they believed that You sent Me. I pray for them. I am not praying for the world, but for those You have given Me, for they are Yours. All I have is Yours, and all You have is Mine. And glory has come to Me through them. I will remain in the world no longer, but they are still in the world, and I am coming to You. Holy Father, protect them by the power of Your Name, the Name you gave Me, so that they may be one as We are one. While I was with them, I protected them and kept them safe by that Name you gave Me. None has been lost except the one doomed to destruction so that Scripture would be fulfilled."
>
> —John 17:6–12 (NIV)

Jesus' prayer that day was for all who accept Jesus, and that includes us today. Tears come to my eyes when I realize Jesus prayed to the Father for us. His concern was for us—the ones who would have to remain in this world. He cares about us. "Protect them," He asked. He knows this world is harsh; He knows we will need God to protect us by the power of His Name. Know that Jesus continues to intercede for you today.

> Who then is the one who condemns? No one. Christ Jesus who died—more than that, who was raised to life—is at the right hand of God and is also interceding for us.
>
> —Romans 8:34 (NIV)

# May 30

"My prayer is not for them alone. I pray also for those who will believe in Me through their message, that all of them may be one, Father, just as You are in Me and I am in You. May they also be in Us so that the world may believe that You have sent Me. I have given them the glory that You gave Me, that they may be one as We are one—I in them and You in Me—so that they may be brought to complete unity. Then the world will know that You sent Me and have loved them even as You have loved Me.

Father, I want those You have given Me to be with Me where I am, and to see My glory, the glory You have given Me because You loved Me before the creation of the world.

Righteous Father, though the world does not know You, I know You, and they know that You have sent Me. I have made You known to them, and will continue to make You known in order that the love You have for Me may be in them and that I myself may be in them."
—John 17:20–26 (NIV)

These last few words of Jesus' prayer tells us every believer throughout time was included in that prayer. Know that the same love that the Father has for His Son, He has for you. Jesus wants you to be with Him—in His glory. He wants us to persevere so that we can see His glory and be with Him in heaven. Be brave—for the Son of God and the love of the Father lives in you.

# May 31

Have you ever been lost while driving, and afraid to get out of the car to ask for directions? Imagine being lost and your phone won't connect to make a call or even navigate for you. Your only hope is to continue driving until you see a familiar landmark. Then, when you think it couldn't get any worse, you're stopped by a train and the railroad crossings hold you hostage as you wait. Your mind begins to carry you away, thinking, "What if someone comes up to my car? How will I escape?" Fear could overtake you. Then, you look up and someone you know is knocking on your window. You finally take a deep breath and sigh in relief as you explain your predicament. Your friend graciously offers to ride with you to navigate your way home, as his friend in their car follows you. Safe, comforted, protected, guided.

I know this probably isn't a scenario that could easily happen to you. But this gives a good picture of how the Holy Spirit works in your life. You're lost, scared, and all alone; and He comes alongside you, comforting you, protecting you, and guiding you home. You're safe with Him.

_____
_____
_____
_____

# June

We also have joy with our troubles, because we know that these troubles produce patience. And patience produces character, and character produces hope.
—Romans 5:3–4 (ESV)

# Joy in the Mourning

> Why are you cast down, O my soul,
> and why are you in turmoil within me?
> Hope in God; for I shall again praise him,
> my salvation and my God.
> —Psalm 43:5 (ESV)

# June 1

> For those God foreknew He also predestined to be conformed to the image of His Son, that He might be the firstborn among many brothers and sisters. And those He predestined, He also called; those He called, He also justified; those He justified, He also glorified.
> —Romans 8:29–30 (NIV)

Before the creation, God knew the beauty and the consequences of creating people. He knew we would be added to His family as His children.

All that has happened before and since that first moment when God created Adam and Eve, is under God's control— even though it may not seem so at times. Since God controls everything, and you are His child, and He loves you, then be sure that God will take care of the details of your life.

Consider a river—at times the current is rough and the river runs rapid; other times it is so serene you can hardly see the current of the water moving by ever so slowly. If you were to step out into the waters until you can no longer touch the river bottom, the current could carry you wherever it chooses. You can swim to the side, stop and take notice along the shores if you like. But the river flows on. Living life knowing God is in control allows you to live in peace. You will not, however, be at peace if you are constantly fighting the current.

As you glide with the current of life that God has predestined, gently moving in the direction God creates for you, life becomes a joy and exciting; sometimes hard work is needed, but you will feel exuberated when you hit your mark!

God has the power, wisdom, and love to help you. Whether you can see the current or not, He is moving on your behalf providing new opportunities and endless possibilities, which can give you hope for a promising eternal future.

# June 2

> The LORD reached down from above and took me; He pulled me from the deep water.
> —Psalm 18:16 (NCV)

Pain. It causes a ripple effect. Through pain, you are made stronger. From pain, you experience brokenness. Before you are aware, depression can set in. Depression can fall so deeply that you begin to lose yourself in a dark place of hopelessness and fear; thoughts of despair come like waves crashing all around you, as you begin to sink in deep waters.

No one wants to feel pain. Bad news comes, and it hurts. We fret over it; we struggle to understand it, or even know what to do about it. It becomes difficult to see anything but that what we face. Thoughts begin to shout, "God will not save me; I'm too far gone. I don't deserve His help." I've been there. Though it's hard to believe I thought those things, I did at one point. I felt as though I had questioned God just one too many times. I can testify that God still loves you and wants to lift you up. Open your eyes and look up. Your God is reaching for you to lift you out of these deep waters. God has a wonderful plan, and He will equip your spirit so that you will be able to endure the pain through His strong arms and grace.

# June 3

> Therefore, there is now no condemnation for those who are in Christ Jesus, because through Christ Jesus the law of the Spirit who gives life has set you free from the law of sin and death.
> —Romans 8:1–2 (NIV)

The black cloud of sin no longer hangs over us. The power of sin is overcome by the power of the Spirit through Jesus Christ. Like a strong wind, Jesus has magnificently cleared the skies, freeing us from the fateful lifetime of brutal tyranny at the hands of sin and death. Watch the sky the next time there is a storm. Watch how the wind moves the clouds. Can you see the wind? No. You can only feel it, and see what it does to the objects in its path. Just as the wind moves the clouds, God's Spirit moves and removed the cloud of sin. And just as the wind clears the clouds from the sky and reveals the sun, God's Spirit gives life—a bright future in God's kingdom.

# June 4

> For what the law was powerless to do because it was weakened by the flesh, God did by sending His own Son in the likeness of sinful flesh to be a sin offering. And so He condemned sin in the flesh, in order that the righteous requirement of the law might be fully met in us, who do not live according to the flesh but according to the Spirit.
>
> —Romans 8:3–4 (NIV)

A deep wound cannot be healed with a band-aide. A wound so deep needs great medical attention. Just the same, no sacrifice—no "fix" —man could offer would be enough to remedy sin. Only the Son of God could remove the sting of sin and death by sacrificing His own life. Once and for all, what was needed to save us is accomplished in Jesus.

    I like to fix things. I like to be self-sufficient. But, this is one area I will not be able to resolve on my own. No matter how hard I try to be right, I will never be good enough to pay the debt of sin. And God knew this to be true—only the justified, pure and righteous soul can enter into heaven. And Jesus made us just that—perfect through His sacrifice.

_____
_____
_____
_____

# June 5

> Those who live according to the flesh have their minds set on what the flesh desires; but those who live in accordance with the Spirit have their minds set on what the Spirit desires. The mind governed by the flesh is death, but the mind governed by the Spirit is life and peace. The mind governed by the flesh is hostile to God; it does not submit to God's law, nor can it do so. Those who are in the realm of the flesh cannot please God.
> —Romans 8:5–8 (NIV)

We all want to know how to live the abundant life. And as we read here, we cannot please God if we are focusing on what we want—things to satisfy our flesh—material things. Choices we make determine if we are focusing on self, or focusing on God. A new and unconquerable principal of life and holiness is implanted in us by God! Yes, the living and breathing, awe-inspiring God *is* life and peace.

You will be limited in your own strength. But when you trust in God, your life mirrors God's strength and not your own. And how will you know the strength of God, unless your own strength is tested and found to be weak. Set your mind on the things that the Spirit desires—things that will last forever. Trusting in, believing in, and counting on His way of life will bring peace. With peace, life is good no matter the material means.

# June 6

> You, however, are not in the realm of the flesh but are in the realm of the Spirit, if indeed the Spirit of God lives in you. And if anyone does not have the Spirit of Christ, they do not belong to Christ. But if Christ is in you, then even though your body is subject to death because of sin, the Spirit gives life because of righteousness. And if the Spirit of Him who raised Jesus from the dead is living in you, He who raised Christ from the dead will also give life to your mortal bodies because of His Spirit who lives in you.
>
> —Romans 8:9–11 (NIV)

Have you ever moved in and lived with a relative, or someone move in to live with you? If you have, I'm sure you found out more about that person than you had known before. Some things you may not have wanted to know. There's no escaping their presence, so best be on your guard to show hospitality and kindness as you co-mingle. This is how our God is. He wants to take up residence in your life. You will see Him daily, and you will be able to see things on His terms—knowing this same God who raised Jesus from the dead is the same God who has moved into your life. He will do the same for you, by pointing you in the way of righteousness, and bringing you back to life. Our bodies may be failing, but our spirits are very much alive.

# June 7

> Therefore, brothers and sisters, we have an obligation—but it is not to the flesh, to live according to it. For if you live according to the flesh, you will die; but if by the Spirit you put to death the misdeeds of the body, you will live.
> For those who are led by the Spirit of God are the children of God.
> —Romans 8:12–14 (NIV)

God's Spirit calls to you—a beckon to come with Him and see His heart, so that you will respond and find life according to what He has given you. Set aside the things of the world, which shall perish, and follow the Spirit of God, which is eternal.

"That's not easy," you might say. And you're right. Crucifying the flesh (putting to death the misdeeds of the body) is not a quick task. It's a constant, every-day, battle between flesh and spirit. Our body wants more for itself—more money, bigger houses, better cars, more stuff; but the spirit wants more of what God has to offer—more peace, grace, mercy, hope, godly wisdom and so much more. When you give up the greediness of the flesh, you will find what God has is much better and then will multiply as He works *through* you. Does that mean you should sell your home, your car and all you have and live with nothing material? Of course not! But, you need to be careful not to place too much value on these things that they ultimately get in the way of what God wants for you.

# June 8

> The Spirit you received does not make you slaves, so that you live in fear again; rather, the Spirit you received brought about your adoption to sonship. And by Him we cry, *"Abba,* Father." The Spirit Himself testifies with our spirit that we are God's children. Now if we are children, then we are heirs—heirs of God and co-heirs with Christ, if indeed we share in His sufferings in order that we may also share in His glory.
> —Romans 8:15–17 (NIV)

God's Spirit connects with our spirit and confirms who we really are. Our new relationship is with God, as His sons and daughters—co-heirs with Christ. If we go through hard times with Jesus by our side, know that we will certainly share in His glory.

Through the Holy Spirit, we cry out, "Father, dear Father."

As you walk through difficult times, remember the promise our Father has given—you will see His glory. Sometimes, God shows just a glimpse of His glory right here on earth so that we are reminded of our relationship as Father-child. We see His glory when someone receives healing of a sickness, though the doctors said there would be no cure. We see His glory when broken relationships are restored; and lives rebuilt after a disaster. These times of suffering and restoration are but short stories and glimpses of His glory that remind us of His glory yet to come. Then, we will one day see the fullness of His glory when we cross over into heaven—no more suffering; we will be in our permanent restored body, soul, mind and spirit.

# June 9

> For I consider that the sufferings of this present time are not worth comparing with the glory that is to be revealed to us. For the creation waits with eager longing for the revealing of the sons of God. For the creation was subjected to futility, not willingly, but because of Him who subjected it, in hope that the creation itself will be set free from its bondage to corruption and obtain the freedom of the glory of the children of God.
> —Romans 8:18–21 (ESV)

Your pain is real. It hurts and you need a Father to answer your cry for help. He will. You will find hope when you realize the greatness of God's glory to come is much more powerful than the immensity of your pain. Hope that cannot be quenched. The suffering we endure through this life will strengthen us and bring joy as we anticipate the glory that will come. Your story can be one that gives Him glory. His glory may go unnoticed when there is no struggle, and no need for miracles. But, when there is a great need and the need is met, that is the moment when you see God's glory. When a child is abused and removed from the home, then placed in a new home—a Christian home, the child is redeemed; and not only is the child adopted into a new family who will show love and kindness, but the ripple effect of what will happen in that child's life going forward will be changed. This shows a beautiful picture of the glory of God. Good things happen. And then there are the bad things that happen where redemption is given in a miraculous way. Give Him the glory in all things.

# June 10

> For we know that the whole creation has been groaning together in the pains of childbirth until now. And not only the creation, but we ourselves, who have the firstfruits of the Spirit, groan inwardly as we wait eagerly for adoption as sons, the redemption of our bodies. For in this hope we were saved. Now hope that is seen is not hope. For who hopes for what he sees? But if we hope for what we do not see, we wait for it with patience.
> —Romans 8:22–25 (ESV)

If you've ever experienced it, you remember the nine months waiting for a little one to be born. For me, this waiting was not one of fear, but joy and anticipation. Though a high-risk pregnancy, and doctors bringing bad news each week, I couldn't help but feel the joy of being a mommy to my soon-born baby. The fear of losing her catapulted me closer to the hope that she would live. The hope, though I couldn't see her yet, kept me moving forward. Even the day she was born, and the doctor came to tell me that she would die that night (yes, it was said that brutally), my hope held on to the idea she may survive—because I knew God could bring life back into a baby's body that was failing. I know it could have played out differently, but my premature little girl became a miracle of life showing God's glory in a beautiful way.

As children of God, our heart cries out to our Father. His heart connected to ours. Our life connected to His. The day we see Him face-to-face is a day we look forward to, and we are not afraid. We do not lose hope in thinking it may not happen. We hope—we are confident, that we will see Him. We press forward in that hope, believing.

# June 11

> Meanwhile, the moment we get tired in the waiting, God's Spirit is right alongside helping us along. If we don't know how or what to pray, it doesn't matter. He does our praying in and for us, making prayer out of our wordless sighs, our aching groans. He knows us far better than we know ourselves, knows our pregnant condition, and keeps us present before God. That's why we can be so sure that every detail in our lives of love for God is worked into something good.
> —Romans 8:26–28 (MSG)

Just as the Spirit of God gives hope for eternal life in glory, the Spirit also helps in our lives while here on earth, waiting—in our weaknesses, our insecurities and pain so deep we're lost for words. When you haven't the words to speak and only tears fall, the Spirit will intercede for you. He knows your heart, and sees your pain. Amidst the evils of life, you will not fall to dangers piercing in around you. For His Word is true—we know that nothing falls undetected by God. Trouble is but an instrument to be used by God to bring about good.

When you have no words to express your deepest sorrows; when your heart is overwhelmed, the Spirit will speak for you. The Holy Spirit will search your heart and pray according to God's will for you.

You do not have to rely on your own strength, or your own words to save you. Let the strength of God encourage you.

# June 12

> And we know that all that happens to us is working for our good if we love God and are fitting into his plans.
> For from the very beginning God decided that those who came to Him—and all along He knew who would—should become like His Son, so that His Son would be the First, with many brothers. And having chosen us, He called us to come to Him; and when we came, He declared us "not guilty," filled us with Christ's goodness, gave us right standing with Himself, and promised us His glory.
> What can we ever say to such wonderful things as these? If God is on our side, who can ever be against us?
> —Romans 8:28–31 (TLB)

If God is for us—which He is—we have nothing to fear.

I have had experiences where I wondered if I would get through them. I wondered how such ugly things, horrible pain, enormous disasters, broken relationships, could work together for good—that the end result would glorify God. I can certainly understand that, in times of trouble, our greatest pain, we wonder and even argue the idea that God will use it for His glory.

I can see how beautiful things can be associated with God's purpose and ultimately show His glory. But, the ugly things? A troublesome neighbor who is being unreasonable; an unfaithful spouse—broken marriage; an alienated family member. God has the power to turn around what was intended for evil. He can change things. And He may choose to use things to show His power. No matter the "thing" it is, God will use it for His purpose. We can be sure that every detail in our lives of love for God is worked into something good.

You may wonder, too. The Lord will give you courage when you have no courage. Believe the words of encouragement in the scripture. You will be able to look back on this day and say, "I made it. By the grace of God, I made it!" This moment will develop character. So, take a deep breath and relax in His presence. Knowing He will make beauty from ashes makes the suffering bearable.

No matter what you do, no matter what road you're on today, God will use it for good as we follow His plan. Rejoice! Even if you fall down again and again, if you call out to Him, He will pick you up and set you back on His plan.

# June 13

> What, then, shall we say in response to these things? If God is for us, who can be against us? He who did not spare His own Son, but gave Him up for us all—how will He not also, along with Him, graciously give us all things? Who will bring any charge against those whom God has chosen? It is God who justifies. Who then is the one who condemns? No one. Christ Jesus who died—more than that, who was raised to life—is at the right hand of God and is also interceding for us.
> —Romans 8:31–34 (NIV)

The eighth chapter of the book of Romans has clearly spoken of God's ever-present help—first we realize a power within, bringing righteousness to which the final victory is assured, glorifying us in His presence; then, the reminder of an inheritance far surpassing the present evil which awaits us; and finally, to understand that everything that befalls us is still governed by God, and that everything is worked together for good, and God will give to His children all that they need. What, then, is there to fear? God has made us joint heirs with His Son. We are His children. He loves His Son; and He loves us so much that He gave up His Son. He loves you more than you can fathom.

Anything you may be concerned with today—any hurt, any fear, any loss—is in the hands of God. Such an incredible sacrifice was given on your behalf, so trust God with whatever you lack, or whatever is holding you hostage. Replace fear with faith. He will make sure you have what you need and He will break the shackles holding you back; He *will* set you free.

_____

_____

_____

_____

# June 14

> Can anything ever separate us from Christ's love? Does it mean He no longer loves us if we have trouble or calamity, or are persecuted, or hungry, or destitute, or in danger, or threatened with death? (As the Scriptures say, "For your sake we are killed every day; we are being slaughtered like sheep." No, despite all these things, overwhelming victory is ours through Christ, who loved us.
> —Romans 8:35–37 (NLT)

This day—wherever you are, whatever you come against, you are more than conquerors through God who loves you. You win!

Divorced, rejected, no hope for a future? No. You are not alienated, but are His children. You are not rejected, but accepted. You are not hopeless, but full of promise of a future. Your Father loves you and is taking care of you.

Broken, your life threatened, lost your strength? God Restores, promises eternal life, and is strong when you are weak. I'll say it again, your Father loves you and is in control.

Don't give up! Nothing—not anything—can separate you from God's love. He will not let things go undone for His own. He will finish the work He has started in you and His plan. Let this day mark the beginning of a new life! I know it's not New Year's Day, but every day can be a new day with God. If you have begun a journey away from pain and brokenness to a renewed heart and transformed life, then you're starting a new way of living. I pray all will be restored to you by the Father of love and that you can rejoice.

God loves you, not for what you bring to Him, not for who you are or what you have done, but, in spite of it all—brokenness, a shameful past, shattered dreams, illnesses, or any other titles this world has given. Nothing can stop His amazing love. And nothing surprises Him.

# June 15

> Then Jesus told His disciples a parable to show them that they should always pray and not give up.
> —Luke 18:1 (NIV)

A giant predator, called Fear, crouched in the shadows, taunting, and waiting for the opportunity to attack in a moment of weakness and vulnerability. Prey to fear, the outcome can be deadly—destroying relationships, joy, peace, your talents, resources. The only hope of survival is to call out to God. He has provided the shield of faith and His mighty sword of Truth, so that you can defend yourself and fight the enemy. Faith allows you to face that fear with confidence and assurance that God is in charge. The sword of Truth destroys the enemy, bringing you freedom, peace, a sense of belonging and purpose.

Jesus told a parable to show them that they should pray and not give up. It was the parable of the persistent widow who finally found justice. She persistently went to the judge of the city asking, "Grant me justice against my adversary." Her rights were violated, and she asked for protection. The judge did not care about God or the people of God, but finally granted it.

God, who hears your persistent cries for protection, will bring justice.

If you are on the run, and you feel alone with the darkness closing in on you, remember to call on His Name—Jesus. He is the Truth. He is our weapon and our shield. You will see that His presence is all that you need. Remain faithful. Keep calling out to Him. Don't give up.

# June 16

But those who hope in the LORD will renew their strength. They will soar on wings like eagles; they will run and not grow weary, they will walk and not be faint.
—Isaiah 40:31 (NIV)

Like an eagle that stirs up its nest and hovers over its young, that spreads its wings to catch them and carries them aloft.
—Deuteronomy 32:11 (NIV)

In the above excerpt from the book of Deuteronomy, Moses described God to be like an eagle, when the eagle lifts the young into the air and teaches them to fly—that this is how God led Jacob. God is watching and teaching you. As you are being stirred up, and removed from your comfort, trust that He is strong enough to carry you. As you are plunging, look up and see Him.

When the mother eagle teaches the young to fly, she will nudge them out of the nest and then the father will swoop down and catch the young eagle. It may look pathetic on the first flight, unable to fly, frantically flapping its wings. But the eagle is only falling, not failing.

You are learning, not losing. You are learning to fly!

# June 17

> The cords of death entangled me, the anguish of the grave came over me; I was overcome by distress and sorrow. Then I called on the name of the Lord:
>
> "Lord, save me!"
>
> The Lord is gracious and righteous; our God is full of compassion. The Lord protects the unwary; when I was brought low, He saved me.
> —Psalm 116:3–6 (NIV)

Horatio Spafford was a prominent lawyer and businessman who lived in Chicago in the late 1800s. He was happily married and the proud father of four daughters and a four-year-old son. The Spafford family was well known in Chicago for their hospitality, their involvement in the abolitionist movement, and their support of Christian evangelists, including D. L. Moody. Horatio was heavily invested in Chicago real estate, the market was expanding, and life was good.

Then tragedy struck. In 1870, he lost his four-year-old son to scarlet fever. Just a few months later, the great Chicago fire hit, and destruction came to his investments. Two years later, the family decided to vacation in Europe. The day came for them to go on the ship, but at the last moment, Horatio was detained by real estate business. So he sent his wife and four daughters ahead on the ship *S.S. Ville de Havre,* intending to join them later.

After several days, he received a now-famous cable from his wife. It began, "Saved alone. What shall I do…" He soon learned the horrifying news: the ship bearing his family had collided with another ship in the open sea. Within twelve minutes, the *Ville de Havre* had gone under. All four daughters drowned. The only thing he knew to do now was to get on the next ship over to console his wife. As the ship's captain notified Horatio that they had reached the place where the *Ville de Havre* had gone down, where he had lost his daughters to the sea, he began to write. What he wrote has become one of the most loved hymns of all time.

When peace, like a river, attendeth my way,
When sorrows like sea billows roll;
Whatever my lot, Thou hast taught me to say,
It is well, it is well with my soul.

Though Satan should buffet, though trials should come,
Let this blest assurance control,
That Christ hath regarded my helpless estate,
And hath shed His own blood for my soul.
My sin—oh, the bliss of this glorious thought!—
My sin, not in part but the whole,
Is nailed to the cross, and I bear it no more,
Praise the Lord, praise the Lord, O my soul!

For me, be it Christ, be it Christ hence to live:
If Jordan above me shall roll,
No pang shall be mine, for in death as in life
Thou wilt whisper Thy peace to my soul.

But, Lord, 'tis for Thee, for Thy coming we wait,
The sky, not the grave, is our goal;
Oh, trump of the angel! Oh, voice of the Lord!
Blessed hope, blessed rest of my soul!

And Lord, haste the day when the faith shall be sight,
The clouds be rolled back as a scroll;
The trump shall resound, and the Lord shall descend,
Even so, it is well with my soul.

It is well with my soul,
It is well, it is well with my soul.

—It Is Well With My Soul, Horatio G. Spafford, 1873

Joy while in mourning. How is it possible? Peace. Hope. Though troubles come, we know and proclaim, "It is well with my soul."

# June 18

> I love the Lord, for He heard my voice; He heard my cry for mercy. Because He turned His ear to me, I will call on Him as long as I live.
> For you, Lord, have delivered me from death, my eyes from tears, my feet from stumbling, that I may walk before the Lord in the land of the living. I trusted in the Lord when I said, "I am greatly afflicted"; in my alarm I said, "Everyone is a liar." What shall I return to the Lord for all His goodness to me?
> —Psalm 116:1–2, 8–12 (NIV)

David longed to find acceptance—to be able to walk in public without fear of disapproval and evil plots. David lived in hiding, to escape King Saul's plan to kill him. David cried out and the Lord heard him. David knew His deliverance came from the Lord, and vowed to call on Him for the rest of his life and fulfill his vows to the Lord.

Like David, we long to find acceptance. When rejected, insecurity sets in. We are afraid of losing and failing. If insecurity takes its course, it can lead to bitterness, and we become angry at the one who betrayed us, and eventually blame the world for our losses! We don't trust anyone.

Rather than fall into self-pity and downhill run of panic, call out to the Lord, just as David did. Have faith in God's love, and through the moment of pain, let worry dissipate. The need to control everything around you can be handed over to Him, as you allow your heart to be moved by what moves God's heart—mercy, forgiveness, love, compassion, peace, joy.

# June 19

> The Lord *is* my light and my salvation; Whom shall I fear? The Lord *is* the strength of my life; Of whom shall I be afraid?
>
> —Psalm 27:1 (NKJV)

Who is the strength of your life? What do you see as your safety net? Jesus does not want you to forget that you were created to be like Him. Life is a gift and anything or anyone else that may be a part of your life, is just that—a gift. Each part is like filling in fancy chocolates—like Forest Gump would say, "Life is like a box of chocolate. You never know what you're gonna get". Family, friends, job, home or anything else—all part of the life planned for you. But in all of the beauty and wonder of it all—life—we cannot find our strength in it. Security is not found there. The Lord is your light, your salvation and your strength. When placed where it belongs, there is nothing to fear when these gifts are shifted, replaced or removed.

---
---
---
---

# June 20

> For the Spirit God gave us does not make us timid, but gives us power, love and self-discipline.
> —2 Timothy 1:7 (NIV)

The world may think Christians are weak and needy. And in a sense, that is true—when we compare to the power of God. Are we stronger than God? No, we are inferior to His power. That makes us the weaker vessel. Do we need God? Yes. Without Him, we perish. So, we are needy. But that does not make us voiceless, timid Christians afraid to stand up for what's right and to tell others of God's love. With His love and power in us, we can be bold and strong.

_____

_____

_____

# June 21

> Do not be afraid of those who kill the body but cannot kill the soul. Rather, be afraid of the One who can destroy both soul and body in hell. Are not two sparrows sold for a penny? Yet not one of them will fall to the ground outside your Father's care. And even the very hairs of your head are all numbered. So don't be afraid; you are worth more than many sparrows.
> —Matthew 10:28–31 (NIV)

Don't fear people—fear God. In reverence to God, we acknowledge Him; we follow Him; we honor Him.

If you come face-to-face with a decision to either honor God or honor man, it should be an easy choice. But it seems to cause many to fall short. When confronted with a choice to sin so that you are accepted by others, choose to be accepted by God and honor Him. Don't be afraid of what people can do or say. Don't let the fear of losing a friendship or job or anything else cause you to sin. Diseases can cripple and sometimes it ends in death. Natural disasters can destroy all that you have. Divorce hurts. Loss hurts. But do not be afraid. Remember that whatever this is, it will not destroy your soul. No one and not one thing can take your salvation away. Only God has charge over your soul's future. And it is your choice as to whether you will accept or reject God's grace and salvation of your soul.

The Father reminds us that He will take care of us, so there's nothing to fear.

# June 22

> Wait patiently for the LORD. Be brave and courageous.
> Yes, wait patiently for the LORD..
> —Psalm 27:14 (NLT)

People look for comfort is so many places. Some seek peace in alcohol, hoping that they can forget their troubles. Some look to people for comfort, hoping they will be affirmed. Some go as far as to immerse themselves in a lifestyle of sin to absorb the pain. But there is only one kind of peace that will truly comfort you, and it comes from Jesus. Jesus will not abandon you; He will comfort you; He will reaffirm you.

# June 23

> May the God of hope fill you with all joy and peace as you trust in Him, so that you may overflow with hope by the power of the Holy Spirit.
> —Romans 15:13 (NIV)

The world is searching for hope and peace. There is no greater hope and sense of accomplishment except that found in trusting God. You may think you trust Him. And I hope you do. But listen to your words, and make sure you speak the words of faith. Rather than say, "I hope we can find a home," say, "I trust God has the perfect home for us." Rather than say, "I don't know what I'm going to do. I have to get that job!," say, "I know God will take care of me. If this is not the job for me, I will wait for God, and trust He will provide for us." Turn your anxiety into peace, and your panic into joy. Trust Him.

Trusting God, you believe all things work together for good. Trusting God, you believe He is alive and working in you and through you. Trusting God, you find hope, joy and peace by the power of the Holy Spirit.

# June 24

> I do not hide Your righteousness in my heart; I speak of Your faithfulness and Your saving help. I do not conceal Your love and Your faithfulness from the great assembly.
>
> —Psalm 40:10 (NIV)

Your testimony means something. Your story within God's story is unique and filled with the faithfulness of God throughout your life.

So, think about where you would like to be in ten years from today. What goals have you set in place? Interestingly, many people who achieve material goals find that success was not as satisfying as they had hoped it would be. There was something missing. But your goals can be set by following the plan God has for you. Those who forego their own plans in order to pursue God's plan, discover a life full of purpose and abundant in love, hope and wonder—just as David testifies here in the Psalm of God's love and faithfulness.

Try to imagine the great things that could happen when God is the one who does the work. Trust God with your dreams; you will begin a journey full of joy and excitement, because you are working side-by-side with God. Watch what He will do for you, through you and in you—all for His glory and His purpose.

# June 25

> In the morning, as they went along, they saw the fig tree withered from the roots. Peter remembered and said to Jesus, "Rabbi, look! The fig tree you cursed has withered!"
> "Have faith in God," Jesus answered.
> —Mark 11:20–22 (NIV)

Jesus and His twelve disciples have entered Jerusalem. Jesus rides in on a colt as the King of the Jews. Many people were there who spread their cloaks on the road, while others spread branches they had cut in the fields, making a path for their king. They shouted, "Hosanna!" It had been a long day full of excitement, and it was late, so Jesus went out to Bethany with the twelve. The next day as they were leaving Bethany, Jesus was hungry. There was a fig tree. So He went to find out if it had any fruit. When He reached it, He found nothing but leaves, because it was not the season for figs. Then He said to the tree, "May no one ever eat fruit from you again." And His disciples heard Him say it. (Mark 11:7–14) So, when they pass the fig tree again the next morning and it is withered, they are surprised. Really? Were they not there when Jesus cursed the tree? So, wouldn't they expect it to be withered? Did they question His reason for cursing a tree that had no fruit, even though it was not the season to bear fruit? Maybe they figured He should have made the tree bear fruit if He wanted fruit from that tree. They'd seen miracles, so why not this time? Jesus simply responded by saying, "Have faith in God."

We do the same. We know God's power, yet question it. We ask for God's help, and then are surprised when He comes through with the answer. We think we know what God should do and not do in any given circumstance. We think Jesus is bound by our own rules of nature. He is not. Jesus can do anything. We may not understand why He does things the way He chooses to do them, but we must trust His wisdom. We must have faith in God.

Pray, believing God will answer. Though your hopes may seem far away at times, and seems unreachable, believe. Acknowledge that God can answer you with all of His authority behind Him; then fully trust

Him for the answer. Is your tree bare? Is it dry, with no life left? His power is not bound by any circumstance.

When God answers, follow His instructions with a humble heart and with renewed hope. If your request is in God's will, He is faithful to bring it about. If it is not His will, and you have asked for God's will to be done, God may change your desires to mirror His. You will find that having His will done will be so much better than your own will, if your desires differ from His.

# June 26

> So when you, a mere human being, pass judgment on them and yet do the same things, do you think you will escape God's judgment? Or do you show contempt for the riches of His kindness, forbearance and patience, not realizing that God's kindness is intended to lead you to repentance?
> —Romans 2:3–4 (NIV)

I appreciate the management style of leading with positive motivation—to lead with kindness and not a judgmental attitude. That's how I am motivated to work hard; and I've found that people treated with love, kindness and patience will want to do their best for their boss.

But in the same breath, know that my kindness is not a sign of weakness. Like that, God is not weak, though He is kind. In His kindness, He takes us firmly by the hand and leads us to radical change—repentance. His love is an example of how we should treat others. His love does not condemn. Instead, it leads us to repentance. With love, we can point others to Jesus where they can find His love, mercy and patience, which will lead them to repentance.

# June 27

> Surely Your goodness and love will follow me all the days of my life, and I will dwell in the house of the Lord forever.
> —Psalm 23:6 (NIV)

This verse of scripture is the end thought of the twenty-third Psalm. You may recognize it, because it is the well-known and often used Psalm of David, "The Lord is My Shepherd". For goodness and love to follow you all of the days of your life, and even through the dark days, and through the suffering, we need to first trust our Shepherd. We will still go through the valleys, and face giants as enemies, but with the Lord as our Shepherd, His love and beauty will chase after you everywhere you go.

# June 28

> Being confident of this, that He who began a good work in you will carry it on to completion until the day of Christ Jesus.
>
> —Philippians 1:6 (NIV)

Paul's letter to the Philippians begins with encouragement. He reminded them that God will continue His work until it is finally finished on the day when Jesus returns. He never stops, even if we slow down. He never tires like we do. He doesn't give up. He is relentless in His love and diligently at work to finish His plan. It's not over yet, so you can be sure He is working on your behalf just as well. Be confident. Be brave. As you trust God for your life, He will continue the good work He began.

---
---
---
---

# June 29

> They disciplined us for a little while as they thought best; but God disciplines us for our good, in order that we may share in His holiness.
> —Hebrews 12:10 (NIV)

My mom taught me manners; she taught me godly standards and how to live a life for God—a good life. She protected me and did so with love and compassion, so that I would be safe in this life. No one enjoys discipline—it's painful! But as we are trained in the ways in which we should go, we become stronger and better finding peace in right living. God wants to teach us for our own benefit. And the benefit will be that we live a better life here and now and will share in His holiness for eternity!

# June 30

> How abundant are the good things that You have stored up for those who fear You, that You bestow in the sight of all, on those who take refuge in You. In the shelter of Your presence You hide them from all human intrigues; You keep them safe in Your dwelling from accusing tongues.
>
> —Psalm 31:19–20 (NIV)

David began this psalm calling out to God for rescue and protection. He didn't want to be disgraced by his enemies. David looked to God as his fortress—his safe place. Have you ever been in a place where you're afraid? Maybe you feel alone—worthless. Maybe you're afraid of losing your life. The enemy, Satan, wants you to give up. He will say your worth lies in labels of this world—divorced, homeless, alcoholic, broken, ugly, widowed. He wants you to believe you have no place to turn in your time of trouble. But he is a liar. God sees your troubles, and He knows the anguish of your soul. He notices your tears as you sob in pain—in grief. He will not allow the enemy to take hold of you and leave you hopeless and devastated. Are you tired—worn out by the anxious thoughts? God is faithful in His love. You can trust Him. Your name is not "unworthy", but "redeemed". Your name is "forgiven", "holy", "free", "delivered", "beautiful". Your name is "child of God". Your future lies in the hands of the Father. This world can be cruel and leave you feeling beaten and alone. But our soul finds rest in His shelter. Cry out to Him, just as David did, and find hope in the Lord!

# July

You have allowed me to suffer much hardship,
but You will restore me to life again
and lift me up from the depths of the earth.
You will restore me to even greater honor
and comfort me once again
—Psalm 71:20–21 (NLT)

# Restored

# July 1

Listen…

    Can you hear the birds singing again, a song you heard before the night began?
    Look out the window; through the blinds; see the sunrise, the warmth that it finds.
    In your heart, there is a tune that I'm sure you used to know;
    A sweet, sweet melody of long ago.

Larene Sanford

# July 2

When I am afraid, I put my trust in You.
—Psalm 56:3 (NIV)

Remember, God is all-powerful, all-knowing, and complete love. Have faith that our Father will meet all of your needs. He gave us the best gift—His Son, Jesus. Knowing this, that our Father did not withhold His Son, why would we ever allow fear to settle in our souls?

# July 3

Jesus came and brought immediate restoration when He died on the cross. You are complete in Him. God continues to restore in many ways as a reminder that He is the God who restores.

Once Restored, Don't Resort

Collins English Dictionary [2] defines Resort as this (American definition):

Verb intransitive

1.
To go; esp., to go often, customarily, or generally
2.
To have recourse; go or turn (to) for use, help, support, etc.
To resort to harsh measures
Noun
3.
A place to which people go often or generally, esp. one for rest or recreation, as on a vacation
4.
A frequent, customary, or general going, gathering together, or visiting
A place of general resort
5.
A person or thing that one goes or turns to for help, support, etc.
6.
A going or turning for help, support, etc.; recourse
To have resort to relatives

Once you have learned to trust with a child-like faith, don't let circumstances distract you and cause you to disbelieve, and return to your old ways of resolve. Don't resort to trusting in something or someone else to bring joy back into your life. Your security is in God. Remain in faith. Believe in the life that God has established for you.

Fight the good fight of the faith. Take hold of the eternal life to which you were called when you made your good confession in the presence of many witnesses.
—1 Timothy 6:12 (NIV)

# July 4

Immediately after this, Jesus insisted that His disciples get back into the boat and cross to the other side of the lake, while He sent the people home. After sending them home, He went up into the hills by Himself to pray. Night fell while He was there alone.

Meanwhile, the disciples were in trouble far away from land, for a strong wind had risen, and they were fighting heavy waves. About three o'clock in the morning Jesus came toward them, walking on the water. When the disciples saw Him walking on the water, they were terrified. In their fear, they cried out, "It's a ghost!"

But Jesus spoke to them at once. "Don't be afraid," He said. "Take courage. I am here!"

—Matthew 14:24–27 (NLT)

Notice when the disciples cried out in fear that Jesus immediately calmed their hearts. Before He calmed the waves and wind, He calmed their hearts. Jesus will make sure you know that He is present in time of trouble, and He doesn't want you to be afraid. Hear His calming voice and listen when He tells you, "Don't be afraid. Take courage. I am here." You're not alone. He is with you. The storms may be raging all around you, but close your eyes to the storm, and look for Jesus.

# July 5

"Lord, if it's You," Peter replied, "tell me to come to You on the water."
"Come," He said.
—Matthew 14:28–29 (NIV)

Peter wanted assurance that it was Jesus out on the water. He asked Jesus for something that would require a miracle—to walk on the water. And Jesus provided that miracle for Peter.

When we make requests to Jesus, He will prove Himself to us. I have asked Jesus to show Himself real to me and, at times, He showed me with miracles—so many times that I've lost count. Why do you suppose Jesus did that? Only to prove Himself to be who He was? It did, in fact, prove Jesus could do great things, including walk on water, and enabled Peter to walk on water. But I believe it was more than that. It showed Peter that day, that Jesus really loved him enough to show him a miracle. He wanted to help Peter believe. He cared enough to answer Peter intimately—it was between Peter and Jesus. In all of the chaos, in all of the commotion of the storm and frightened crew, Jesus picked Peter out of the crowd and answered his cry.

Sometimes, we feel so insignificant, but Jesus wants us to know that we are not unimportant to Him and that He loves us—love that shows us miracles to help us believe; love that we can share with the Son of God!

---
---
---
---

# July 6

> Then Peter got down out of the boat, walked on the water and came toward Jesus. But when he saw the wind, he was afraid and, beginning to sink, cried out, "Lord, save me!"
> Immediately Jesus reached out His hand and caught him. "You of little faith," He said, "why did you doubt?"
> —Matthew 14:30–31 (NIV)

When Peter saw the wind and how boisterous it was, it scared him! Why? Peter believed Jesus could cause him to walk on the water, but he couldn't believe that Jesus could make him *stay* on top of the water if the winds case as strong as *this*. Did the winds pick up? Or did Peter finally come to notice how strong the wind was? Whatever the case, Peter initially believed—yes, even to the point of seeing and being a part of a miracle; but, at some point, he could not believe he could walk on water in the horrible wind. Peter was in the middle of a miracle, when doubt came swooping in, and he questioned the power of God.

We hear from Jesus, and even see a miracle and believe. But then things change—the course of the wind, the strength of the wind, or maybe even an addition of rain, snow or hail, and we ask, "Can God still work in that?"! Yes! When the oceans rage, is God big enough to calm *that* storm? Absolutely! When you see trouble headed your way, and it appears God's plan has been somehow altered, leaving you questioning if God is bigger or even in it at all, don't let your mind carry you away in disbelief. Have faith that God's plan cannot be destroyed or even tampered with, unless God allows it. He is in ultimate control—of the boat you travel in; of the water you walk on; the wind; the rain; the storm; the rainbow; the sun—all of it!

---
---
---

# July 7

> And when they climbed into the boat, the wind died down. Then those who were in the boat worshiped Him, saying, "Truly You are the Son of God."
> —Matthew 14:32–33 (NIV)

Jesus saved Peter. He reached down and caught him, and helped him climb back into the boat.

Jesus will come when we call for help. He is a compassionate God. He cares about *you* first—not what you can become, or what you can offer Him, but He cares about you. He wants to take away your fears.

Even when we doubt or have trouble believing, He reaches down and saves us. Do you think it a coincidence that the winds died down when Jesus got in the boat? I don't believe that for a minute. First Jesus got Peter to safety, then the storm calmed. Jesus will remove that which causes you fear—even if it takes place after He saves you from what you fear.

# July 8

> After they had crossed the lake, they landed at Gennesaret.
> 
> —Matthew 14:34 (NLT)

Don't move too quickly past this moment. Realize, they made it to the other side of the lake. Before they headed out into the lake, and before the storm when they all panicked, and before Peter walked on water, Jesus told them to get in the boat and cross over to the other side of the lake. So, why would He tell them to cross over to the other side, if they were going to die? Jesus knows the future. He knew they would make it. Peter wasn't sure. He was afraid as he began to sink in the water. If he would have trusted that Jesus knew he would survive the storm, his fear would not have taken over. When Jesus caught him, He said, "Why did you doubt?"

Fear can make everything in your life fall apart. God will rescue you in your time of trouble, and free you from the power of fear—even if your fear has caused destruction, as well as the predicament you are in. Call out to God, trust that He is able to save you, and He will come through on your behalf.

# July 9

"Now then," Joshua continued, "honor the LORD and serve Him sincerely and faithfully. Get rid of the gods which your ancestors used to worship in Mesopotamia and in Egypt, and serve only the LORD. If you are not willing to serve Him, decide today whom you will serve, the gods your ancestors worshiped in Mesopotamia or the gods of the Amorites, in whose land you are now living. As for my family and me, we will serve the LORD."

—Joshua 24:14–15 (GNB)

Don't be terrified of whatever happens in life. Fear God—show Him reverence.

Don't fear your future ~ fear God.

Don't fear your past ~ fear God.

Don't fear trouble ~ fear God.

Don't fear your circumstances ~ fear God.

Don't fear the enemy ~ fear God.

When we fear God, we fear nothing else, because we know that God is on our side and nothing can defeat God. Therefore, nothing can defeat us as we stand next to Him.

Imagine a grizzly bear cub being chased by a lion. Grizzlies are, in fact, very large and powerful creatures. They can also be very aggressive and the lion would have pretty much no defense against them should they attack. An adult male grizzly will weigh around 400–790 lbs., and females around 290–400 lbs.. They also tend to be around 6.50 ft long, and a little more than 3 feet at the shoulder. Some giant individuals are occasionally found. Some have been found weighing in at around

1,500lb.. Females will rear their cubs for 2–3 years. When a female grizzly bear leaves her mother, they often set up their home range quite close to their mother's home range. Males will typically range further, but may also remain close by. But a young bear cub is weak, and the lion can devour the cub. The lion thinks the cub is an easy target. But the bear cub knows just where to go—run to mama bear! The lion now faces her with all her force against the lion to protect her cub. Should the lion consider the fight, he will pay the cost. History has shown that the grizzly bear will conquer the lion when they are involved in a fight. A mama bear is not weak. She will defend her young.

The enemy comes in different sizes and personas, and represents danger if we don't submit to his forces. History tells us that Jesus conquered the enemy when He paid the price on the cross. The enemy may have thought that He was weak when He was dying. But He was in the most powerful state of all time. He was conquering death and sin! God is bigger. He is stronger. Faithfully stand next to the One who can defend you in all circumstances.

# July 10

Plans fail for lack of counsel, but with many advisers they succeed.
—Proverbs 15:22 (NIV)

To God belong wisdom and power; counsel and understanding are His.
—Job 12:13 (NIV)

God allows us to make our own choices in life. He gives us the free will to live as we will. At times, our desires may differ from His will and then it is up to ourselves to decide whether we are going to do His will or our own. We have access to God's wisdom and direction. The first counsel we need to inquire is the advice from God. Seeking wise counsel from strong believers in Christ will also help confirm what you understand to be wisdom from the Lord. You would be wise to seek answers in the scriptures and in prayer first, as well as relying on your experience with the Lord, then consult with others.

# July 11

> Consequently, faith comes from hearing the message, and the message is heard through the word about Christ.
> —Romans 10:17 (NIV)

If faith comes from hearing the message, and the message through the Word, then it is obvious that, when we need faith to believe even though we cannot see any evidence of things hoped for, we need to stop, look, and listen. Just as we learned in grade school how to watch for traffic before crossing the road, we need to stop (stand still), look (to God for direction and wisdom and courage), and listen (to God's Word, His voice and His guidance). Then we will have faith—faith to believe in God; faith to believe what God says is true; and faith to persevere.

# July 12

> But He said to me, "My grace is sufficient for you, for My power is made perfect in weakness." Therefore I will boast all the more gladly about my weaknesses, so that Christ's power may rest on me.
> —2 Corinthians 12:9 (NIV)

Are you tired? Do you feel the anxiety rising in your heart, at the thought of possible failure? Your weakness is an opportunity for God to show Himself strong. His power can bring success when failure seemed sure. And if you do fail, God's power can sustain you. He will see you through it. No matter how inadequate you may feel, God is much higher than your shortfalls.

# July 13

> That is why, for Christ's sake, I delight in weaknesses,
> in insults, in hardships, in persecutions, in difficulties.
> For when I am weak, then I am strong.
> —2 Corinthians 12:10 (NIV)

Don't give up hope when everything seems dark. God will make you strong. He will restore you. That truth is the reason we can have joy through our weakest moments. Not a masked joy, which covers up the pain; but a joy deep within that sees us through the difficult moments. It is not to say we enjoy the weakness, or insults or hardships. It is to say that we no longer focus on the weakness or hardship, and instead take the opposition in stride. And so we take joy in the knowing that the weaker we get, the stronger we become.

# July 14

> Now the Lord is the Spirit, and where the Spirit of the Lord is, there is freedom. And we all, who with unveiled faces contemplate the Lord's glory, are being transformed into His image with ever-increasing glory, which comes from the Lord, who is the Spirit.
> —2 Corinthians 3:17–18 (NIV)

The only reason we will see the Lord's glory with the veil removed is because of Jesus and what He did for us on the cross. It's time we realize that the law of sin cannot be rectified by our own righteousness. We cannot make ourselves pure by good deeds. The veil cannot hide our true selves when we stand face to face with God. We must recognize that God is a living, personal presence; not a god made of stone or jewels. Nothing remains between us and God—like a veil between the bride and groom lifted up so to see each other face-to-face. As God transforms our lives, we become more like Him—just as God intended when He said in the beginning, "Let Us make man in Our image." (Genesis 1:26)

# July 15

> Remember that at that time you were separate from Christ, excluded from citizenship in Israel and foreigners to the covenants of the promise, without hope and without God in the world. But now in Christ Jesus you who once were far away have been brought near by the blood of Christ.
> —Ephesians 2:12–13 (NIV)

In Christ Jesus alone, there is hope for an everlasting life, made possible through His sacrifice. Let's not forget. Let's not think lightly on it. We are no longer without hope. With God and His promises, we can live at peace within ourselves.

---
---
---
---

# July 16

> Come now, let us reason together, says the LORD: though your sins are like scarlet, they shall be as white as snow; though they are red like crimson, they shall become like wool.
> —Isaiah 1:18 (ESV)

Have you ever been called into the boss's office? Were you confident that the reason for the discussion would be positive? Or were you concerned? When the boss calls you into the office, you know that the conversation must be important and very personal. One thing is sure—when you leave the office, you will know why you were called to the discussion, and it will be clear as to how it involves you. God is calling you for a discussion. Are you ready for what He has to say? Do you have an answer—a question for Him, maybe? You don't have to be afraid. God is fair and He loves you and wants the best for you. There is a spiritual restoration waiting for you. He wants to show you what He alone can do.

---
---
---
---

# July 17

> Create in me a pure heart, O God, and renew a steadfast spirit within me. Do not cast me from Your presence or take Your Holy Spirit from me. Restore to me the joy of Your salvation and grant me a willing spirit, to sustain me.
> —Psalm 51:10–12 (NIV)

Restoration of joy comes when we know God is faithful. We will see God's hand at work in our lives, transforming our hearts to mirror His. Simply knowing He is with us is enough to restore hope and joy.

Look up from the pit. It may seem like your story is finished from your point of view in the pit. But your story is not finished! Remain loyal to Him. Wait for the miracle to come. Your miracle requires faith in what you cannot see. Faith is about being at peace no matter how things turn out. Sometimes things don't turn out the way you expected them to. And promises from God seem to be for anyone else but you. But know that every detail of your life of love for God is worked into something good.

# July 18

Heal me, LORD, and I will be healed; save me and I will be saved, for You are the one I praise.

—Jeremiah 17:14 (NIV)

Medicine can heal sicknesses, and heroes save lives, but we will continue to see more sicknesses and lives lost while here on earth. The only one who can provide ultimate healing and eternal salvation is God. And while I'm living, I, like Jeremiah, will trust the Lord for miracles, or the medicines and help that might be used by the Lord to bring a healthier and safer life.

# July 19

> "But I will restore you to health and heal your wounds," declares the LORD, "because you are called an outcast, Zion for whom no one cares."
> —Jeremiah 30:17 (NIV)

God has compassion on those who are outcasts. People can betray you; people can hurt you, leaving you with societies labels. But you are not defined by society and the state of your brokenness. You are defined by what Jesus did on the cross. He is able to restore you—your health and any other brokenness you may have. He may restore you now, or later, or in eternity; but all will be for the glory of God.

# July 20

"In your anger do not sin": Do not let the sun go down while you are still angry, and do not give the devil a foothold.
—Ephesians 4:26–27 (NIV)

Pain can easily turn into bitterness and quickly to anger.

There have been days where the stresses of life are so great that even a stump of the toe can make me angry. So, I understand the natural reaction. That is why it is important to recognize how the stress is affecting you. Anger will only hurt yourself by making you miserable overall. Allow God to heal your wounds and calm your anxiety so that bitterness and anger will not settle into your heart.

# July 21

> You intended to harm me, but God intended it for good to accomplish what is now being done, the saving of many lives.
> —Genesis 50:20 (NIV)

God can restore what was stolen from you, and the loss you've experienced as He determines necessary. He, too, can use what was lost to meet a greater purpose. What was intended for evil, God can turn around and use it for good. Just as Joseph answered, we too can answer the same when calamity comes knocking.

# July 22

> But when they said, "Give us a king to lead us," this displeased Samuel; so he prayed to the Lord. And the Lord told him: "Listen to all that the people are saying to you; it is not you they have rejected, but they have rejected Me as their king. As they have done from the day I brought them up out of Egypt until this day, forsaking Me and serving other gods, so they are doing to you. Now listen to them; but warn them solemnly and let them know what the king who will reign over them will claim as his rights."
> —1 Samuel 8:6–9 (NIV)

Rejection hurts. It causes insecurity, depression, and even frustration. Samuel felt rejected when the people asked for a king to rule over them, rather than listen to Samuel or accept his appointed sons as leaders. But, God made it clear that they were not rejecting Samuel, but God, Himself. And, Jesus was also rejected when He came and dwelt among people.

If you have been rejected, know that God understands; He was rejected by His own people; and people continue to reject God even today.

> The stone that the builders rejected is the one that has become the chief cornerstone.
> —Psalm 118:22 (NIV)

That's plain enough, isn't it? You're no longer wandering exiles. This kingdom of faith is now your home country. You're no longer strangers or outsiders. You *belong* here, with as much right to the name Christian as anyone. God is building a home. He's using us all—irrespective of how we got here—in what He is building. He used the apostles and prophets for the foundation. Now He's using you, fitting you in brick by brick, stone by stone, with Christ Jesus as the cornerstone that holds all the

parts together. We see it taking shape day after day—a holy temple built by God, all of us built into it, a temple in which God is quite at home.
—Ephesians 2:19–22 (MSG)

# July 23

> Humility is the fear of the LORD; its wages are riches and honor and life.
>
> —Proverbs 22:4 (NIV)

Have you ever wondered what your reward is for humility and fear of the Lord? Well, now you know. Sometimes, you may feel that you are only paying for humility and for doing the right thing because of your faith. But His word is true—you will have plenty, honor, and a satisfying life. You won't regret it. Choose humility; choose to give reverence God.

# July 24

> But when you pray, go into your room, close the door and pray to your Father, who is unseen. Then Your Father, who sees what is done in secret, will reward you.
> —Matthew 6:6 (NIV)

This scripture is a lead-in to the well-known prayer that Jesus taught, called, *The Lord's Prayer*. In the next few days, let's look at the Lord's Prayer together and learn how we should pray.

All Christians should pray at all times—to keep in communication with the Lord throughout each day. However, He also wants some special time with you. We need this time with Him, and it is a time where we need to get away from all of the noise, in a quiet, solitude location to pray and listen. The Father wants quality time with you, and your undivided attention—not a prayer that *looks good in public*. In the business of life (motherhood, fatherhood, jobs, ministry, recreation), it may be difficult to find a place and time with no distractions, but try and find that moment where you can listen and share your heart with Him.

# July 25

> And when you pray, do not keep on babbling like pagans, for they think they will be heard because of their many words. Do not be like them, for your Father knows what you need before you ask Him.
> —Matthew 6:7–8 (NIV)

Be honest. Speak to Him with your deepest thoughts. He knows them anyway, and God wants your sincerity. Tell Him what's really on your heart, whether good or bad. He wants you to bring it to Him. Are you afraid to tell Him how you feel? Ask yourself why. What are you afraid will happen if you are honest with Him? Afraid you will feel you've failed Him? He already knows and Jesus already paid the debt for the failures. Afraid you will lose the relationship you have with Him? Nothing can separate you from His love—not even your feelings. Do you think it is a sign of weakness? Then let your weakness show God's power—in your weakness, He is strong. Whatever it is, tell Him. He can help with whatever it is.

# July 26

"This, then, is how you should pray:
'Our Father in heaven, hallowed be Your name, Your kingdom come, Your will be done, on earth as it is in heaven.'"
—Matthew 6:9–10 (NIV)

In your time with the Lord, acknowledge who God is, which in turn you are proclaiming who *you* are—His child. He is the Father and His Name is holy. Ask that His desires and His will might become yours and that His purpose for His kingdom will be fulfilled.

With your heart, your desires, and purpose in this life mirroring that of Gods, you will open up possibilities beyond your own dreams.

# July 27

"Give us today our daily bread. And forgive us our debts, as we also have forgiven our debtors."
—Matthew 6:11–12 (NIV)

When you pray, be humble. He knows what we need today, and every day that follows. Pray for your needs, believing He can meet them. Humility will remind us that we are not better than others—or God. We will remember to pray for forgiveness for any wrong doing. When Jesus sacrificed His life on the cross, we were immediately forgiven. All who were sinful, became sinless. So, this act of humility is not because we are not forgiven, but that we realize we need His forgiveness. God may speak to you about someone who you need to forgive for their sins against you. Be ready to forgive them, as God gives you the heart of forgiveness. There are some who do not deserve your forgiveness, but that is where grace comes in. God's grace covers our sins, and also covers theirs. Remember, their sins are not only against you, but against God. Find the heart of God in you, and forgive others, and accept forgiveness for yourself. You are forgiven.

# July 28

"And do not cause us to be tempted, but save us from the Evil One.' [The kingdom, the power, and the glory are yours forever. Amen.]
—Matthew 6:13 (NCV)

Who can save you from the Evil One? God. He has the kingdom, and all the power and glory, to conquer any evil, and to do anything and everything you can ask of Him. Are you in a dry place? Do you feel empty? Do not allow the temptation to take hold and fill the emptiness with things that don't belong. The Lord will help you in your desert place. He can fill your emptiness with His love and peace. He will save you.

# July 29

> The LORD is close to the brokenhearted and saves those who are crushed in spirit.
> —Psalm 34:18 (NIV)

The Lord restores the heart that is broken. He brings life and hope. Jesus has already restored you completely. Restoration took place on the cross. He is not bound by time; therefore, what He did "then" on the cross has accomplished restoration in me and you in this very moment, in the "now", just as you and I will be restored "then" in heaven. He rescues, reaffirms, reassures, renews and restores. There is nothing He can't fix.

There may be a time when you need someone close by to comfort you, and to let you know you are not alone. Feeling crushed and broken, cry out to the Lord. He is near and He will save you from the despair that could destroy your peace and hope.

_____

_____

_____

_____

# July 30

> But He said to me, "My grace is sufficient for you, for My power is made perfect in weakness." Therefore I will boast all the more gladly about my weaknesses, so that Christ's power may rest on me.
> —2 Corinthians 12:9 (NIV)

The grace that Jesus gives you is sufficient for any situation you may face. The way He answers you in grace may look different than someone else's answer; but, it will be enough, and it is personalized for you in this very moment. Grace to one may be deliverance from a life-threatening disease, while grace to another may be the strength to persevere through the pain of the disease even to the last days of life. Both beginning in weakness, and both ending with deliverance because of God's grace.

_____
_____
_____
_____

# July 31

You may have been waiting for God to answer your prayers, and finally an answer comes. The moment the long awaited little red caboose appears at the end of the locomotive, and then passes you by in an instant, the gates swing open and off you go to the other side. You made it. You are finally moving. You realize a smile returned to your face, then laughter—shockingly and almost unrecognizable. You are ready to start your journey on the other side of the tracks—from this side of tragedy to the other side of restoration.

# August

Say to God, "How awesome are Your deeds!
So great is Your power
that Your enemies cringe before You.
—Psalm 66:3 (NIV)

# Rejoice!

# August 1

> The righteous will rejoice in the LORD and take refuge in Him; all the upright in heart will glory in Him!
> —Psalm 64:10 (NIV)

When you need help, I have good news! You have a place of refuge in the Lord. Notice how the psalmist said to *rejoice* and take *refuge*. So, it is understood that in the moment when you are hurting or struggling and need a place of refuge, you can also rejoice. Why? Because, your help is here. God is your sanctuary. So, let all the good-hearted people praise the Lord.

# August 2

Of David. When he pretended to be insane before Abimelek, who drove him away, and he left.
I will extol the LORD at all times; His praise will always be on my lips. I will glory in the LORD; let the afflicted hear and rejoice. Glorify the LORD with me; let us exalt His name together.
—Psalm 34:1–3 (NIV)

The scripture began with deceit. David was pretending to be insane. Yet, he calls us to glorify the Lord in the psalm, with a call to praise the Lord with him. David condemned deceit, yet his actions were that of a deceiver. This time of David's life was not one of spiritual vitality and personal piety, but one of instability and fear. David was to be king of Israel. How could his actions be conceived as one with dignity and honor? It can't.

In 1 Samuel, we hear the full story. When Saul became jealous of David because of David's heroic achievements and praise of the people, he sought to kill him. And deception became David's way of dealing with danger. David was running from Saul; he instructed his wife to lie to Saul (her father); he told his friend, Jonathan, to lie to Saul when he was expected at a feast; in Nob, he lied to the priest Ahimelich as to why he was alone and asked for provisions and a weapon. The priest gave him consecrated bread and the sword he had taken from Goliath—remember, he told the Israelites, he didn't need a weapon to conquer the Philistines for the Lord was on his side. But now he does need a weapon? Because of his lies, Ahimeleh and eighty-four other priests were executed at Saul's command. David said later that he was morally responsible for the slaughter. David had the heart of vengeance when he intended to kill Nabal and every male heir. He would have if not for the godly intervention that took place there.

Ultimately, he landed in Gath—the home of Philistines, looking for an alliance with Israel's enemies. He was willing to join the forces with Achish and fight against the Israelites. His escape to Gath was in hopes that Saul would not search for him in that territory. No hope in God, no hope in the Lord's strength and protection. Deception and violence was his way of coping with danger. Achish refused and did not form a reliance with David. David feared Achish king of Gath.

Now David resorted to faking insanity. And the king drove him out of the city. David's actions were not noble, and his predicament was not grounds for dishonesty and murder. His actions were not reasonably acceptable. So, it leaves to question how we can harmonize the situation with deceit and praise. The answer is found in Psalm 56. Reflecting on what had happened, David had found the answer to his running, "When I am afraid, I will put my trust in Thee. In God, whose word I praise, in God I have put my trust; I shall not be afraid. What can mere man do to me?" He was not running from man, but his own fear. Fear of Saul, fear of kings, priests, and prophets, became his reason for poor actions. And this is where he renewed His trust in God (a fear of God) and realized that "mere man" can do nothing against him while God is his defense. David was forgiven and restored as a result of his experience.

In your time of trouble; and in your time of victory, you can praise Him. You can stop running, and trust the Lord. Rejoice, for He is our refuge. Learn from David (a man after God's own heart), that fear is the true enemy. And do not fear; instead, exalt the Name of the Lord; proclaim He is God and our trust is in Him alone.

You called out and God heard your cry. Praise Him, even when evildoers plot against you; in the middle of the battle!

---
---
---
---

# August 3

> Dear friends, now we are children of God, and what we will be has not yet been made known. But we know that when Christ appears, we shall be like Him, for we shall see Him as He is. All who have this hope in Him purify themselves, just as He is pure.
>
> —1 John 3:2–3 (NIV)

Did you think you had lost your smile? Did you think your days of tears would never end? Remember the days of childhood, when you were dared to do something you were afraid to do. Did you take the dare? Most children do. Children have an amazing faith that gives them the fearlessness to step out and dare to see if they can make it.

Today, you may want God to bail you out of your trouble; but God wants you to trust Him to see you through it. You are His child and you can have that child-like faith to be brave and persevere through it. There is a bigger picture that is not yet known to us. Don't give up. He will see you through it.

_____
_____
_____
_____

# August 4

> Hear my prayer, LORD God Almighty; listen to me, God of Jacob. Look on our shield, O God; look with favor on your anointed one.
> LORD Almighty, blessed is the one who trusts in You.
> —Psalm 84:8–9, 12 (NIV)

David remembered his place. He was the anointed one. He remembered who he was. The Lord is Almighty; He is our shield; we are His children; we are blessed as the ones who trust in Him.

Almighty (defined) by Merriam-Webster: [3]

**1** *often capitalized*: having absolute power over all
- *Almighty* God

**2 a**: relatively unlimited in power
- an *almighty* board of directors

**b**: having or regarded as having great power or importance
- the *almighty* dollar

**3** *informal*: MIGHTY —used as an intensive
- an *almighty* shock

He is greater than any circumstance. He is in front of you and behind you, and everywhere you turn. He is in complete control, unstoppable, and has power over all. You can trust this omnipotent God.

_____
_____
_____
_____

# August 5

> Shout for joy to God, all the earth! Sing the glory of His name; make His praise glorious. Say to God, "How awesome are Your deeds! So great is Your power that Your enemies cringe before You.
> All the earth bows down to You; they sing praise to You, they sing the praises of Your name."
> —Psalm 66:1–4 (NIV)

Joy. He turns your mourning into dancing, and your tears fade as the smile returns. See what awesome things He has done for you because of His love, and all for His glory. Wipe the tears from your eyes and see how God has delivered you. He stayed close by you, held you in times of trouble. He showed you His love in ways you'd never seen before—His love is fierce, relentless in His pursuit. He chases after you when you are running away in fear. He found you when you were deep in the pit of despair and hopelessness—you are no longer lost. Your faith is stronger now. Your love is deeper. Let your heart cry out in praises, for He has done, and will do, great things!

# August 6

Come and see what God has done, His awesome deeds for mankind! He turned the sea into dry land, they passed through the waters on foot—come, let us rejoice in Him. He rules forever by His power, His eyes watch the nations—let not the rebellious rise up against Him.
—Psalm 66:5–7 (NIV)

Today, let us remember what God has done. He did not leave you in the desert—in your place of desolation; but, He made a way for you to go forward. His eyes have stayed on you and He will never leave your side. Rejoice in Him; give thanks to Him for what He has already done!

# August 7

> Praise our God, all peoples, let the sound of His praise be heard; He has preserved our lives and kept our feet from slipping. For You, God, tested us; You refined us like silver. You brought us into prison and laid burdens on our backs. You let people ride over our heads; we went through fire and water, but You brought us to a place of abundance.
> —Psalm 66:8–12 (NIV)

First comes the fire, and then the water. And then the place of abundance. Are you in the fire? Are you still struggling through a difficult time? Remember the hope you have in God. He is the one who will set you on the road to life. Have you finally crossed over to the other side of your desert place? You made it! The refining fire burned; it hurt. Now, you are refined—through trials and pain, you made it. Now, remember what once was done, He will do again. He restores; He makes new; He forgives, justifies and frees us from the bondage of sin. Whatever may have held you back before, no longer has a grip on you. He makes us stronger and better. His rewards are much more than we expect.

_____

_____

_____

# August 8

> I will come to your temple with burnt offerings and fulfill my vows to You—vows my lips promised and my mouth spoke when I was in trouble. I will sacrifice fat animals to You and an offering of rams; I will offer bulls and goats.
>
> —Psalm 66:13–15 (NIV)

In times of trouble, we often make vows to God that, if He saves us, we promise we will repay Him; with sacrificial gifts and offerings of ourselves. But what happens after the salvation of the Lord? Do we keep our promises? Do we actually offer more to the Lord and His mission? Sadly, many fall away from their commitments.

What have you promised the Lord? After all that He has done, is it too much of a sacrifice? I don't believe so. Whatever the Lord requires of you today, freely give. Let it be a sacrifice of praise, honor and thanksgiving to God who has saved you time and time again.

# August 9

Come and hear, all you who fear God; let me tell you what He has done for me. I cried out to Him with my mouth; His praise was on my tongue. If I had cherished sin in my heart, the Lord would not have listened; but God has surely listened and has heard my prayer. Praise be to God, who has not rejected my prayer or withheld His love from me!

—Psalm 66:16–20 (NIV)

See what incredible love the Father has given us. Blessed with His love and saving hand, we can trust Him. No longer living in fear, we can believe. Believe even when bad news comes and words of defeat shout in your ears. When you are tested, let your faith be deeply rooted in the foundation of God's Word—and how will this happen unless you are reading God's Word daily to know the truths of it? Believe when life's worries cloud your mind, when you see others with so much and are happy with all that they have, and you have so little. Know God does have a plan—a good plan and one that matters.

Tell *your* story. Tell them what God had done for you. You called out to Him and He answered. Shout it! Say with me, "Rejoice, my soul, rejoice!"

# August 10

Let us hold unswervingly to the hope we profess, for He who promised is faithful.
—Hebrews 10:23 (NIV)

Are you hurting? Jesus loves you so much that He gave His life for you. He always tends to your heart first. If you are lost, or have loss in your life, your mourning will not last forever. Your morning will come, just as that first morning when Jesus rose from the dead after the brutal death on the cross. You will rejoice as life returns to your broken state. Remember, we have hope and security in God knowing that He is here—to the rescue. He brought hope into the world when He was born, and He can bring hope in your situation too. Better than a hero of this world; better than any security system or walls we can build for protection; He is here to save your soul, mend your heart, heal your mind and restore your peace.

# August 11

> And if the Spirit of Him who raised Jesus from the dead is living in you, He who raised Christ from the dead will also give life to your mortal bodies because of His Spirit who lives in you.
>
> —Romans 8:11 (NIV)

Is your heart in need of a transplant? Is your heart giving you problems? Rejoice, for the one who gives life and who is able to perform the operation is here. He can, and will, make your heart brand new, removing the imperfections and replacing them with the works of the Spirit. He can remove the sin and the hurt, and make you pure and whole again.

There may be heart issues that need to be addressed. At some point in life, you will find this to be true. There is, was, or will be a time for the need to transform your heart. As you come to the Great Physician, God will heal you and then deal with the deeper issues. As the Holy Spirit convicts you of these things, allow God to resolve them for you. Praise God, though we are convicted of our sins, we are not condemned by them. What a gentle God we have. He is the Physician that understands our needs—He created us.

# August 12

> You are the God who performs miracles; You display Your power among the peoples.
> —Psalm 77:14 (NIV)

Do you need a miracle? Does your family need a miracle? Your neighborhood, country? Be still and know that He is God and He is the one who can perform miracles for His children in order to meet their needs. As you wait for the Lord to bring it to you, rejoice!

---
---
---
---

# August 13

> My sheep listen to My voice; I know them, and they follow Me.
>
> —John 10:27 (NIV)

Draw near to the Shepherd. As you draw near to God, He will draw near to you. If you are lost, He will find you. He will stay with you wherever you go. You can talk to Him, no matter where you are and He will speak to you. As a child of God, you will know His voice. You will not mistake others to be Him. Know His Word—know what His voice sounds like. Do not be deceived, when you hear voices of others that contradict the scriptures. When you hear His voice, rejoice!

# August 14

> Please, God, rescue me! Come quickly, LORD, and help me.
> May those who try to kill me be humiliated and put to shame.
> May those who take delight in my trouble be turned back in disgrace.
> Let them be horrified by their shame, for they said, "Aha! We've got him now!"
> But may all who search for You be filled with joy and gladness in You.
> May those who love Your salvation repeatedly shout, "God is great!"
> But as for me, I am poor and needy; please hurry to my aid, O God.
> You are my helper and my savior; O LORD, do not delay..
> —Psalm 70:1–5 (NLT)

Rejoice while still in distress; while you wait for God to answer; with the same breath you cry out for help, shout out how awesome your God is. We know who can save, and are filled with joy and gladness, because we know He will. We know God is a mighty God!

_____

_____

_____

_____

# August 15

Jesus—the Divine Christ! He experienced a life-giving birth and a death-killing death. Not only birth from the womb, but baptismal birth of His ministry and sacrificial death. And all the while the Spirit is confirming the truth, the reality of God's presence at Jesus' baptism and crucifixion, bringing those occasions alive for us. A triple testimony: the Spirit, the Baptism, the Crucifixion. And the three in perfect agreement.

—1 John 5:6–8 (MSG)

The Holy Spirit bears witness directly to our spirit confirming the truth—the reality of God's presence, bringing truth to life for us that the Father, the Son and the Holy Spirit are one. And He is alive and is working in us His purpose for His kingdom.

_____
_____
_____
_____

# August 16

Thrilling, then terrifying.

Enjoyable, then exasperating.

Anxious, then audacious.

Definite, then doubtful.

This journey we travel is exciting, and sometimes exhausting. So, rejoice while still weak; be brave when you face your fears; be faithful in the midst of doubt; persistent in trial; steadfast and immovable against sin and the enemy. Plant yourself near the water. Let your roots be grounded and firmly planted. Look for truth when winter's winds and the cold extremes take the life from your branches. Spring will come, and you will feel the warmth of the sun, and the calm breeze through the branches, returning the evidence of life.

_____

_____

_____

> Hope deferred makes the heart sick; but when dreams come true at last, there is life and joy.
> —Proverbs 13:12 (TLB)

The Lord gives good gifts. He transforms your dreams into reality. Though your heart may ache for a time, He will stay with you until what He has promised and that you have hoped for finally becomes the reality and you rejoice again!

_____

_____

# August 18

But this precious treasure—this light and power that now shine within us—is held in a perishable container, that is, in our weak bodies. Everyone can see that the glorious power within must be from God and is not our own.

We are pressed on every side by troubles, but not crushed and broken. We are perplexed because we don't know why things happen as they do, but we don't give up and quit. We are hunted down, but God never abandons us. We get knocked down, but we get up again and keep going. These bodies of ours are constantly facing death just as Jesus did; so it is clear to all that it is only the living Christ within who keeps us safe.

We boldly say what we believe, trusting God to care for us, just as the psalm writer did when he said, "I believe and therefore I speak."

—2 Corinthians 4:7–10, 13 (TLB)

I believe, therefore, I speak.

Are you afraid to step out and do what the Lord has called you to do? I have two words for you: Be brave. Jesus often told others, "Take courage," and "Don't be afraid." He can move mountains. He can move the wind, and calm the storm with one word. Trust Him to move you. Paul and his friends faced death. He understood what it meant to speak and risk his own life. But he understood too that it resulted in eternal life for those who heard and believed. We may not be facing death when we speak out, but we will face resistance. Don't be afraid of the resistance, or ridicule, or fear that you may fail. Struggles of life gives us constant opportunities to show others the power of Jesus Christ. When you get knocked down, get up again and keep going. You can do this.

Speak boldly. Believe, trusting God to take care of you. Keep in mind those who will be won to the Lord, and the more the Lord will be glorified.

# August 19

> Early on the first day of the week, while it was still dark, Mary Magdalene went to the tomb and saw that the stone had been removed from the entrance. So she came running to Simon Peter and the other disciple, the one Jesus loved, and said, "They have taken the Lord out of the tomb, and we don't know where they have put Him!"
> —John 20:1–2 (NIV)

Only a couple of days before, Mary watched while Jesus was brutally beaten, tortured and then crucified. It was still dark when she arrived at the tomb, and she found it empty—a miracle. Jesus was alive! She couldn't believe it, and feared someone had moved Him. But the truth was that He rose from the dead.

In your darkest hour, while it is still dark, know that He is with you and your morning is near. Rejoice!

# August 20

Be alert and of sober mind. Your enemy the devil prowls around like a roaring lion looking for someone to devour. Resist him, standing firm in the faith, because you know that the family of believers throughout the world is undergoing the same kind of sufferings.

And the God of all grace, who called you to His eternal glory in Christ, after you have suffered a little while, will Himself restore you and make you strong, firm and steadfast. To Him be the power for ever and ever. Amen.

With the help of Silas, whom I regard as a faithful brother, I have written to you briefly, encouraging you and testifying that this is the true grace of God. Stand fast in it.

—1 Peter 5:8–12 (NIV)

Though your hope is lost and your life may be shattered, there is a God who restores. Rejoice! He will supply you with grace which is sufficient for your situation.

One day as I was driving to work, I pulled up to stoplight. A man driving behind me did not stop in time and hit my car. I got out of my car and walked around to the back of my car to see what the damage was. The man got out of his car and began apologizing as I was inspecting my car. When I turned to look at him, he was covered from shoulders to feet with what looked like a blended green breakfast drink, which I found out from him that was the case. He said when he hit my car his drink splattered everywhere. He was on the way to work and obviously would not be able to go to work looking like that. I then had pity on him—and tried not to laugh. I saw him not for what he had done to my car at that point, but what he had done to himself. He showed me the front seat and dashboard of his car and it was also covered in the mess. I told him not to worry about my car and acknowledged his need to clean up the car—and himself. He thanked me profusely and got back in his car.

That is how Jesus sees us. He does not see us as the ones who put

Him on the cross. Although it is true. He sees what we have done to ourselves—with the mess we have made. And He has compassion and love and gives us grace and mercy and forgiveness.

I had the power that day to make a claim and make him pay for the damages. Grace and mercy showed up when I saw the man in his own mess. We are forgiven because Jesus sees us through His eyes of compassion.

Though life can leave you feeling mangled, Jesus can come in and give you life. He can put you back together again and make you new—as if you had never been broken. All that the enemy steals from you, God will take back. He will restore to you all that was lost—He will bring it back, replace it, or make it so that you no longer need what was lost. You will be whole no matter the path it may take. You will be free of fear, and again rejoice!

---------------
---------------
---------------
---------------

# August 21

> Rejoice in the Lord always. I will say it again: Rejoice!
> Let your gentleness be evident to all. The Lord is near.
> —Philippians 4:4–5 (NIV)

Celebrate God every day and all day long. Let all those around you know what the Lord has done for you; share hope with them. Let them know God is near and He cares. Encourage them to wait for Him.

One day, my sisters, Lanette and Sharon, were reminiscing of our hike up a mountain. I was struggling at this time of my life. Thinking of the hike, I remembered how we couldn't see an end with each turn we took on the path. It seemed endless and unreachable, but we made it. We encouraged Lanette to keep moving forward, and she did. Her act of perseverance was an inspiration to us all. And Lanette encouraged me in my time of struggling as she told me, "You can do it! And sometimes it will be a huge struggle like it was for me, but keep going and you'll get there!" She reminded us, "It was really difficult, just like things are for you right now. It was a miracle that I made it, because at least the last half of the *climb* was brutal. For every step, I had to push myself and take the next step with faith that I would make it. Faith as big as a grain of mustard seed was all I had for each step."

The higher you get, the more difficult the climb. Just a small amount of faith—even if it's simply to say, "You are God, and I believe that you are"—will be all that it will take for you to keep moving forward ... pushing through in the strength of the Lord. Don't be ashamed to admit your weakness. You may feel you should be stronger through this, but God knows your weaknesses and understands you more than you understand yourself. It may take a miracle, and that takes God to move, and He will. He is near.

# August 22

> Do not worry about anything, but pray and ask God for everything you need, always giving thanks. And God's peace, which is so great we cannot understand it, will keep your hearts and minds in Christ Jesus.
> —Philippians 4:6–7 (NCV)

Instead of worrying, pray. When you feel your anxiety rising up within you, stop; call out to God, and pour out your heart to Him. When you have prayed to the point of peace in your heart, you have prayed through—through the storm. Such a peace that cannot be explained or understood will now overwhelm you—not the circumstances. You find peace in the middle of the storm.

In Jesus we find hope and the power of His Spirit to keep moving heavenward. In Jesus we have purpose in this great plan of His. So put before the Lord your plans, praying and believing He presented the plan to you. As you go in the direction God has planned, He goes with you. And the hopes and dreams we have must come from God—as we are one with God, we ask only what is in the will of God.

# August 23

God, have mercy on us and bless us and show us Your kindness so the world will learn Your ways, and all nations will learn that You can save.

God, the people should praise You; all people should praise You. The nations should be glad and sing because You judge people fairly. You guide all the nations on earth.

God, the people should praise You; all people should praise You. The land has given its crops. God, our God, blesses us. God blesses us so people all over the earth will fear Him.

—Psalm 67 (NCV)

# August 24

Let God rise up and scatter His enemies; let those who hate Him run away from Him. Blow them away as smoke is driven away by the wind. As wax melts before a fire, let the wicked be destroyed before God. But those who do right should be glad and should rejoice before God; they should be happy and glad.

Sing to God; sing praises to His name. Prepare the way for Him who rides through the desert, whose name is the Lord. Rejoice before Him. God is in His holy Temple. He is a father to orphans, and He defends the widows. God gives the lonely a home. He leads prisoners out with joy, but those who turn against God will live in a dry land.

God, You led your people out when You marched through the desert. Selah

—Psalm 68:1–7 (NCV)

He is the Father to fatherless; He protects the widows. Are you lonely? He will be the father, the husband, the caretaker; He will give you a home. Are you in bondage—to fear, sin? He will set you free.

There may be happenstances that will break you. You may be left feeling that you are unlovable, useless, unworthy, and unfit for any ministry or even to be called a child of God. You may believe that anything you could have done before and all of the plans you may have made up to this point have now been destroyed. But God has placed you on a particular journey. And what you have thought impossible, He can make possible. Truly His grace is sufficient in every conflict, in every moment. His love is stronger. Even when things go wrong, even when surrounded with trouble, God is still with you, and that's all you need to know. New dreams can be created, and they come from His heart, not of your own making.

# August 25

Praise the Lord, God our Savior, who helps us every day. Selah

—Psalm 68:19 (NCV)

Every day. Not some days, but every day. God will carry your burdens. He will help you with each and every task set before you. Allow Him to carry the weight and walk with Him in your journey throughout the day.

# August 26

God, order up Your power; show the mighty power You have used for us before.

God, You are wonderful in Your Temple. The God of Israel gives His people strength and power.

Praise God!

—Psalm 68:28, 35 (NCV)

As God has done before, may He show His strength and power again. For He is an awesome God!

I know sometimes the pain and emptiness can seem so long, and as dry as the season with nothing but what looks dead. But, the day comes when redemption comes and your broken heart is mended, and all that was once dead comes to life much more beautiful than it was before the harsh, cold season. Look up. He is near.

---
---
---
---

# August 27

Praise the Lord.

Praise the Lord, my soul.

I will praise the Lord all my life; I will sing praise to my God as long as I live. Do not put your trust in princes, in human beings, who cannot save. When their spirit departs, they return to the ground; on that very day their plans come to nothing. Blessed are those whose help is the God of Jacob, whose hope is in the Lord their God.

—Psalm 146:1–5 (NIV)

Though your heart is weak, and the sin and weight of the world has left you broken, let His love and grace fall on your head like rain, and praise Him. Even when you have nothing left, and no words to express how you feel, praise Him. Let Him take the mountain of weight and wipe the tears from your eyes. Even when nothing makes sense, and the world does not understand how you can praise Him, give Him praise. Sing until your miracle comes. Praise Him in the trouble; praise Him when the battle is over and won; praise Him as you enter into eternity.

Our souls—the very core of who we are, knows God and sings praises to the Lord. Remember where our help comes from. The help from friends, family, wealth or stature (even like that of a prince), will only provide temporary help. Rather, hope in the Lord. He is the one who knows your heart and understands everything you are made of. He can change you or the circumstances around you. He is your refuge and your every source of help.

# August 28

He is the Maker of heaven and earth, the sea, and everything in them—He remains faithful forever.
He upholds the cause of the oppressed and gives food to the hungry. The LORD sets prisoners free, the LORD gives sight to the blind, the LORD lifts up those who are bowed down, the LORD loves the righteous.
—Psalm 146:6–8 (NIV)

Has anyone ever wronged you? God will defend you. Are you in need? He will supply all of your needs. Do you feel trapped in sin or a situation caused by sin against you? God will set you free. Do you need healing? He is the Great Physician. Have you fallen away from the ways of the Lord? He will lift you up. He loves you. He will protect you.

While you wait, do not be afraid. Let your faith remain. Hope in the things not yet seen. As the curtain was torn in two when Jesus made a way on the cross, let the glory of God be revealed as He opens the way between you and your place of brokenness, to the place of His glory and forgiveness, where you will see the fullness of His love, child of God face to face with Him. Be lost in the wonder of His love and beauty. Oh, how He loves you!

# August 29

The LORD watches over the foreigner and sustains the fatherless and the widow, but He frustrates the ways of the wicked.

The LORD reigns forever, your God, O Zion, for all generations.

Praise the LORD.

—Psalm 146:9–10 (NIV)

God is always in charge; and as His child, He is on your side. He will block the way of the wicked and protect His own. God cannot be manipulated. He cannot be fooled. He knows the hearts of His children and knows the ways of the wicked.

# August 30

> Therefore, since we have a great high priest who has ascended into heaven, Jesus the Son of God, let us hold firmly to the faith we profess. For we do not have a high priest who is unable to empathize with our weaknesses, but we have one who has been tempted in every way, just as we are—yet He did not sin. Let us then approach God's throne of grace with confidence, so that we may receive mercy and find grace to help us in our time of need.
> —Hebrews 4:14–16 (NIV)

If you question whether God has directed you one way or the other, remember God is bigger than your misunderstanding. When the time comes, God will lead the way. God will reveal things that need to be revealed. Some things you may not know until the race is finished. You can live a life restored and yet still be broken. What an oxymoron this is. When the rain keeps pouring and life continues to diminish, trust God.

You may wonder why you are where you are, frustrated by the events you're going through or tired of the constant changes and negative circumstances. You may be wondering where God is and why He isn't moving. But God is in that place with you. He was there before this long journey began, has been with you on the journey through difficult times, and will be with you when you are on the other side of it. So don't lose heart. Keep believing. He is still on the throne and still rules over every minute detail of your life. Keep moving forward.

# August 31

You give life; You are love; You bring light to the darkness. You give hope; You restore every heart that is broken. Great are You Lord!

—Great Are You Lord
Song Lyrics By Jason Ingram, Leslie Jordan and David Leonard

God wants to restore every area of your life. He will redeem lost years. As you allow God to rule and reign over your life, He will restore your soul to life, and will replace good with what was stolen by the enemy.

# September

Living on the other side of the railroad crossings ~ the journey continues.

# Restored to Believe

# September 1

> You have multiplied, O Lord my God, Your wondrous deeds and Your thoughts toward us; none can compare with You! I will proclaim and tell of them, yet they are more than can be told.
> —Psalm 40:5 (ESV)

Let me remind you of how awesome God is, and the incredible things He has done. You made it! You were once destined to destruction, and now you are redeemed. Now you believe! Though you faced tragedy and though the pain seemed overwhelming, you made it to the other side—He brought light, hope, restoration! God has been faithful and will remain true until the end of days.

Praise Him! You will remember this day—a day when God reached down and saved you.

Our hearts will cry out, "Great is Your wondrous love, oh God!"

# September 2

> Give praise to the LORD, proclaim His name; make known among the nations what He has done. Sing to Him, sing praise to Him; tell of all His wonderful acts.
> —1 Chronicles 16:8–9 (NIV)

Tell others what the Lord has done for you. Remember the miracles and how He has saved you.

Even when we cannot see the answers to our questions, and even if He answered in a way we didn't expect, He showed up. Our hope is in God alone. The people around you need to know that today. What's your story of restoration, redemption and hope?

# September 3

> Be careful to follow every command I am giving you today, so that you may live and increase and may enter and possess the land the Lord promised on oath to your ancestors. Remember how the Lord your God led you all the way in the wilderness these forty years, to humble and test you in order to know what was in your heart, whether or not you would keep his commands.
> —Deuteronomy 8:1–2 (NIV)

The children of Israel were in the desert forty years. They were tested to show their true heart. When you are in the middle of a difficult situation, your true heart will be known. When you trust God in these times, your heart will show humility and right-standing with God. In tough times, you will be tempted to complain, or act out of your anger, or give in to sin. But, stay strong in the Lord. Know that this is only temporary and God is creating an eternal character in you for His eternal purpose.

___
___
___
___

# September 4

> I want to know Christ and experience the mighty power that raised Him from the dead. I want to suffer with Him, sharing in His death, so that one way or another I will experience the resurrection from the dead!
> —Philippians 3:10–11 (NLT)

Can you share that desire? To know Jesus; to experience the mighty power that raised Him from the dead? I'm sure you do. Then comes the next question: Do you want to suffer with Him, sharing in His death? That's not the easy part, to say the least. But, Paul understood it was a matter of perspective. He knew that one day he would experience the resurrection from the dead! One day, He would see Jesus. One day, all of the suffering, the sicknesses, the death, would end. So, we can say, too, "I want to know Jesus; I want to experience His power; I want to suffer through this, because one day I will be restored to life!"

# September 5

> But whatever were gains to me I now consider loss for the sake of Christ. What is more, I consider everything a loss because of the surpassing worth of knowing Christ Jesus my Lord, for whose sake I have lost all things. I consider them garbage, that I may gain Christ and be found in Him, not having a righteousness of my own that comes from the law, but that which is through faith in Christ—the righteousness that comes from God on the basis of faith.
> —Philippians 3:7–9 (NIV)

Accomplishments are rewarding. You feel good when you succeed. Like Paul, though, we know Jesus is worth so much more than any earthly success. Seek to know more about Jesus—through prayer and the reading of the Bible, and by fasting. You will find treasures in Him that are much more valuable than the accomplishments and successes of this world. Don't let commercialism and the need for popularity be your motivation in what you do. To seek the intangible things will require a change in perspective and determination. It won't be easy to give up on everything the media, and maybe even your family, is pushing you to do, but that is why it is called "crucifying the flesh." If you have lost much, He will restore much. But be ready to let go of anything that God deems no longer necessary or beneficial for you.

---
---
---
---

# September 6

Now the Jordan is at flood stage all during harvest. Yet as soon as the priests who carried the ark reached the Jordan and their feet touched the water's edge, the water from upstream stopped flowing. It piled up in a heap a great distance away, at a town called Adam in the vicinity of Zarethan, while the water flowing down to the Sea of the Arabah (that is, the Dead Sea) was completely cut off. So the people crossed over opposite Jericho.

For the LORD your God dried up the Jordan before you until you had crossed over. The LORD your God did to the Jordan what He had done to the Red Sea when He dried it up before us until we had crossed over. He did this so that all the peoples of the earth might know that the hand of the LORD is powerful and so that you might always fear the LORD your God."
—Joshua 3:15-16 and 4:23-24 (NIV)

Remembering the Dry Ground

Joshua and Caleb were present forty years earlier, when God parted the Red Sea so that the Israelites could escape the Egyptian army. Can you imagine what thoughts were rushing through their minds when the Jordan River stopped flowing from upstream and parted as the feet of the priests carrying the Ark touched the edge of the water? Notice the Jordan was at flood stage, so the people must have watched in awe of this phenomenon. They knew God was present and that the hand of the Lord was powerful.

Do you ever feel you are right back up against the same wall that hindered you before? When you are reminded of God's presence, and remember how you witnessed His power to set you free, God wants you to revere Him and know how powerful He is. Remembering what God has done in the past as you saw His power unfold, should not cause you to fear He will never move as mighty as to match such an experience again.

Do not become frozen in fear; but, instead His presence and knowledge of His power can give you the courage to step out in faith and trust God to lead you through again—through whatever the rapid rivers of circumstances you face, that is keeping you from moving forward. He parted the way before; He'll do it again.

# September 7

> "Go, find out where he is," the king ordered, "so I can send men and capture him." The report came back: "He is in Dothan." Then he sent horses and chariots and a strong force there. They went by night and surrounded the city.
>
> When the servant of the man of God got up and went out early the next morning, an army with horses and chariots had surrounded the city. "Oh no, my lord! What shall we do?" the servant asked.
>
> "Don't be afraid," the prophet answered. "Those who are with us are more than those who are with them."
>
> —2 Kings 6:13–16 (NIV)

Elisha's servant, Gehazi, must have thought Elisha was speaking in metaphor or had suddenly lost all sense of reality. Gehazi counted two—Elisha (one), himself (two). As he was looking around to see if there was anyone else with them and finding no one else that had come to their rescue, he didn't understand the prophet, Elisha. But Elisha saw something that Gehazi couldn't see. And Elisha prayed, "Open his eyes, Lord, so that he may see." Then the Lord opened the servant's eyes, and he looked and saw the hills full of horses and chariots of fire all around Elisha. (2 Kings 6:17 NIV)

Not alone, but surrounded by forces sent by God!

You may not see it, but you are not alone. God is present and can call upon His armies if necessary to defend you.

---------
---------
---------
---------

# September 8

> For I know the plans I have for you," declares the LORD,
> "plans to prosper you and not to harm you, plans to give
> you hope and a future.
> —Jeremiah 29:11 (NIV)

Just as God promised the Israelites then, He still promises you today, that He has a plan—plans to prosper you. Trust Him today, for His plan is good.

A walk of faith will require you to go all in! Take all of what you have and place in a "bucket." Then watch as God takes what He has and places it in that bucket. Can you see how minimal your portion is now compared to His riches? He promises to supply all your needs from His riches in glory because of what Christ Jesus has done for us. (Philippians 4:19 TLB). His ability to supply all of what we need for today or the future does not depend upon what we have in the bucket. God did not say, I will supply all of your needs according to what is in your savings account or what you can provide, but what *He* has and what *He* provides. So why do we worry about our little portion? The fear sets in when we can't see it, or we don't know if it's enough for the future. Don't look at your portion—look at His! His portion is enough to ensure His plan turns out exactly the way He intended.

# September 9

> Now to Him who is able to do immeasurably more than all we ask or imagine, according to His power that is at work within us, to Him be glory in the church and in Christ Jesus throughout all generations, for ever and ever! Amen.
> —Ephesians 3:20–21 (NIV)

Can you dream big? I'm sure you can. As you draw close to God, His desires will become your desires. What you had dreamed up will be outdone by God's dreams for you. And, He has all the power to work this plan in us, so that in this plan, God is glorified.

Do you feel as if your dreams have been crushed? Just as Jesus did not stay in the grave after His horrific death on the cross but was gloriously resurrected, your dreams that have died can be revived again.

People have said, "Keep your eyes on the prize'." It's a catchy phrase, but I have to say, your prize must be Jesus, and any other prize/gift is given by Him. So keep your eyes on Jesus, the one who is our gift and the one who gives good gifts.

_____
_____
_____
_____

# September 10

> And my God will meet all your needs according to the riches of his glory in Christ Jesus. To our God and Father be glory for ever and ever. Amen.
> —Philippians 4:19–20 (NIV)

God will not leave you helpless. If you are afraid of losing something, know this: God knows what you need, and if you need it, He will supply it for you. And if you lose it, and need it, He will restore it back to you. Whether it be a job, your home, your spouse, or anything else, God knows and He is able—He has all the riches of His glory at His fingertips. Your loving Father will take care of it.

# September 11

Some of my fears are real; some of them are imaginary. Some of physical; others, psychological or emotional. Some are for loved ones. Whatever the fear, it is keenly felt—an unpleasant experience. And, invariably, the bridge between despair and hope looks awesome and precarious when I am looking down at myself—my circumstances, my feelings, my emotions—instead of looking up and trusting Him whom my soul loves.
—Gigi Graham Tchividjian

Focus on Faith—Not fear; not feelings.

> Many of the people scolded him and told him to be quiet. But he shouted even more loudly, "Son of David, have mercy on me!"
> —Mark 10:48 (GNT)

Don't let your fears control you. Fear can paralyze your potential and ability to move forward in faith. When we choose fear over faith, we can become skeptical of any new ventures. It causes us to look inward, become self-centered and selfish; and thus afraid to keep our commitments with others and God. We are unable to press forward; instead, we focus on the past failures or losses, when we should be looking at the past only to see that God was there and helped us through it.

The blind man in this story wouldn't give up, even when others told him to be quiet. The devil will whisper things like that to us. When we are afraid, our thoughts can scream, "God doesn't care! He isn't here! You need to take control and do something about it yourself!" But God is asking you to depend on Him completely—to trust Him. It can be scary, but you can press forward in faith, past your fears. Don't go back!

Emotions are important. God made us with emotions. He often gives confirming emotions and will answer the most immature, self-centered prayers. He does this so that you will know He exists. But as you grow in faith, He will teach you to trust Him even when you don't feel Him. He wants you to sense His presence, but not depend on what we feel. There will be situations when life falls apart and God seems to be distant and silent. These are the moments that will grow your faith most. Knowing He is there, even when He is silent shows your faith. When these moments come, tell God exactly how you feel. As I mentioned, He created us with emotions, so He understands them. Pour out your heart to Him, with every emotion you are feeling. Then, believe; trust; choose faith.

As I began to live a life of true faith—where I trusted God had control of all things—my perspective changed immensely. My circumstances didn't change who God was and is. The fact that losses in my life were sure to come again did not change God's love for me. In darkness, in times I cannot hear His voice, when God is silent, I can still hold on to what is true and remember all that He has done. I can remember the life I live is only because of Jesus. I am a child of God—forever. My soul is secure. And in time, His light breaks through those dark times. God was teaching me how to live abundantly even in the dark moments—in moments when bad news comes from the doctor, from family, or from the boss.

---
---
---
---

# September 12

### Live the Life of Faith

> Since, then, you have been raised with Christ, set your hearts on things above, where Christ is, seated at the right hand of God. Set your minds on things above, not on earthly things. For you died, and your life is now hidden with Christ in God. When Christ, who is your life, appears, then you also will appear with Him in glory.
>
> —Colossians 3:1–4 (NIV)

Live this new life you have been given. Why would you ever go back to the old way of living—in your own strength and your own set of rules? This new life is lived by a supernatural transformation of God. In all you do, apply that supernatural, heavenly perspective. Ask the question, is what you do glorifying God? Where you go, will it honor Him? Sure, you need to take care of earthly business, but ask yourself why you do what you do. Isn't it, too, for an eternal purpose? As you care for yourself and others so to provide for a better "you" and better family and community, you can do so for the sake of the kingdom.

The Word says to "Work willingly at whatever you do, as though you were working for the Lord rather than for people." (Colossians 3:23 NLT) That means we need to give it our best—building character in us that is pleasing to God, so that God can be glorified in all we do and all that we become. What responsibilities do you have that could be used to honor God?

_____
_____
_____
_____

# September 13

> In this new life, it doesn't matter if you are a Jew or a Gentile, circumcised or uncircumcised, barbaric, uncivilized, slave, or free. Christ is all that matters, and He lives in all of us.
>
> Since God chose you to be the holy people He loves, you must clothe yourselves with tenderhearted mercy, kindness, humility, gentleness, and patience.
> —Colossians 3:11–12 (NLT)

If you are not of Jewish decent, maybe you have wondered if God's promises are for you. Now you know. As Jesus made a way for all people, all nations, from generation to generation, we are now God's chosen people, holy and dearly loved. When God speaks of His children—His people—He is speaking of you. With that being known, rejoice! And in that thought, we can humbly accept this adoption. How can we not then respond with compassion, kindness, humility, gentleness and patience? Who am I but a humble gentile that God would choose me? Whether Jew or Gentile, you and I are now brothers and sisters sharing in the inheritance and promises of God, the Father.

# September 14

> Make allowance for each other's faults, and forgive anyone who offends you. Remember, the Lord forgave you, so you must forgive others. Above all, clothe yourselves with love, which binds us all together in perfect harmony.
> —Colossians 3:13–14 (NLT)

There will come a time, if it hasn't come already, where you will have a grievance with someone who also is a brother or sister in the Lord. And, at times, it may be difficult to know what to do in these instances—whether to defend yourself or let it go. The answer is this: apply love. Ask yourself if what they have done is causing physical harm to one of you, or to someone else; or if it is causing eternal damage to their soul or character, or to your own soul. If the answer is *yes*, then it needs to be addressed. If not, then the conflict may be something of a selfish nature, and you can let it go. People have faults. People are selfish, and though we do need to learn from our mistakes, the key to any response is that we are acting in the best interest of others—in love.

# September 15

### Two Builders

Anyone who hears and obeys these teachings of Mine is like a wise person who built a house on solid rock. Rain poured down, rivers flooded, and winds beat against that house. But it did not fall, because it was built on solid rock.
Anyone who hears My teachings and doesn't obey them is like a foolish person who built a house on sand. The rain poured down, the rivers flooded, and the winds blew and beat against that house. Finally, it fell with a crash.
—Matthew 7:24–27 (CEV)

I love how Jesus speaks in parables. And in this story, Jesus explains how building a house on the rock is like listening to Jesus' Words and putting them into practice.

To live a life of faith, we must listen and put it into practice; and the foundation is what will make a difference. It must be founded on the rock, Jesus. The foundation of Christ is the only foundation that will be secure when the storms of life come. When the storm rages, you will remember the words Jesus spoke, and you will find peace and hope.

Building a tower right next to the water was a fun game I played as a child, and it also is a reminder of how quickly things can come crashing down when they are built with our hands and on a foundation that is weak. Tragedy and loss can leave you feeling weak and powerless. It can bring everything crashing down. You may feel you no longer have control over the circumstances of your life. And that might rightly be so. This hopelessness and loneliness can devastate you. But, in Christ, you are not alone. He will never leave you or forsake you. This sure foundation of hope in Jesus Christ is the only foundation that will withstand any tragedy and remain secure. And on that rock—Jesus—the church will be built.

And why must we build the tower? Why do we work hard to build a life of faith? It is not for others to see. It is not for them to see how great God is, though some would tell you so; and though it may be true that they *will* see how great God is. It is not to show God how faithful you are. No. We build—grow spiritually—for ourselves so that we can become what we are meant to be for the building of the kingdom and for eternity. Then we can be used for a purpose meant to grow the kingdom. Then, yes, others will see the greatness of God as we become a representative of His grace.

_____
_____
_____
_____

# September 16

> When neither sun nor stars appeared for many days
> and the storm continued raging, we finally gave up all
> hope of being saved.
> —Acts 27:20 (NIV)

"We," Paul said. Paul said, "We finally gave up all hope of being saved." There will be storms of this life that will beat you up to the point of giving up all hope—feeling you will not be saved from the storm. Losses will happen in that storm, just as it was for Paul and his shipmates, but finally Paul stood up and proclaimed, "Not one of you will be lost." He found faith and hope again. Why the newfound faith? Because an angel of God had visited him the night before and told him so, and Paul believed.

> So keep up your courage, men, for I have faith in God
> that it will happen just as He told me.
> —Acts 27:25 (NIV)

Are you tired? Do you need strength? Look to God for strength. He holds all power in heaven and earth and has promised to shower you with power and strength, even when the pouring rain of tragedy hits. Believe it. God is with you in the storms of life.

> You, God, are awesome in Your sanctuary; the God of
> Israel gives power and strength to His people.
> Praise be to God!
> —Psalm 68:35 (NIV)

_____

_____

_____

_____

# September 17

> As you come to Him, the living Stone—rejected by humans but chosen by God and precious to Him—you also, like living stones, are being built into a spiritual house to be a holy priesthood, offering spiritual sacrifices acceptable to God through Jesus Christ. For in Scripture it says:
>
> "See, I lay a stone in Zion, a chosen and precious cornerstone, and the one who trusts in Him will never be put to shame."
>
> Now to you who believe, this stone is precious. But to those who do not believe,
>
> "The stone the builders rejected has become the cornerstone," and, "A stone that causes people to stumble and a rock that makes them fall."
>
> They stumble because they disobey the message—which is also what they were destined for.
>
> —1 Peter 2:4–8 (NIV)

Any builder, even a child working with building blocks, learn that the foundation is what will hold the structure together and make it strong. If the foundation is weak, it will ultimately fail. So, let us be grounded firmly in Jesus by trusting Him completely. If you are unsure of the stability of your marriage, home, finances, job, or life, then look to Him who can be the foundation you need. What kind of foundation have you laid before your home, your spouse, your life? Is it time to build a new foundation where Jesus is the basis of all you do? Let everything you do begin with Jesus in mind; then build from there.

I don't know the story of where you are today or what you may be facing, but I do know that God has orchestrated this plan of life and He wants you just where He has planted you. With bold faith, trust Him and His plan.

# September 18

> The weapons we fight with are not the weapons of the world. On the contrary, they have divine power to demolish strongholds. We demolish arguments and every pretension that sets itself up against the knowledge of God, and we take captive every thought to make it obedient to Christ.
> —2 Corinthians 10:4–5 (NIV)

Are your thoughts, emotions and actions based on God's ways? Does love motivate what you do?

If your home was invaded by thieves, wouldn't you call the police, and hope to have the criminal captured and taken out of your home? Of course you would! Just the same, the negative or anxious thoughts can enter your mind and begin destroying your attitude, your marriage, your home, your life and will determine how you respond to things. So, take those thoughts captive with the divine power given to you by God to destroy the hold it has on you. Replace the lies with God's truths. Replace the pain and anxiety with the hope and peace that is found in the fact that Jesus is Lord of your life. Release them to the Lord and replace them with God's Word.

We hold weapons made by God (not of this world)—such as the sword of the Spirit, which is the Word of God (Ephesians 6:17 NIV). We can take every thought captive (your thoughts, or the thoughts of others), and make it obedient to Christ.

People tend to argue with themselves. We wonder if God is real. We wonder if God is present. We wonder if God cares. Our thoughts against the truth (God) can destroy us. But, the Word of God can stop the questioning.

Are your thoughts born of your own desires, or fears, or sin? Take control of those thoughts and replace them with the truth and promises of the Lord. Take on the whole armor of God so that you can stand against the devil's schemes.

# September 19

> My dear children, I write this to you so that you will not sin. But if anybody does sin, we have an advocate with the Father—Jesus Christ, the Righteous One. He is the atoning sacrifice for our sins, and not only for ours but also for the sins of the whole world.
> —1 John 2:1–2 (NIV)

We fail. We struggle; we stumble; we fall.

No matter how hard I try, I will not be able to keep myself *clean*. The world's ugly sin tempts, it taunts, it traps. This is why I need Him. You need Him. I write so much of how we can refrain from sinning, remain faithful, and believe God for restoration; yet, I still find myself needing the same lesson to be learned over and over again.

We can be broken, but still be used by God for His glorious purpose. We can be cast aside, but we are worthy to be God's son and daughter. We can fail, yet God still accepts us and loves us and will keep His promises. God looks at the heart, and if we are sincerely trying to do God's will, that doesn't end the work God had started in us. Others may abandon and criticize when we fail, but God knows our intentions and is able to look past the failure or inadequacies. He lifts us back up and moves on with the plans He has for us.

---
---
---
---

# September 20

> One day as Jesus was preaching on the shore of the Sea of Galilee, great crowds pressed in on Him to listen to the word of God. He noticed two empty boats at the water's edge, for the fishermen had left them and were washing their nets. Stepping into one of the boats, Jesus asked Simon, its owner, to push it out into the water. So He sat in the boat and taught the crowds from there.
>
> When He had finished speaking, He said to Simon, "Now go out where it is deeper, and let down your nets to catch some fish."
>
> "Master," Simon replied, "we worked hard all last night and didn't catch a thing. But if you say so, I'll let the nets down again." And this time their nets were so full of fish they began to tear! A shout for help brought their partners in the other boat, and soon both boats were filled with fish and on the verge of sinking.
>
> —Luke 5:1–7 (NLT)

Peter (then called Simon) told Jesus that they had tried and tried, but to no avail. And Jesus told them to try again. The difference? Jesus was involved. Peter listened as Jesus spoke, and did what Jesus said to do. I don't think they expected the results they actually got; otherwise, they might have taken more boats out, and more men to help.

When it makes no sense, trust Jesus and do what He says to do, and be prepared for much more than you expect. Even when it doesn't make sense, believe it. Note the story of Daniel in the lion's den. Daniel was faithful and did not defile himself (Daniel 1:8), and when he was thrown into the lion's den, God was faithful to him and the lion's mouths were shut by the hand of God. You too can remain faithful and not allow fear, doubt, and uncertainty to cloud your vision. Stand firm. Remain confident and sure. Remember Moses, who felt inadequate to speak on God's behalf. Yet, God called him to lead His people out of bondage. Though you may feel inadequate in your ability to do what God asks of you, believe He will give you what you need to carry it out. And it was faith that brought the walls of Jericho tumbling down after the people of Israel had walked around them seven days as God had commanded them. It didn't make sense that walking around the walls of Jericho, then blowing trumpets and shouting that the walls would fall. But it happened. Let's not forget the people of Israel who trusted God and walked on dry ground through the Red Sea. But when the Egyptians chasing them tried to follow, they all were drowned.

If God asks you to go, then go. He will not ask you to do anything and then allow you to fail.

---
---
---
---

# September 21

> For God so loved the world that He gave His one and only Son, that whoever believes in Him shall not perish but have eternal life.
> —John 3:16 (NIV)

What life are you living? Are you living the life that God intended for you? There is an everlasting life—and it's found in faith—believing in Jesus. Let your view be set on His eternal kingdom and truly live.

Strive for success and you may succeed. Look for love and you may find it. Work to obtain what you dream of having, and you may have it. But, think about why you strive for these things—it's about happiness, and finding peace once we arrive. So, if you think about it, if we're all looking for something to find peace, then all we need to do is find Jesus and trust that all is in His hands. Our lives are in His control, and that brings you peace if you believe it to be so. And that, friends, is a life of happiness.

---
---
---
---

# September 22

> But now that you have been set free from sin and have become slaves of God, the benefit you reap leads to holiness, and the result is eternal life. For the wages of sin is death, but the gift of God is eternal life in Christ Jesus our Lord.
>
> —Romans 6:22–23 (NIV)

This life—eternal—is not earned. It's not won or rewarded by great accomplishments. It is a gift which we can accept through faith. The benefit of this gift is freedom which leads to holiness and eternal life. We cannot wait until we are worthy to accept this gift. Instead, we accept the gift, and He makes us holy by His righteousness living in us.

# September 23

> "I have told you these things, so that in me you may have peace. In this world you will have trouble. But take heart! I have overcome the world."
> —John 16:33 (NIV)

Jesus said there'd be days like this. Our life—this path we are on—can be challenging. You might find yourself in a place you hadn't planned—whether it happened because of choices you made or by unforeseen circumstances beyond your control. But, here you are nonetheless. Jesus reminds us, "Take heart! I have overcome the world."

# September 24

For this *is* God,
Our God forever and ever;
He will be our guide,
*Even* to death.

—Psalm 48:14 (NKJV)

In victory, God is our God. In trial or pain, He continues to be our God. On mountains, in valleys, in oceans and deserts—yes, He is our God. We can follow God even to the end!

# September 25

Jesus Calms the Storm

> Then Jesus got into the boat and started across the lake with his disciples. Suddenly, a fierce storm struck the lake, with waves breaking into the boat. But Jesus was sleeping. The disciples went and woke Him up, shouting, "Lord, save us! We're going to drown!"
>
> Jesus responded, "Why are you afraid? You have so little faith!" Then He got up and rebuked the wind and waves, and suddenly there was a great calm.
>
> The disciples were amazed. "Who is this man?" they asked. "Even the winds and waves obey Him!"
>
> —Matthew 8:23–27 (NLT)

A life that is directed under God's umbrella will still have rain and winds; but protected. There is peace. Have you ever been in the rain and wind and your umbrella snaps and rain comes pouring on your head? I have. And this comes to mind when I think of umbrellas in heavy storms. This is what happens when you place your trust in earthly *umbrellas*. Our source of security cannot be in the things of this world. Our source of help must be God. The one we need to pour our heart out when we are hurting is God. Remember the God you serve, with all of the power at His hands. This is the God who loves you and protects you. Don't be afraid. His umbrella will not break. "Even the winds and waves obey Him!"

_____
_____
_____
_____

# September 26

Delight yourself also in the Lord,
And He shall give you the desires of your heart.

Commit your way to the Lord,
Trust also in Him,
And He shall bring *it* to pass.
He shall bring forth your righteousness as the light,
And your justice as the noonday.
—Psalm 37:5–6 (NKJV)

To delight yourself in the Lord, is to desire to be in His presence and to take great joy in what He has for you. When you place your delight—your joy in Him, you will act on what the Lord wants for you. Can you trust God with your hopes and dreams?

_____
_____
_____
_____

# September 27

If I can stop one heart from breaking,
I shall not live in vain;
If I can ease one life the aching,
Or cool one pain,
Or help one fainting robin
Unto his nest again,
I shall not live in vain.

—Emily Dickenson (1830-1886)

# September 28

> Give all your worries and cares to God, for He cares about you.
> —1 Peter 5:7 (NLT)

Let God handle it. There will be times when you are unable to control the situation—especially if it involves someone else.

Have you ever skipped a rock across the lake? I remember learning how to skip the rocks, as my brother, Chris, taught me how to hold the rock, direct it in line with the water and toss it. I was so excited when I final skipped my first rock across the water. I also remember learning how to fish, as my dad taught me how the cast the line out into the water. I had to learn how to control the rod, press the release button at the right time, and watch the line so that I could toss it in the right direction. I learned that I needed to let go of the button on the line for the hook to land where I intended. Giving your worries and cares to God is like tossing the rock. You have to let it go. It's like casting a fishing line. You need to press the button—let the line go and let the worries land with Jesus.

# September 29

> "Come to me, all you who are weary and burdened, and I will give you rest. Take My yoke upon you and learn from me, for I am gentle and humble in heart, and you will find rest for your souls.
> —Matthew 11:28–29 (NIV)

You don't have to be perfect to come to Jesus. You don't even have to be a good person to come to Him for rescue. In fact, you can be worn out, and broken, and Jesus will come, accept you, and will give you rest. He offers spiritual rest—to cease from striving. Tired? Feel like you can't take another step forward? Are you struggling? Let go of the things you are trying to control and experience His sweet, easy rest. A big sigh of relief comes as you get away with Jesus.

I've heard people say, "I am not in the right attitude to pray right now." My response is this: "This is when you need to pray the most." You need God because you are not *good enough*, or strong enough. And we come to Jesus because we realize we need Him; not to show Him how good we are.

# September 30

### Believe It

God is who He says He is—The beginning, and the end; the almighty, all-powerful, omnipresent, infinite God. Creator.

God is in control of all things, including your life. You are His child.

He loves you—so much that He sent His own Son, Jesus, to die in our place.

It's all about Jesus—not me, you, or anything or anyone else.

We will live in Eternity with Him—He has a place for you and for me. The spiritual world is more the reality than the physical world we live in today. And the things unseen are more significant than the things seen.

With all of this in mind, we can rejoice! There is peace.

God restores—We are restored, and He reminds us of His character of restoration many times as He restores that which is lost; by returning it, replacing it, or removing the need for it.

With God, there is *nothing* to fear.

_____
_____
_____
_____

# October

Pray for both wisdom and courage—the wisdom to know God's will and the courage to act upon it. With wisdom alone, you will know God's will, yet have no courage to do what you know to do. With courage alone, you will act on a whim, going here or there, not sure of what you are to do.

# Live the Life of Faith

If you're going to make a fresh start with faith in your life, you have to face your fears. Don't let them control you! Fear has an incredible ability to paralyze our potential, to keep us from launching out, to keep us from having faith in our lives.

When we choose fear over faith, it makes us skeptical — we're afraid of trying anything new when we're afraid. It makes us selfish — we're afraid to commit to God and to others. It makes us shortsighted — we focus on the past and not on the future.

—Rick Warren, Pastor of Saddleback Church, Lake Forest, CA and Author

# October 1

> Guard against turning back from the grace of God. Let no one become like a bitter plant that grows up and causes many troubles with its poison.
> —Mark 12:15 (GNT)

There will be times of failure. Don't let that failure cause you to think you are no longer worthy of God's love. Failure refines you. It does not define you. It is not by your successes that you are worthy, but by God's unconditional love and sacrifice, offering grace and mercy to you. Don't give up!

# October 2

The Lord knows the days of the blameless, and their inheritance will continue forever. They will not be ashamed in the time of evil, and in the days of famine they will have plenty *and* be satisfied.
—Psalm 37:18–19 (AMP)

Did you really hear that? Even if there is a famine, God will make sure you have what you need to sustain you. He will protect your character in times when all appears perilous. You will prosper if you remain faithful, delighting yourself in the Lord. So, why worry when we are struggling to pay the bills? Isn't famine worse than struggling with finances? Absolutely. Looking at the extreme, we can see that God will surely take care of us.

# October 3

And when He had removed him, He raised up David to be their king: of him He testified and said, 'I HAVE FOUND DAVID the son of Jesse, A MAN AFTER MY OWN HEART [conforming to My will and purposes], who will do all My will.' From this man's descendants God has brought to Israel a Savior, [in the person of] Jesus, according to His promise.
—Acts 13:22–23 (AMP)

David was a man after God's heart. Did David make mistakes? Sure he did. Even though failure was in his history, God still looked into David's heart and found his faithfulness. When we conform to God's will and purpose, we demonstrate the spirit of a faithful follower of Christ. And, our heart is joined with His. I pray our hearts will mirror the heart of God and belong exclusively to Him.

_____
_____
_____
_____

# October 4

> Be on your guard; stand firm in the faith; be courageous; be strong.
> —1 Corinthians 16:13 (NIV)

Imagine, one man standing in battle, the enemy army before him, yet he stands firm, holding his position, brave and strong. This is how I envision our battles with the enemy. When you want to give up and even consider joining the enemy's side, remember to be courageous and stand your ground. Stand against what seems to be a giant before you. Do what is right to do.

# October 5

> Above all else, guard your heart, for everything you do flows from it.
> —Proverbs 4:23 (NIV)

Everything you do comes from the heart. Actions are based on what is in your heart. Your heart, then, must be guarded—like a vigilant soldier standing guard refusing any danger to pass. Protect and keep a careful watch for possible influence that could damage our innermost being and result in poor character. A poor character will exhibit poor actions such as acting out in anger, jealousy, hurt, bitterness or revenge. Allow the love of God to be the barrier around your heart, so that what flows from your heart will be the fruits of the Spirit: love, joy, peace, forbearance, kindness, goodness, faithfulness, gentleness and self-control.

Yes, even evil flows from our hearts. This is yet another reason to guard your heart. We do what we do because of what comes out of our hearts.

> For the mouth speaks what the heart is full of. A good man brings good things out of the good stored up in him, and an evil man brings evil things out of the evil stored up in him.
> —Matthew 12:34b–35 (NIV)

> Do everything in love.
> —1 Corinthians 16:14 (NIV)

# October 6

This is how love is made complete among us so that we will have confidence on the day of judgment: In this world we are like Jesus. There is no fear in love. But perfect love drives out fear, because fear has to do with punishment. The one who fears is not made perfect in love.

We love because He first loved us.
—1 John 4:17–19 (NIV)

Look to God for strength, direction, hope, security and all that you need to live. Pursue God in all you do. There is a built-in desire to belong, and have meaning and purpose. But, never forget that God pursued us initially. God created us for His glory and purpose. He reached down to us because of His love for us, so that we could be shown His love. He showed us that we belong to Him, and do not have anything to fear. His perfect love casts out all fear of desertion and compete destruction—a love that is complete and cannot grow stronger by what we do, nor can it decay or grow weak because of our failures. His love is not dependent upon our performance.

You, then, can live the life you were created to live and persevere through trial and temptation with the power and strength that comes from knowing God loves you!

# October 7

> For the word of God is living and active, sharper than any two-edged sword, piercing to the division of soul and of spirit, of joints and of marrow, and discerning the thoughts and intentions of the heart. And no creature is hidden from His sight, but all are naked and exposed to the eyes of Him to whom we must give account.
> —Hebrews 4:12–13 (ESV)

Think of a father of a teenage girl standing in front of a boy she brought home to meet the parents and he asks the boy, "What are your intentions for my daughter?" Can you imagine the boy's face turning red and a bead of sweat forming on his forehead? His heart begins to race. If his intentions are anything but respectful and good for her, his body language will certainly show it.

Our heavenly Father already knows the intentions of the heart, and as His living and active Word speaks to our heart, it exposes whether or not our intentions and thoughts are pure and good. Pretending to be anything we are not, is futile with God. Honesty is the only way to respond to His voice—His Word. In all actuality, you are finally being honest with yourself, because, God already knows anything that you might confess to Him. By admitting what is in your heart, you can remove the barrier you may have built between you and God for fear of facing the truth. You can trust Him. He is a good Father.

# October 8

God's Pursuing Heart

> But the Lord God called to the man and said to him, "Where are you?"
> —Genesis 3:9 (ESV)

This was the first time that God asked a question. He sought out Adam and Eve after they had disobeyed Him and now were afraid and hiding. God knew where they were. So, why ask the question? God revealed His heart as a loving Father who pursues, even when we have disobeyed Him.

Jesus told stories of lost things and how people earnestly pursued them: lost sheep, a lost coin, and lost son. He summarized His passion to seek the lost when He was speaking to Zacchaeus and said, "For the Son of Man came to seek and to save the lost." (Luke 19:10 ESV)

Does He know where you are? Sure, He does. What will your response be? Run away or run to Him? Open up your heart and be honest about your fears.

___

___

___

___

# October 9

### The heart of God, the Father

The God who made the world and everything in it is the Lord of heaven and earth and does not live in temples built by human hands. And He is not served by human hands, as if He needed anything. Rather, He Himself gives everyone life and breath and everything else. From one man He made all the nations, that they should inhabit the whole earth; and He marked out their appointed times in history and the boundaries of their lands. God did this so that they would seek Him and perhaps reach out for Him and find Him, though He is not far from any one of us. "For in Him we live and move and have our being." As some of your own poets have said, "We are His offspring."
—Acts 17:24–28 (NIV)

He began with one man—Adam. He created every nation from then until now. God decided when you would live and where you would be born. He wants you to reach out to Him in response to His love, because He is our Father who gave us life and sustenance to live. May you go out with the heart of God shining down on you so that you may find abundant life; and tell the story of His love so that others will may have hope and find life worth living.

> The heart of God loves.
> The heart of God pursues.
> The heart of God protects.
> The heart of God is personal and sensitive.
> The heart of God is full of joy and laughter.
> The heart of God brings peace.
> The heart of God brings life.
> The heart of God restores.
> The heart of God is full of grace.

The heart of God is strong!
The heart of God disciplines.
The heart of God cares.
The heart of God brings light to the darkness.
The heart of God sustains.
The heart of God gives purpose and meaning.
The heart of God is gentle.
The heart of God forgives.
The heart of God provides.
His love is endless, indescribable, and inconceivable to our human minds.

_____
_____
_____
_____

# October 10

> By faith Enoch was taken from this life, so that he did not experience death: "He could not be found, because God had taken him away." For before he was taken, he was commended as one who pleased God. And without faith it is impossible to please God, because anyone who comes to Him must believe that He exists and that He rewards those who earnestly seek Him.
> —Hebrews 11:5–6 (NIV)

The heart of God is to reward those who pursue Him, believing that He can do anything—no matter the seemingly impossible circumstances. Whether great or small, God is able to achieve the impossible. Even when you are unsure of where God's plan will take you, and even if things turned out differently than you had contemplated, there is great reward for obedience to His Word and plan for your life. Look to Him and His direction for your life. It's your turn to look for Him. He first pursued you, and now it's your turn to run back to Him. You can believe God is for you, and find peace that comes with that faith.

_____
_____
_____
_____

# October 11

> Sustain me, my God, according to Your promise, and I will live; do not let my hopes be dashed.
> —Psalm 119:116 (NIV)

The heart of God is to sustain you. When plans fail, so often we sink into a sense of hopelessness—especially when you had believed those plans were of God. Ideas you may have had that were not accepted by others may leave you feeling rejected. But know this: You will find that God is close to you, and will carry you from this moment to the next—sustaining you. And your life will be filled with renewed strength and hope to move forward. And remember, just because someone doesn't agree with you, it doesn't mean that it wasn't God's plan. If you are living according to God's Word, that is what is important; not the opinions of others.

# October 12

> When will you ever learn that "believing" is useless without *doing* what God wants you to? Faith that does not result in good deeds is not real faith.
> —James 2:20 (TLB)

Faith is active, never passive. Faith is not simply a frame of mind, as some might believe. Some Christians are waiting to see what God will do before they do anything. But that's not what faith is all about.

### Live Your Faith
### By Israel Marshall

> For as the body without the spirit is dead, so faith without works is dead also.
> —James 2:26 (NKJV)

We say we have faith, but what good is it to us? Does it possess value? Can faith save anyone? Faith without works is dead and meaningless. Think of someone you know that is in need. Your response should not be one of spiritual cliché in the form of an, "I'm praying for you, sister." This does nothing for the needy individual and is dwarfed in comparison to what Jesus does for the people He comes into contact with. James challenges us to show our faith by what we do, not by what we think or say. The challenge, if we choose to accept it, is to live our faith; to befriend the one at work that acts as if they hate you; to parent the orphan who needs you; to be an ear to listen when that person keeps rambling on about how terrible their life is; to feed the dirty guy you pass by every single day; to protect the vulnerable; to tend to the needs of the addict. If you want a faith with meaning and a life of immeasurable value, you must live your faith.

# October 13

> That night the Master appeared to Paul: "It's going to be all right. Everything is going to turn out for the best. You've been a good witness for me here in Jerusalem. Now you're going to be my witness in Rome!"
> —Acts 23:11 (MSG)

Taking just a few words of scripture can mean so many different things to so many different people. His Word is incredible that way. Some have said that we should only think about today, because His Word says this: "So don't worry about tomorrow, for tomorrow will bring its own worries. Today's trouble is enough for today." (Matthew 6:34 NLT) They think we should never give a thought to tomorrow and to stop asking what God has for the future. But that is just not true. Though we should not fret about the future, God often will show us a bit of the future to bring us comfort, or faith, or hope—to know He has a plan for us, gives direction and motivation to move toward that goal.

God told Paul he was going to Rome. It wasn't the first time God told people about their future. He told King Nebuchadnezzar of the fall of his kingdom (Daniel 2–4). He told the people about the Promised Land; and Joseph was given dreams that only he could interpret. God foretold the birth of Jesus through the prophets and to Mary and Joseph (the greatest story to be foretold). And he has given us a glimpse of what heaven will be like. Several times, God foretold the future. It is a way that God increases our faith. It's okay to ask God what He has for you and where you should go. If all you see is one step in front of you, then take that step. But if God reveals a bigger goal, then get moving.

Of course we should not worry about tomorrow—about our provision, and what we will do, or where we will go; however, we can also look to tomorrow with anticipation and determination as God leads us in the way we should go.

Paul set out for Rome. Where are you headed?

# October 14

### The Armor of God

Finally, my brethren, be strong in the Lord and in the power of His might. Put on the whole armor of God, that you may be able to stand against the wiles of the devil. For we do not wrestle against flesh and blood, but against principalities, against powers, against the rulers of the darkness of this age, against spiritual *hosts* of wickedness in the heavenly *places*. Therefore take up the whole armor of God, that you may be able to withstand in the evil day, and having done all, to stand.

    Stand therefore, having girded your waist with truth, having put on the breastplate of righteousness, and having shod your feet with the preparation of the gospel of peace; above all, taking the shield of faith with which you will be able to quench all the fiery darts of the wicked one. And take the helmet of salvation, and the sword of the Spirit, which is the word of God; praying always with all prayer and supplication in the Spirit, being watchful to this end with all perseverance and supplication for all the saints—and for me, that utterance may be given to me, that I may open my mouth boldly to make known the mystery of the gospel, for which I am an ambassador in chains; that in it I may speak boldly, as I ought to speak.

—Ephesians 6:10–18 (KNJV)

Living a life of faith will be a battle. Knowing that there is a real battle—an unseen war between you and the rulers, authorities and powers of this dark world and spiritual forces of evil—should cause you to remain alert. If the battle was physical, you would not let your guard down. And a physical battle is for the body and this lifetime alone. If a soldier boasted about his mighty weapons, but never picked them up, he would parish in the fight. You need to pick up your weapons and use them. Our fight to save souls is much more important; this spiritual war will be one that will win victory for eternity, if you do not give up. So, keep in communication with the commander and chief, Jesus. Take up your weapons, believe in truth, righteousness, the gospel of peace, faith, and salvation.

---
---
---
---

# October 15

I will not look with approval on anything that is vile.
—Psalm 101:3a (NIV)

Are you mindful of what you look at? When you see things that are not acceptable, do you turn away? Movies, pictures, books you read, places you go—you know in your heart what is pleasing to God and what would dishonor Him. There will be moments when unacceptable things are placed in front of you unexpectedly. And, when that happens, you will need to make a choice as to whether to keep it or remove it. It may not be easy, but it will be critical that you do, so that nothing becomes an obstacle between you and the Lord, and what He wants for you. Make the right choices and you won't be disappointed.

# October 16

> Set a guard over my mouth, LORD; keep watch over the door of my lips.
> —Psalm 141:3 (NIV)

You may not be able to control all that you hear, but you *can* control what you say or repeat. Your words can set a course in action for your whole body, and your life. They cannot be taken back. Once leaving your lips, the words are spoken and heard.

> In these you too once walked, when you were living in them. But now you must put them all away: anger, wrath, malice, slander, and obscene talk from your mouth.
> —Colossians 3:7–8 (ESV)

The new *self* you are called to be will change the way you used to think, act and talk. Sticks and stones may break your bones, and words *can* really hurt you. The hurt is unseen; it's deep; and it leaves a mark. Many people suffer from emotional distress because of verbal abuse. So, guard your tongue—for your own sake and that of others.

_____
_____
_____
_____

# October 17

> Be very careful, then, how you live—not as unwise but as wise, making the most of every opportunity, because the days are evil. Therefore do not be foolish, but understand what the Lord's will is.
> —Ephesians 5:15–17 (NIV)

Can you imagine if everyone, including yourself, would live wisely, seeking the Lord's will, and making the most of *every* opportunity? I know the reality is that this type of world will only be in heaven, because we, in fact, are very human and will make mistakes. But we can certainly try to be careful of how we live.

Being careful is an interesting thing. I don't see it every day and, most often than not, I instead see carelessness. People speed on the freeway; they eat whatever they want, then try crash diets; they do whatever they want without considering the consequences or repercussion of their behavior. Many now or will suffer with severe health issues or tragic accidents that may have been avoided if they had been careful.

In this same mindset, we can consider the outcome of our actions and plan with the application of wisdom and the knowledge of the Lord's will in everything we do. What an incredible concept!

# October 18

He who goes about *as* a talebearer reveals secrets;
Therefore do not associate with one who flatters with his lips.

Do not say, "I will recompense evil";
Wait for the Lord, and He will save you.

—Proverbs 20:19, 22 (NKJV)

Do you remember the children's song that says, "O be careful little eyes"? The song reminded children to be careful of what they see, hear, do and say. It reminded them that there's a Father up above, who's looking down in love. Though we are now adults, maybe we need a quick reminder as well.

You don't need to listen to gossip, and you don't need to retaliate when you feel wronged. Too many times, I have resorted to actions in which I knew would not be right. And if I had remembered that God was watching, I would have done things differently.

# October 19

> So faith comes from hearing, that is, hearing the Good News about Christ.
> —Romans 10:17 (NLT)

How do we stand firm in faith? It all begins with listening. We need to know God's Word—read and study the Bible. Then, we need to take His Word and put it into action: listen to the Lord's instruction; accept His open arms; understand what His will is; apply and obey His instruction.

# October 20

> Whatever you do, work at it with all your heart, as working for the Lord, not for human masters, since you know that you will receive an inheritance from the Lord as a reward. It is the Lord Christ you are serving.
> —Colossians 3:23–24 (NIV)

Jesus is now your boss! And the pay is much more rewarding than any paycheck you will receive from your earthly boss.

I've had some great bosses, and I've had some very difficult bosses. Some days I've dreaded going into work, when I knew I was going to work to face another challenging day. But, even in those days, it is important to remember that God is the one we ultimately report to. He is a kind boss, and gives a reward for staying faithful, especially when it's not easy to do.

Sometimes suffering is God's will for your life, because it makes you more like Jesus. It deepens your faith, and builds your character. Sometimes suffering is simply because this world is not perfect, and all are subject to its trouble. Sometimes suffering comes because of sin—either by your own actions or the sins of others. Making poor choices in life can also result in suffering later on.

The Bible says in 1 Peter 4:19 (NIV), *"Those who suffer according to God's will should commit themselves to their faithful Creator and continue to do good."*

If you find life difficult because you're doing what God said, remain faithful. Trust him. He knows what He's doing. I understand, it may not be easy. But it will be worth it.

# October 21

### Our Final Victory

Now this I say, brethren, that flesh and blood cannot inherit the kingdom of God; nor does corruption inherit incorruption. Behold, I tell you a mystery: We shall not all sleep, but we shall all be changed—in a moment, in the twinkling of an eye, at the last trumpet. For the trumpet will sound, and the dead will be raised incorruptible, and we shall be changed. For this corruptible must put on incorruption, and this mortal *must* put on immortality. So when this corruptible has put on incorruption, and this mortal has put on immortality, then shall be brought to pass the saying that is written: "Death is swallowed up in victory."

"O Death, where *is* your sting?
O Hades, where *is* your victory?"

The sting of death *is* sin, and the strength of sin *is* the law. But thanks *be* to God, who gives us the victory through our Lord Jesus Christ.

Therefore, my beloved brethren, be steadfast, immovable, always abounding in the work of the Lord, knowing that your labor is not in vain in the Lord.
—1 Corinthians 15:57–58 (NKJV)

The stresses and pressures of life can move you, if you allow them to. As issues and complications come your way, choose to stand firm in what you believe. Do not give up and give in to the negative emotions and reactions to the struggles. Let your response be a reflection of your true self—your heart, which will be of God if you have given yourself completely to God's will.

It won't last forever. Think of it this way: You are at work, and the job seems overwhelming and almost unbearable. You look at the clock and see that only one hour has past and you release a sigh of exhaustion. But, you push through knowing the day will eventually come to an end and you will finally be able to go home. Though the minutes seem like hours, and the hours seem to pass by slower than you think, you watch as the countdown finally reaches the time to go home. That's how it will be for us as we wait on earth anticipating the moment when we finally go home to heaven. So, when life is getting tough, stay strong. Keep doing what you know is right to do—keep working for the Lord. Nothing you do for Him is a waste of time or effort. And there will be a day of victory.

# October 22

This is what the Lord says:

"Cursed is the one who trusts in man, who draws strength from mere flesh and whose heart turns away from the Lord. That person will be like a bush in the wastelands; they will not see prosperity when it comes. They will dwell in the parched places of the desert, in a salt land where no one lives.

But blessed is the one who trusts in the Lord, whose confidence is in Him. They will be like a tree planted by the water that sends out its roots by the stream. It does not fear when heat comes; its leaves are always green. It has no worries in a year of drought and never fails to bear fruit."

—Jeremiah 17:5–8 (NIV)

When you don't get the job you applied for; when you don't get that promotion you had hoped for; when your energy is low, or your bank account looks bleak, or you've lost someone you love; keep your roots planted in God's Word and trust Him. There is no need to worry. Your confidence is not based on the acceptance of others, and it is not in that job or the money, but it is in the Lord. Think about it—the tree is by the river, so even if no rain comes, and the heat is blistering hot, the tree will survive because the roots are by the stream of water.

One day, The Lord showed me a vision of a tree—a large tree full of green leaves, rounded and still. Then the wind came and began to blow the leaves away slowly. And birds that had been hidden in the tree also began to leave the tree and fly away, leaving the tree barren but firmly grounded. God did not interpret the vision in words, but as I watched I sensed the tree was a representation of myself. A tree that had once flourished now stood with only its branches. The birds that once depended on the tree for shelter and protection would no longer find shelter in this tree. At first the vision was sad—to lose its beauty, its splendor, and even sustenance and shelter for the little birds. I turned my eyes to the trunk of the tree and knew that I must stay grounded in Him. I didn't want to believe I would begin to lose everything, but if it was to happen, I knew I would still be standing in the end. I would be able to say, "It is well with my soul," as I remained firmly planted and nurtured by God, who sustains life.

> Let your roots grow down into Him, and let your lives be built on Him. Then your faith will grow strong in the truth you were taught, and you will overflow with thankfulness.
> —Colossians 2:7 (NLT)

The Lord calls you to be like a tree that is well grounded in the His Word. When trials come, keep your eyes on the trunk of the tree, and know the trunk has deep roots that are connected to the river—and don't look at the branches where all of the leaves have blown away. The trunk has deep roots. And the river will not run dry.

_____
_____
_____
_____

# October 23

> I've told you all this so that trusting me, you will be unshakable and assured, deeply at peace. In this godless world you will continue to experience difficulties. But take heart! I've conquered the world."
> —John 16:33 (MSG)

Jesus had just told His disciples that He would soon be betrayed, denied, and then He would die and be resurrected to life and be glorified. And Jesus comforted them saying, "Do not let your hearts be troubled. Trust in God, trust also in Me. I go to prepare a place for you and I will come back for you."

He promised them that the Holy Spirit would come and comfort them, teach them, and remind them of everything Jesus said.

You, too, will experience hard times, where it feels impossible to remain faithful. But just as Jesus comforted the disciples that day, hear His voice speak to you today, and take heart—Jesus has overcome the world!

# October 24

> God saved you by His grace when you believed. And you can't take credit for this; it is a gift from God. Salvation is not a reward for the good things we have done, so none of us can boast about it. For we are God's masterpiece. He has created us anew in Christ Jesus, so we can do the good things He planned for us long ago.
> —Ephesians 2:8–10 (NLT)

From the first moment man was created, we have been called to be something different than any other creation that God made—to bear the image of God. As a human, we are able to reason; we are able to love; and we have a desire built in us to want to belong and have meaning and significance. We have a part in the grand scheme of God's plan of eternity. He treats us like a Father does His beloved children. When a child falls, He picks them back up. He shows His love and grace each time we fall.

As a parent, you are called to raise them up according to the Lord's instruction—bearing God's image. To be a reflection of God, children should see love, and grace, and receive sound advice an training.

> Fathers, do not provoke your children to anger by the way you treat them. Rather, bring them up with the discipline and instruction that comes from the Lord.
> —Ephesians 6:4 (NLT)

_____
_____
_____
_____

# October 25

> Come to me, all you who are weary and burdened, and I will give you rest. Take My yoke upon you and learn from Me, for I am gentle and humble in heart, and you will find rest for your souls. For My yoke is easy and My burden is light.
> —Matthew 11:28–30 (NIV)

This world is full of examples of fathers and mothers. Some are great examples of loving parents taking on the heart of God by teaching, with sound doctrine and discipline. And there are parents that do not reflect love, who will beat a child for forgetting to do their chores; or who takes advantage of their children; or who scream and belittle and cause their children to become resentful and angry. Some will abandon their children and leave them fatherless, motherless or orphaned.

Of course we must realize that it's not easy for parents to raise children without struggling with frustration and the feeling of defeat. Discipline must come in some measure, but the extremes happen too often in our society. As the hateful abusive actions continue, it creates a wounded generation as the young children struggle through the abusive years and on into adulthood. The lonely, broken hearts run away from any father figure—even God.

But God, in His relentless love reaches down and is faithful to the broken-hearted. He can be trusted. You are not forgotten; you are not alone or abandoned. He is a good Father—one who will come by your side and teach you gently. It is time to take hold of the hand of a Father whose heart is *for you.*

I've mentioned this passage in Matthew several times throughout our journey this year. I hadn't noticed it until this moment—in the fourth quarter. I believe there is a purposeful reason the Lord has done this. Just as our bodies need rest from time to time, our souls do as well—in fact, often. He cares about you. In the last quarter, when you're tired, when you need that refreshing drink, keep moving forward—in step with

Jesus. Move with Him as you press forward side-by-side. And remember to take the needed time to refresh your souls.

# October 26

> Keep your lives free from the love of money and be content with what you have, because God has said, "Never will I leave you; never will I forsake you."
> —Hebrews 13:5 (NIV)

Do you find it interesting that the love of money and the presence of God is mentioned together here? The truth here is that, when you truly understand God's promise that He will never leave you or forsake you, money and the desire for more stuff becomes trivial. Your trust and security is then not in the things money can buy; instead, it is in God and His presence.

When you live in fear of losing what you have, you will have a tendency to hoard what you have and strive to collect more and more, adding as much as possible to your treasure. The end result is that you love the money that makes the life you've created possible. There will be no peace in a life based on what you have and don't have.

You can live fearless, by believing that God will not forget you, abandon you, or desert you. Without fear, you will be content with your current state and with what you already have.

Now you know. Money is but a tool to be used for God's purposes—to supply you with what you need and also to help others in need. You can build things eternal when used for His kingdom. Love people and not money. You can use money, not people. And if you love money, you will soon realize that you also use people. It's a matter of trust—as you love God, and not money, you will understand what He meant when He said, "I will never leave you or forsake you." You will be content when you know and believe that He is with you, and that He will not abandon you.

# October 27

The Great Commission

> Then the eleven disciples went to Galilee, to the mountain where Jesus had told them to go. When they saw Him, they worshiped Him; but some doubted. Then Jesus came to them and said, "All authority in heaven and on earth has been given to Me. Therefore go and make disciples of all nations, baptizing them in the name of the Father and of the Son and of the Holy Spirit, and teaching them to obey everything I have commanded you. And surely I am with you always, to the very end of the age."
>
> —Matthew 28:16–20 (NIV)

Jesus rose from the dead just as He said He would. But some doubted. And again Jesus comforts them with His words. And what He said to them was meant for us. Their commission has become our commission. As you can see, Jesus said, "Make disciples of all nations."

There will be days of doubt, when you're unsure if you have what it takes to do what you are called to do, or to be the person you know you should be. But be encouraged—all, yes all, authority in heaven and earth has been given to Jesus and He is with you no matter where you are.

When you can't hear His voice; when you feel afraid—remember, He said, "Surely I am with you always, to the very end of the age."

_____
_____
_____
_____

# October 28

> Now if we are children, then we are heirs—heirs of God and co-heirs with Christ, if indeed we share in His sufferings in order that we may also share in His glory.
> —Romans 8:17 (NIV)

Staying true to your faith will bring challenges at times—even suffering, because we share in Christ's sufferings. He was misunderstood, rejected, betrayed, tempted, abandoned, wounded, tortured and sentenced to death on the cross. If you have suffered, remember His suffering was greater. And we share in this unbelievable inheritance in heaven. The will is already written and you're in it. Be strong and courageous. We are restored completely as God intended from the beginning of creation and through all time until we see Him face to face.

# October 29

> I consider that our present sufferings are not worth comparing with the glory that will be revealed in us. For the creation waits in eager expectation for the children of God to be revealed.
> —Romans 8:18–19 (NIV)

We have our place in the family of God. Other believers are now our brothers and sisters. We have an identity and sense of belonging in God, the Father. You may have an earthly brother or sister, and you may have a husband or wife, or have been blessed with children. Though these family members can be blessings (gifts from God), and though we can find a part of our identity in each relationship and our ancestry tree, they are temporary. The family of God will last forever. Do you have a wife, a husband, or sister or brother? Then, build that relationship for eternity. Decide that what matters are the things that will last. Start thinking like a creature that will live forever.

# October 30

> Yet God has made everything beautiful for its own time. He has planted eternity in the human heart, but even so, people cannot see the whole scope of God's work from beginning to end. So I concluded there is nothing better than to be happy and enjoy ourselves as long as we can. And people should eat and drink and enjoy the fruits of their labor, for these are gifts from God.
> —Ecclesiastes 3:11–13 (NLT)

> Now all has been heard; here is the conclusion of the matter: Fear God and keep His commandments, for this is the duty of all mankind.
> —Ecclesiastes 12:13 (NIV)

This is your purpose: To be the spiritual "You" that will live forever. The writer here had come to the conclusion that the meaning of life was to fear God and to keep God's commandments. That's it! He concludes that all the actions of men are vain, futile, meaningless, temporary, transitory, fleeting or mere *breath* since the life here on earth will end. So, by dedicating your life to God's Word and direction, your purpose is fulfilled. And since this life, as it relates to everything else, is senseless, then seeking pleasures, wisdom and self-gratification is futile. Keeping it simple, he proclaimed, was wise—to enjoy the simple pleasures of life, while being obedient to God.

So live it. Live the life abundantly by living the life of faith and obedience to His Word. The time spent here on earth is a practice field to get ready for eternal life in heaven.

_____

_____

_____

_____

# October 31

> Behold, You desire truth in the innermost being, and in the hidden part [of my heart] You will make me know wisdom.
> —Psalm 51:6 (AMP)

God has birthed a new, and true life in you. He knows your heart and everything you need. He created you. He has given good things to you and has sustained you. Your heart, then belongs to Him and your innermost sincerity is what He deserves. No need to hide who you really are, or to be afraid of losing what you have. Remember, He has given them to you as gifts in the first place. Everything you have was made possible by Him. Be honest about who you are, and what you feel, so that God can work in you and through you. Go deeper with God. He can handle the real "You".

# November

"Meaningless! Meaningless!"
Says the Teacher.
"Utterly meaningless!
Everything is meaningless."

Philosophers can debate the meaning of life, but you need a Lord who can declare the meaning of life."
—Max Lucado, Traveling Light: Releasing the Burdens You Were Never Intended to Bear

# Look Up!

# November 1

> God is our refuge and strength, an ever-present help in trouble. Therefore we will not fear, though the earth give way and the mountains fall into the heart of the sea, though its waters roar and foam and the mountains quake with their surging.
>
> There is a river whose streams make glad the city of God, the holy place where the Most High dwells. God is within her, she will not fall; God will help her at break of day.
>
> —Psalm 46:1–5 (NIV)

Have you ever been in a dark place, grasping for something to hold onto—unsure of what to do, where to go? In the same way, we grasp in the dark places of our lives. We search for something to regain our stability and ability to move forward.

We tend to place our security in earthly things—family, friends, home, career, church, wealth, community, national resources. But what happens when your security system fails? When these things tremble or crumble? What can you depend on when the thing you believed in and trusted is lost?

You will experience broken dreams—like pebbles crashing from the waves of the river. Ernest Hemingway said this: "The world breaks everyone and afterward many are stronger at the broken places." It does. We are. And the only security that is sure, is found in God. Who is our refuge and strength in time of trouble? Our bank account? The shoulder of a friend? Family? These are all gifts of God to be cherished, but they belong to God. I cannot control them, I cannot look to them to bring me joy and peace—though they may bring happy moments and I enjoy life when finances aren't a burden. But this world will bring losses. In the loss of finances, a spouse, a sibling, parents, and even health—even in the loss of self-worth, hope or peace, God is my refuge. Rest in knowing His plan and eternal purpose in your life is being worked out—even through the trials.

As I read the scriptures in the beginning, remember these words when there seems to be a security breach:

1. God is near—He is our ever present help in time of trouble.
2. Don't worry—we will not fear.
3. You will find peace in your heart—we are safe in the city of God.

Psalm 46:10 goes on to say this: "Be still, and know that I am God; I will be exalted among the nations, I will be exalted in the earth."

# November 2

> Blessed are the merciful, for they will be shown mercy.
> —Matthew 5:7 (NIV)

The people listening to the message Jesus spoke that day heard this as a new way of thinking. The people showed no mercy. Sin was punished. Then, Jesus came with a new message. He sought out the sinners and the broken to show mercy.

Mercy is compassion or forgiveness shown toward someone whom it is within one's power to punish or harm. Mercy requires action. God has the power to destroy, but instead shows mercy.

My son-in-law, Steven, shared a message one Sunday about a time when he was engaged to my daughter, Rebecca. Rebecca and I were out for a mom-n-daughter day and Steven wanted to do something special for Rebecca and surprise her when she would return home. He saw some laundry and decided to wash her clothes for her. Though not an expert, and the only practice was his college days, he dove in with all-heart to accomplish this wonderful gift for her.

He divided the clothes into two loads and began the first load. He tossed the load into the washer and, looking at all of the bottles for laundry detergent, he added one of the many choices—choosing Clorox. When the first load was finished in the wash, he then added the load to dry and proceeded with the second load to wash.

When finished, he folded each item and placed them neatly in a pile for her to see how well he had done. He noticed the look of the material was a bit "off", but wasn't sure why. But he was full of smiles and anticipation as he waited for Rebecca to return home and see how much time he had saved her.

When she returned home and went upstairs to her room, she saw it! She shrieked with shock—all of her clothes nicely folded were bleach stained and ruined. At this point Steven thought she screamed in excitement. But when she came downstairs and he saw the look on her face, his smile turned into "uh-oh". He had made a mess of things— even though his intentions were good. He was at the mercy of a scorned woman whose wardrobe was destroyed. But she showed mercy. No punishment. No pay-backs.

> We mess things up. Even when we don't intend to. We ruin things, break things, and even completely lose things. We even mess ourselves up. And Jesus has compassion on us. His mercy finds us even while we are broken. Jesus turns the messes into something beautiful.
> —Steven Rose, Youth Pastor of Community Christian Church Hemet, California

# November 3

> Jesus once again addressed them: "I am the world's Light. No one who follows Me stumbles around in the darkness. I provide plenty of light to live in."
> —John 8:12 (MSG)

One of the ways to describe darkness can be dark moments in life. The darkness of this world can represent itself in many ways, such as loss of health, sustenance, home, and life. And when losses happen, we have Jesus as our light to show us the way through the darkness. The moments of darkness here in this life remind us of the spiritual darkness over all of us that sin has caused. As Jesus lights the way through the trials of life, He is resembling the grander factuality of darkness and light. Spiritual darkness is much more dangerous than physical darkness. While physical darkness can cause pain, suffering, and loss, spiritual darkness can destroy the soul. And Jesus paved the way, removing the darkness from our lives. He is victorious over sin and death.

As you make your way through this life, Jesus provides guidance and direction to press through the difficult moments. These times of light through the darkness can be a reminder of His provision of light through the most difficult of all challenges—sin and death, as He lights the way to eternal life.

# November 4

> Three times I pleaded with the Lord to take it away from me. But He said to me, "My grace is sufficient for you, for My power is made perfect in weakness." Therefore I will boast all the more gladly about my weaknesses, so that Christ's power may rest on me.
> —2 Corinthians 12:8–9 (NIV)

At some point in my life, I realized I was waiting for God to finish making me whole before I could tell others how God restores lives. That is when God revealed to me that, sometimes, brokenness remains so that God's power can be shown. Are you waiting for your life to be a better testimony before you testify of God's goodness and grace?

Paul had a thorn in his side that would not be taken from him. He would take this to the grave. It could be said his ailment was physical, or it could be that the struggle was against spiritual warfare and be taken metaphorically. Most scholars tend to believe that this was directly pertaining to being trapped in the world of flesh as spiritual beings. He was challenged, threatened, beaten, and imprisoned because of the opposition from those who refused to believe. We are essentially cursed here on Earth until that glorious day when we are freed from our earthly shells.

John the Baptist spoke of repentance. Repentance relates to a complete transformation of our mind! It is all about our perspective. Jesus spoke of this, then Paul makes the point clear.

> And it is one of King David's descendants, Jesus, who is God's promised Savior of Israel! Before He came, John the Baptist preached that all the people of Israel needed to repent of their sins and turn to God and be baptized.
> —Acts 13:23–24 (NLT)

Even if Paul suffered from a physical ailment, the fact is that he wanted to be released from it. And the answer the Lord gave was this:

"My grace is sufficient." In repentance we find rest for our souls. Peace in our minds.

I was, and am, broken, yet God showed me He is strong in the very place I am broken.

# November 5

> The Jewish leaders were infuriated by Stephen's accusation, and they shook their fists at him in rage. But Stephen, full of the Holy Spirit, gazed steadily into heaven and saw the glory of God, and he saw Jesus standing in the place of honor at God's right hand. And he told them, "Look, I see the heavens opened and the Son of Man standing in the place of honor at God's right hand!"
>
> Then they put their hands over their ears and began shouting. They rushed at him and dragged him out of the city and began to stone him. His accusers took off their coats and laid them at the feet of a young man named Saul.
>
> As they stoned him, Stephen prayed, "Lord Jesus, receive my spirit." He fell to his knees, shouting, "Lord, don't charge them with this sin!" And with that, he died.
>
> —Acts 7:54–60 (NLT)

Stephen was in the middle of a mob. The Jewish leaders surrounded him—but he looked up. He saw the glory of God. He saw Jesus. Can you imagine his boldness when He saw Him? Stephen's death was brutal. Yet, he was able to forgive them even as they stoned him. He knew he was going to be with Jesus, who was waiting there. Look up. God is with you; and He is for you.

---
---
---

# November 6

> Study to shew thyself approved unto God, a workman that needeth not to be ashamed, rightly dividing the word of truth.
> —2 Timothy 2:15 (AKJV)

We live in a culture where people worship and praise and reward higher education—a college degree, for example—more than the knowledge and application of the Word of God. With more employers hiring those with higher education, students are pushing themselves to achieve these goals in hopes for success.

With God, success and eligibility for approval is not based on your education or degree earned with certificates and awards to prove it. Rather, His approval comes by doing your best to live a godly life, applying God's word in your daily practices.

I am not implying that you shouldn't strive for an education to better equip yourselves, so that you are an asset to society and your families; but, I am, in fact, saying that you will need to keep your priorities straight. God may use your education to fulfill His purpose, and then again, may use your life circumstances regardless of whether you have an education in the field, or the lack thereof.

> Education without values, as useful as it is, seems rather to make man a more clever devil.
> —C.S. Lewis

# November 7

> The LORD says, "I will guide you along the best pathway for your life. I will advise you and watch over you.
> —Psalm 32:8 (NLT)

Are you open to whatever God has planned for you? It may not be what you planned, and it may not happen on your timetable, but you can trust God's perfect plan for your life. Don't give up on God. Let go of the worry, anxiety and fear. Nothing is too difficult for God.

Think of it this way: If you have a personal friend or family member who is a financial guru, would you ask them for financial advice? It certainly would be beneficial that you would, especially if you are considering financing of a home, or car or a large transaction. Wouldn't you want the best deal? That's how we can view God's direction. He is the one who knows the best route for anything you can face, and you can ask for His advice and guidance for all that you do.

God allows us to do what we will. There are times that He does not have a specific calling for us to go or do a certain thing—such as moving to the right location, or accepting the right job offer. But, the fact that He knows the best places and best jobs, I prefer to go to Him and ask for His opinion.

# November 8

> Do not conform to the pattern of this world, but be transformed by the renewing of your mind. Then you will be able to test and approve what God's will is—His good, pleasing and perfect will.
> —Romans 12:2 (NIV)

I expect you've heard the phrase, "God's perfect will." Have you wondered what that might be? This passage of scripture will lead you to that answer. Are you tired of being everything for everyone else? Fix your attention to God. You will be molded into what God wants you to be—changed from the inside out.

The world will drag you down; God brings out the best in you. Poor choices will reap poor consequences; godly choices will bring renewal, restoration. God's perfect will for you brings life—abundant life. You will have a new attitude toward life with a new outlook. You will then recognize what God's perfect will is, as you place every day, every thought, before God as an offering to Him. Your thoughts will conform to what He says in His Word. And as your thoughts are transformed, your actions will follow—godly, sound decisions that will build, and not tear down. Marriages could be renewed. Relationships could heal. The results are endless as you remain in the will of God.

# November 9

> The world and its desires pass away, but whoever does the will of God lives forever.
> —1 John 2:17 (NIV)

Jesus wants you to be willing to let go of anything that gets in the way of living the life of abundance He wants to give you. He wants you to have a full life of healthy relationships with people who want to encourage and love one another. And that means you may have to leave some people or some stuff behind if people or stuff is standing in your way. You may feel it is expensive to live for God, but it's worth it.

As you offer yourself to God as a living sacrifice, you are allowing God to work through you—this is God's will for you. And the will of God will last forever. Living for the world, the desires of the world will not bring you complete satisfaction—and, in fact, ultimately weigh you down. Material things will not last forever. Your soul, the souls of others, love, relationship with God—these are the things that will last for eternity.

# November 10

> If any of you lacks wisdom, you should ask God, who gives generously to all without finding fault, and it will be given to you. But when you ask, you must believe and not doubt, because the one who doubts is like a wave of the sea, blown and tossed by the wind.
> —James 1:5–6 (NIV)

When you ask God for wisdom, and for direction, let go of your worries. Do you hold onto your back-up plan just in case God doesn't come through? God does not look down at you with condescending eyes when you ask for help. He wants to help you. Let God answer your questions. If you're holding onto your plan just in case, then you are doubting God, and He will not force His plan on you as long as you hold onto yours.

# November 11

> At this the man's face fell. He went away sad, because he had great wealth.
> —Mark 10:22 (NIV)

Are you willing to let go of something you hold valuable or dear to your heart, so to follow Jesus? It just may come to that at some point when Jesus asks you if you are willing to change the direction you are headed so to follow Him and His plan for your life. If and when you are confronted with this decision, choose Jesus. Don't turn away sad, like the wealthy man did. The man chose his wealth over Jesus when he went away.

Jesus may need you to acknowledge the importance of placing Him before these things of value. And if you choose not to be willing to let go of these things you think will bring you happiness, you will ultimately end up unhappy. Choose Jesus and you will be choosing genuine abundant life. Abundant life is not about stuff. It's about living at peace with God and yourself as you live out the life He has chosen for you.

# November 12

### The Burial of Jesus

> As evening approached, there came a rich man from Arimathea, named Joseph, who had himself become a disciple of Jesus. Going to Pilate, he asked for Jesus' body, and Pilate ordered that it be given to him. Joseph took the body, wrapped it in a clean linen cloth, and placed it in his own new tomb that he had cut out of the rock. He rolled a big stone in front of the entrance to the tomb and went away. Mary Magdalene and the other Mary were sitting there opposite the tomb.
> —Matthew 27:57–61 (NIV)

It is true that you cannot serve God and money (Matthew 6:24); and that the love of money is the root of all evil (1 Timothy 6:10). And it is difficult for a rich man to enter the kingdom of heaven (Mark 10:23). But here is an excellent example displayed by this rich man, of how a wealthy man can become a follower of Christ and give of his wealth to the kingdom. This man, Joseph, made sure the body of Jesus was laid in a tomb properly—a tomb he had made for himself. By doing so, he became a part of the story of Jesus' death and resurrection. Then he went away—no request for notice or recognition; without seeking reward. He simply did it and walked away. Riches do not exclude you from being able to serve the Lord. It can enable you, and be used as a tool to help you do things others may not be able to do.

# November 13

> Cast but a glance at riches, and they are gone, for they will surely sprout wings and fly off to the sky like an eagle.
>
> —Proverbs 23:5 (NIV)

Money comes, and money goes. The check comes in and before you know it, the funds are already spent on the things you need—as if your hard-earned dollar sprouted wings and flew away. It is any wonder that our security falls apart when we put our faith in our finances? Money is not stable. Its value changes often and there are often unexpected expenses that come up, then depleting our savings. But there's nothing to fear—God is our true security. Trusting in God is not measured by our bank account balance. His resources cannot diminish or be lost or stolen. He can supply all our needs according to the riches of His glory in Christ Jesus (Philippians 4:19).

# November 14

> Those who love money will never have enough. How meaningless to think that wealth brings true happiness!
> —Ecclesiastes 5:10 (NLT)

Those who *live to get more* will only continue to strive to get even more—never satisfied with what they have because there is always something they don't have; and therefore they must have. Money will never satisfy the thirst for success. At some point, after years of striving, most people look back to see how the love of money made their lives miserable. They realize how their choices have hurt themselves and others, and think *if only* they had done things differently, they would not be in the situation they are in today.

Instead, love God. Loving and chasing after God will bring more satisfaction than any worldly prize. You will find a better life—one of incomprehensible peace and unexplainable joy.

_____
_____
_____
_____

# November 15

> Then He said, "Beware! Guard against every kind of greed. Life is not measured by how much you own."
> —Luke 12:15 (NLT)

I remember seeing a bumper-sticker that said, "The one who dies with the most toys, wins." And the truck that the bumper-sticker was on had ATV's in the bed of the truck, and it was pulling a large boat on its trailer. Seriously? This is the value of a man's life? More stuff = more value = winner.

No. On the contrary, the Bible tells us, "Your life is not measured by how much you own." Jesus' love = the cross = your worth.

Your worth is measured by the price that was paid by Jesus on the cross. And so, because of His sacrifice of life, we are rewarded heaven and living in the presence of God forever. That's a true winner. Wouldn't you agree?

_____
_____
_____
_____

# November 16

> Don't store up treasures here on earth, where moths eat them and rust destroys them, and where thieves break in and steal. Store your treasures in heaven, where moths and rust cannot destroy, and thieves do not break in and steal. Wherever your treasure is, there the desires of your heart will also be.
> —Matthew 6:19–21 (NLT)

These words are a part of *the Sermon on the Mount*. It is the first and longest sermon of Jesus that we have in the gospel. Jesus had been announcing that the kingdom of heaven was at hand, and He had been calling for people to repent. And in this sermon, Jesus teaches the ethical guidelines for life in His kingdom; and the guidelines point to the quality of righteousness and characterizes life in the kingdom, now in part and then fully in the future. He tells us that we are to store our treasures in heaven.

How? What you do with your time and money will show what is in your heart. Where time and money are spent will show what you love most, and what you treasure, believe in, and trust most. Where do you invest? It's absolutely acceptable, and even encouraged, to invest time and money in things here on earth, like relationships, family, home and savings; but keep in mind, if you find you are investing a great portion of time and money into things that don't make a difference (for yourself and selfish desires), you may want to reconsider your values and create a new plan. Create a table of what you do and how much time you spend on each. Take a look and ask the Lord to help you prioritize properly.

---
---
---
---

# November 17

> Give thanks to the Lord, for He is good; His love endures forever.
> —Psalm 107:1 (NIV)

Life is a gift, and all good things that become a part of our lives are gifts from God. Let us journey from this moment, from now until eternity, giving thanks to God, with contentment in all that we have. For, in just a little while, we will enter the gates of heaven, and this life will seem so very short, and the trials so dim.

# November 18

> Every third year you must offer a special tithe of your crops. In this year of the special tithe you must give your tithes to the Levites, foreigners, orphans, and widows, so that they will have enough to eat in your towns.
> —Deuteronomy 26:12 (NLT)

God brought the children of Israel out of Egypt, showed them signs and wonders, and led them to a place He had promised them—a land flowing with milk and honey (Exodus 3:8). When they arrived, they were instructed to give a portion of their goods to others. Everything they received was a gift promised by God and it is God's heart to take care of those who have very little or nothing. When you give to others in the name of the Lord, you are essentially giving forward what belongs to God. What you give to them, you are giving to Him (Matthew 25:40).

# November 19

"Bring the whole tithe into the storehouse, that there may be food in My house. Test Me in this," says the Lord Almighty, "and see if I will not throw open the floodgates of heaven and pour out so much blessing that there will not be room enough to store it.
—Malachi 3:10 (NIV)

Woe to you, teachers of the law and Pharisees, you hypocrites! You give a tenth of your spices—mint, dill and cumin. But you have neglected the more important matters of the law—justice, mercy and faithfulness. You should have practiced the latter, without neglecting the former.
—Matthew 23:23 (NIV)

I've heard some say that tithing is not for today. But, Jesus made it very clear that tithing remains important. Jesus scolded the scribes and Pharisees as being hypocrites for neglecting to show justice and mercy and faithfulness—these being more important than tithing. Remember, though, that Jesus said they should have done both—not neglecting the tithing.

Tithing is still important today. Your tithes and offering should not be held back for yourself or for hoarding. It should be given to the works of the Lord—to seek the lost, and help grow the church and ready them for the kingdom. Give and expect a blessing. It may not be in the form of money, but it will be from God who has all of the riches in heaven and on earth to give how He desires. He knows how to give good gifts.

---
---
---
---

# November 20

> David praised the Lord in the presence of the whole assembly, saying,
> "Praise be to you, Lord, the God of our father Israel, from everlasting to everlasting.
> Yours, Lord, is the greatness and the power and the glory and the majesty and the splendor, for everything in heaven and earth is Yours. Yours, Lord, is the kingdom; You are exalted as head over all. Wealth and honor come from You; You are the ruler of all things. In Your hands are strength and power to exalt and give strength to all. Now, our God, we give You thanks, and praise Your glorious name.
> But who am I, and who are my people, that we should be able to give as generously as this? Everything comes from You, and we have given You only what comes from Your hand.
> —1 Chronicles 29:10–14 (NIV)

Whatever you have belongs to God.

> Whatever you see belongs to God.
> Whatever you hear belongs to God.
> Whatever you touch, feel, or experience belongs to God.
> Whatever you cannot see belongs to God.

He owns my grieving and He owns my rejoicing. He owns all that I have and all that I need. Nothing is outside of His reach.

# November 21

> Be careful not to practice your righteousness in front of others to be seen by them. If you do, you will have no reward from your Father in heaven.
> —Matthew 6:1 (NIV)

It was a hard lesson to learn as children: Share. Now that we've learned to share, let's continue to do so. Our Father has given to us all that we need and when we share He will reward us. As Jesus continued *the Sermon on the Mount,* He cautioned that we can still be selfish when we give to others. When we want recognition, respect and honor from others, we give with selfish motives. Give without announcing it. Give in secret.

I've often watched my grandchildren at play. And, as any child, they had to learn to share. Then, one day I saw my grandson, Caleb, take what he had and give it to his little brother, Luke. He explained that he was giving it to him because he knew Luke would like what he had. Then Luke followed suit and picked something out of his pile and gave it to his brother, Noah. And Noah gave something of his to his little sister, Elizabeth. They all took turns giving to each other. It brought smiles to their faces and the smiles as they gave was proof they felt good about their generosity. Precious.

It can be learned. And when you experience the joy of giving, you'll want to keep it going—like my grandchildren giving and giving. Trust me when I say, it will bring a great sense of satisfaction to see the smile on their faces, which will be thanks enough.

# November 22

> But love your enemies, do good to them, and lend to them without expecting to get anything back. Then your reward will be great, and you will be children of the Most High, because he is kind to the ungrateful and wicked. Be merciful, just as your Father is merciful. Give, and it will be given to you. A good measure, pressed down, shaken together and running over, will be poured into your lap. For with the measure you use, it will be measured to you."
> —Luke 6:35–36, 38 (NIV)

"Wait a minute!" you might say. "Give to the ungrateful and wicked?" Yes. That's what it said. Just as your Father is merciful, He wants you to be merciful. And when someone who least deserves your kindness receives it none-the-less, this becomes an act of mercy. Your gift may be forgiveness without conditions. It may be kindness to someone who hurt you. As you show mercy, and as you give, it will be given to you.

# November 23

> Anyone who does not provide for their relatives, and especially for their own household, has denied the faith and is worse than an unbeliever.
> —1 Timothy 5:8 (NIV)

I remember how my mom would go to my grandma's house to help her with cleaning and things needed to be done. At the time, I figured it was simply a daughter helping out her mom. Many years later, I was reading the Bible and here was this scripture. My mom has shown to be a living example of God's Word in many ways. And this was one of them. Is there someone in your family who needs help—financially, physically? Do you have the means to help? Take a moment to ask the Lord how you can provide for them. In love and gentleness and kindness of the heart, you can present your gift to them as God has revealed to you.

# November 24

> The King will reply, "Truly I tell you, whatever you did for one of the least of these brothers and sisters of mine, you did for Me."
> —Matthew 25:40 (NIV)

Jesus Asks Us to Pay It Forward

Benjamin Franklin described such a request in a letter to Benjamin Webb dated April 25, 1784. It read like this:

> "I do not pretend to give such a sum; I only lend it to you. When you shall return to your country with a good character, you cannot fail of getting into some business, that will in time enable you to pay all your debts. In that case, when you meet with another honest man in similar distress, you must pay me by lending this sum to him; enjoining him to discharge the debt by a like operation, when he shall be able, and shall meet with such another opportunity. I hope it may thus go through many hands, before it meets with a knave that will stop its progress. This is a trick of mine for doing a deal of good with a little money."

Though Benjamin Franklin said he did not pretend to give, but to lend, he was, in fact, giving it as a gift; because, he was not asking for it to be paid back to himself. However, he was also giving it with a request that it not be perceived as a gift, but as a debt to pay forward—and thus this would be the act of paying back the debt.

Jesus has asked us to pay it forward. And the gifts that we have received from Jesus, that are then given to others, are in turn giving right back to Him. What has God given you in the past, that now you can pay forward?

# November 25

> Daniel, Hananiah, Mishael, and Azariah were four of the young men chosen, all from the tribe of Judah.
>
> Then Nebuchadnezzar flew into a rage and ordered that Shadrach, Meshach, and Abednego be brought before him. When they were brought in, Nebuchadnezzar said to them, "Is it true, Shadrach, Meshach, and Abednego, that you refuse to serve my gods or to worship the gold statue I have set up? I will give you one more chance to bow down and worship the statue I have made when you hear the sound of the musical instruments. But if you refuse, you will be thrown immediately into the blazing furnace. And then what god will be able to rescue you from my power?"
>
> Shadrach, Meshach, and Abednego replied, "O Nebuchadnezzar, we do not need to defend ourselves before you. If we are thrown into the blazing furnace, the God whom we serve is able to save us. He will rescue us from your power, Your Majesty. But even if he doesn't, we want to make it clear to you, Your Majesty, that we will never serve your gods or worship the gold statue you have set up."
>
> —Daniel 1:6, Daniel 3:13–18 (NLT)

King Nebuchadnezzar was sure of his own power. He was sure they would *not* be rescued. The three Hebrew men were willing to go through the fire, even if God wouldn't rescue them. Did you catch that? Even if. They remained faithful even when faced with the threat of death. God showed up, and He *did* rescue them. The king was amazed. Everything changed.

> Then Nebuchadnezzar said, "Praise to the God of Shadrach, Meshach, and Abednego! He sent his angel to rescue his servants who trusted in him. They defied the king's command and were willing to die rather

than serve or worship any god except their own God. ²⁹ Therefore, I make this decree: If any people, whatever their race or nation or language, speak a word against the God of Shadrach, Meshach, and Abednego, they will be torn limb from limb, and their houses will be turned into heaps of rubble. There is no other god who can rescue like this!"

—Daniel 3:28–29 (NLT)

_____
_____
_____
_____

# November 26

> We plan the way we want to live, but only God makes us able to live it.
> —Proverbs 16:9 (MSG)

Seek the Lord's guidance for your future. Make plans. Go ahead and save for the future. Create a budget plan and then execute the plan. It is responsible planning as to how you will live that will set you on a path that is good. Here's the key: Submit your way to Him, follow His lead for the plan and remember, it is only God who makes us able to live it.

# November 27

> The master was full of praise. "Well done, my good and faithful servant. You have been faithful in handling this small amount, so now I will give you many more responsibilities. Let's celebrate together!"
> —Matthew 25:21 (NLT)

One day we will give account to God. Our time as managers here on earth will come to an end and we will graduate into God's eternal kingdom. Let's not hoard all things for ourselves, but, instead, share with those who don't have much.

Life here on earth is not about the money—though many people live as if it is. While it may not be about how much you can make for yourselves, it can be about how much you *can* give to others, and what you do with what you have. What an honor to be given charge over what belongs to God!

# November 28

> So all the elders of Israel gathered together and came to Samuel at Ramah. They said to him, "You are old, and your sons do not follow your ways; now appoint a king to lead us, such as all the other nations have."
> —1 Samuel 8:4–5 (NIV)

"We want what they have!" they said. There is a competitive spirit in all of us. And for some it doesn't become an issue of the heart. Sometimes we will look at others' success when our success looks like it may fail—just as the elders of Israel did. They didn't like what their future looked like, and noticed what other nations were doing, so decided something needed to change to be like the other nations. They took their complaint to Samuel demanding that he give them what they wanted.

Some people will struggle with the fact that they may be missing out on something that someone else has. For fear of having less than their neighbor, they fret and fuss and push themselves to the breaking point—mentally, physically, emotionally and financially, to obtain all they can; even to the point of spiritual damage or bankruptcy. They will try and convince others of their rights to have what they want. Material success, *or keeping up with the Jones'* then becomes more important than relational or spiritual growth.

1 Samuel 8:7 says, "And the LORD told him: "Listen to all that the people are saying to you; it is not you they have rejected, but they have rejected Me as their king."" The elders of Israel were not only rejecting Samuel and his sons; they were rejecting God. When we place anything above God and His plan, we are ultimately rejecting Him.

As you look at your life and what God has for you, let's not say, "It's not good enough. I want more!" Rather, say, "His plans are good; His grace is enough; and I will remain content. He is my God and provider."

# November 29

> When pride comes, then comes disgrace, but with humility comes wisdom.
> —Proverbs 11:2 (NIV)

The English Oxford Living Dictionary[4] defines humility as:

[Noun] The quality of having a modest or low view of one's importance.

Don't let your pride get in the way. Listen to the Lord with a humble heart. When you place God above your circumstances, and above anything you have or know, you have placed yourself beneath Him and His authority; and that's exactly where you need to remain. God's wisdom comes in the place of humility.

With our eyes, we see only what the human eyes can see. We can't see the spiritual world with our human eyes. But it is still very real. In Glory, there are colors of the rainbow that we have never seen. There are gems we've never beheld—like transparent gold and gates made of a single pearl (Revelation 21:21). Our earthly bodies cannot walk through walls or transport, but God can be anywhere and everywhere. Though we marvel at all we are and see, and all we are capable of doing, it is so far beneath the magnificence of God and heaven.

So, when we think of humility in the right manner, we recognize how incredible God is, and that we are no comparison to Him. In the knowledge of that reality, giving reverence to God, we are humbled. And the payoff for this reverent heart is a life of plenty, honor, satisfaction and glory.

Many people have the wrong idea about God and humility. They think it's about groveling in front of Him (or others) or thinking they are no good to Him or anyone else. But with the perspective that He is the mighty God, and in view of the magnificence in all God's creation, we know that is not true. We know we are loved and magnificently created and we know who we are in Christ. We are free from pride and arrogance, and full of grace and humility. We know that we are inadequate in our flesh, because we understand the transformation that will take place in glory when we are with Him.

_____
_____
_____
_____

# November 30

> A very large crowd spread their cloaks on the road, while others cut branches from the trees and spread them on the road. The crowds that went ahead of him and those that followed shouted, "Hosanna to the Son of David!" "Blessed is he who comes in the name of the Lord!" "Hosanna in the highest heaven!"
> —Matthew 21:8–9 (NIV)

Though the people shouted, "Hosanna in the highest," they had no idea what that really meant. They thought it was about a king of that day. But the truth is that He is the forever King that reigns over all. It wasn't about a kingdom in their country alone, as they had thought, but a heavenly kingdom that would last forever.

Believing who Jesus is will take faith. We can't see the kingdom that He speaks about. The kingdom is not about the "here and now" or anything that comes with it—status, success, power, or money. We don't have to be perfect, in control, or to be noticed. It's all about Jesus. Jesus is the one who will bring us to where we need to be and all of these things (status, success, power, money) will be subordinate to seeking His kingdom first, as God sees fit to give or to take away. So, we can say with exuberance, "Hosanna in the highest!"

# December

The story of Jesus is the greatest story ever told. My story—your story— is not possible apart from the story of Jesus' birth, death on the cross, and resurrection from the dead. Because of His story, we can live—truly live.

It's All About Jesus
~ Believe ~

# December 1

And so we know and rely on the love God has for us.

God is love. Whoever lives in love lives in God, and God in them. This is how love is made complete among us so that we will have confidence on the day of judgment: In this world we are like Jesus. There is no fear in love. But perfect love drives out fear, because fear has to do with punishment. The one who fears is not made perfect in love.
—1 John 4:16–18 (NIV)

Peace comes from the freedom from fear, guilt, worry, bitterness, and death. Without fear, you do not have to pretend to be something you are not—for anyone. Because, you are free to be yourself. This kind of freedom is found in God's love. Allow God to love you and trust Him for your life. Anxious thoughts can be replaced with thoughts of God's love for you and His promises.

So if the Son sets you free, you will be free indeed.
—John 8:36 (NIV)

_____
_____
_____
_____

# December 2

> Therefore, since we are surrounded by such a great cloud of witnesses, let us throw off everything that hinders and the sin that so easily entangles. And let us run with perseverance the race marked out for us, fixing our eyes on Jesus, the pioneer and perfecter of faith. For the joy set before Him He endured the cross, scorning its shame, and sat down at the right hand of the throne of God. Consider Him who endured such opposition from sinners, so that you will not grow weary and lose heart.
> —Hebrews 12:1–3 (NIV)

Are you tired of allowing circumstances dictate how your day will go—either in victory or failure? Take your focus off of the circumstances and focus on Jesus. This is how Jesus endured the cross. He focused on *you*. He endured the cross because He knew the joy that was yet to come. When you focus on Jesus, anxiety will subside, fears will be defeated and stress will be lifted. It's not easy to train your mind to do it, but it's the only way you will be able to press forward. In darkness, or when God may be silent, hold onto what is true. You are loved by the almighty God—your Father. Your soul is secure. Your future is solid. Sometimes circumstances may not change, but your perspective can.

# December 3

A miserable heart means a miserable life; a cheerful heart fills the day with song.
—Proverbs 15:15 (MSG)

And again, "Praise the Lord, all you Gentiles; let all the peoples extol him."

And again, Isaiah says, "The Root of Jesse will spring up, one who will arise to rule over the nations; in Him the Gentiles will hope."

May the God of hope fill you with all joy and peace as you trust in Him, so that you may overflow with hope by the power of the Holy Spirit.
—Romans 15:11–13 (NIV)

In Jesus, there is joy. You will have peace as you believe in God, and put your hope in Jesus. Sing praises to the Lord.

Have you ever known someone who was always unhappy? Maybe they had reasons to be disappointed. But, when you put your life in perspective, we don't have to lose hope. There will be days when we will mourn our losses. We may not smile all of the time, but deep down in our soul, there is joy that looks to the future with hope.

There was a next-door-neighbor who I would hear whistling songs throughout the day. When I heard his whistling, I would smile. I didn't even need to know the words to the song. The whistling of a tune was enough to life up spirits.

Who do you want to be? The gloomy one or the whistler?

---
---
---
---

# December 4

### God's Marvelous Plan for the Gentiles

For this reason I, Paul, the prisoner of Christ Jesus for the sake of you Gentiles—

Surely you have heard about the administration of God's grace that was given to me for you, that is, the mystery made known to me by revelation, as I have already written briefly. In reading this, then, you will be able to understand my insight into the mystery of Christ, which was not made known to people in other generations as it has now been revealed by the Spirit to God's holy apostles and prophets. This mystery is that through the gospel the Gentiles are heirs together with Israel, members together of one body, and sharers together in the promise in Christ Jesus.

I became a servant of this gospel by the gift of God's grace given me through the working of his power. Although I am less than the least of all the Lord's people, this grace was given me: to preach to the Gentiles the boundless riches of Christ, and to make plain to everyone the administration of this mystery, which for ages past was kept hidden in God, who created all things. His intent was that now, through the church, the manifold wisdom of God should be made known to the rulers and authorities in the heavenly realms, according to His eternal purpose that He accomplished in Christ Jesus our Lord. In Him and through faith in Him we may approach God with freedom and confidence. I ask you, therefore, not to be discouraged because of my sufferings for you, which are your glory.

—Ephesians 3:1–13 (NIV)

The mystery is revealed. Through the gospel, the Gentiles (that's who I am) are heirs together with Israel (the Jews), and stand together as children of God. We share in all of the promises of Christ Jesus. The wisdom of God is known—His extraordinary plan and eternal purpose is revealed and accomplished in Jesus. You belong to Him! Have faith. Be bold and brave!

# December 5

For God so loved the world that He gave His one and only Son, that whoever believes in Him shall not perish but have eternal life.

—John 3:16 (NIV)

"The virgin will conceive and give birth to a son, and they will call Him Immanuel" (which means "God with us").

—Matthew 1:24 (NIV)

In Jesus, there is love. God's love sent Jesus to be born as a gift to us. God's love is the reason you can live and laugh and love others. His love gives life, and so being the very reason you are breathing. Each breath, each minute, each day and month and year, is a gift. Jesus brings peace—Immanuel; God with us. Because of Jesus, we are never alone.

_____
_____
_____
_____

# December 6

> Once you were alienated from God and were enemies in your minds because of your evil behavior. But now He has reconciled you by Christ's physical body through death to present you holy in His sight, without blemish and free from accusation—if you continue in your faith, established and firm, and do not move from the hope held out in the gospel. This is the gospel that you heard and that has been proclaimed to every creature under heaven, and of which I, Paul, have become a servant.
> —Colossians 1:21–23 (NIV)

Believe it. Don't stray from it. Stand firm in it. Share it. The gospel (the good news of hope) is true! Live it like you believe it.

# December 7

> For I am not ashamed of the gospel, because it is the power of God that brings salvation to everyone who believes: first to the Jew, then to the Gentile. For in the gospel the righteousness of God is revealed—a righteousness that is by faith from first to last, just as it is written: "The righteous will live by faith."
> —Romans 1:16–17 (NIV)

Have you lost hope? Has something happened that left your heart broken? Have you given up on trying to repair your heart? Be still, friend. God is here. In this very moment, even in the darkest corners of this journey in life, God is present and will touch your heart and life, and He will bring healing and restoration. Are you ready for God to reveal Himself to you? Are you willing to live by faith as God unfolds the purpose for your being, and for your pain to bring Him glory? This moment in the dark alleys of your life, is a part of God's story in you. You will receive sufficient grace for your situation.

# December 8

And call on Me in the day of trouble; I will deliver you, and you will honor Me."
—Psalm 50:15 (NIV)

Why are you cast down, O my soul, and why are you in turmoil within me? Hope in God; for I shall again praise Him, my salvation and my God.
—Psalm 42:11 (ESV)

Though I thought I could not be loved, God changed that. Though I thought I had no future, God opened doors to a new future. Though I thought my days of service to Him were a thing of the past, God called me to a new purpose, and reminded me that His work is not finished.

Never say never. God taught me that His grace is sufficient for every conflict, and every moment, and He has something special for each of His children.

# December 9

Just because you claim it, that doesn't mean it's true.

> Saul was told that David had gone to Keilah, and he said, "God has delivered him into my hands, for David has imprisoned himself by entering a town with gates and bars." And Saul called up all his forces for battle, to go down to Keilah to besiege David and his men.
>
> When David learned that Saul was plotting against him, he said to Abiathar the priest, "Bring the ephod." David said, "LORD, God of Israel, your servant has heard definitely that Saul plans to come to Keilah and destroy the town on account of me. Will the citizens of Keilah surrender me to him? Will Saul come down, as your servant has heard? LORD, God of Israel, tell your servant."
>
> And the LORD said, "He will."
>
> Again David asked, "Will the citizens of Keilah surrender me and my men to Saul?"
>
> And the LORD said, "They will."
>
> So David and his men, about six hundred in number, left Keilah and kept moving from place to place. When Saul was told that David had escaped from Keilah, he did not go there.
>
> David stayed in the wilderness strongholds and in the hills of the Desert of Ziph. Day after day Saul searched for him, but God did not give David into his hands.
>
> —1 Samuel 23:7–8, 14 (ESV)

People may want to use God for their own glory and purpose. They may believe things that aren't true. For example, some have said, "All paths lead to everlasting life." But God doesn't do what we tell Him to do, just because we believe it to be true, or because we want Him to do it. He is still God, and He will do what is necessary to bring about what He ultimately plans. God's plan to make David king could not be changed; therefore, Saul could not kill David. Neither will God go against His ultimate plan of salvation—the only path to everlasting life is through His son, Jesus. There is no other way.

Ask God for guidance and wisdom as David did. Saul was sure God had delivered David into his hands, but he was wrong. "God did not give David into his hands."

There are some choices in this life that you can make however you desire without going against God. God allows us our own free will. Then, there are choices we need to make to either do what God is specifically asking of us, or choose to go against His will. His Word will always supersede any desire we may have that contradicts His way. Know Him. Hear Him. Follow Him. Jesus said, "My sheep listen to my voice; I know them, and they follow me." (John 10:27 NIV) We are all called to follow Him and to serve one another in love. That is absolute. What have you committed to do? Are you trying to force your own dream? Or are you asking for God's guidance?

_____
_____
_____
_____

# December 10

You've come to Jesus, who presents us with a new covenant, a fresh charter from God. He is the Mediator of this covenant. The murder of Jesus, unlike Abel's—a homicide that cried out for vengeance—became a proclamation of grace.

So don't turn a deaf ear to these gracious words. If those who ignored earthly warnings didn't get away with it, what will happen to us if we turn our backs on heavenly warnings? His voice that time shook the earth to its foundations; this time—He's told us this quite plainly—He'll also rock the heavens: "One last shaking, from top to bottom, stem to stern."

The words "once more" indicate the removing of what can be shaken—that is, created things—so that what cannot be shaken may remain.

Therefore, since we are receiving a kingdom that cannot be shaken, let us be thankful, and so worship God acceptably with reverence and awe, for our "God is a consuming fire."

—Hebrews 12:24–26 (MSG); Hebrews 12:27–29 (NIV)

Be careful not to forget the covenant of the LORD your God that He made with you; do not make for yourselves an idol in the form of anything the LORD your God has forbidden. For the LORD your God is a consuming fire, a jealous God.

—Deuteronomy 4:23–24 (NIV)

Nothing on earth—including anything in you—should get in the way of trusting God. Not riches or poverty; not success or failure; not religion, the past or future. "Created things" will be shaken. Our hearts will be shaken—our desires will be removed and replaced with what God creates. Is there anything that needs to be shaken from you? Allowing

God to shake what does not belong, and trusting that it will be good, will open the door for Him to work miracles out of messes, and transforming weaknesses into power. He knows what you need and will make sure you have it. Always remember that there is so much more than this material world.

# December 11

Faith Pushes Through Barriers

When Jesus came down from the mountainside, large crowds followed him. A man with leprosy came and knelt before Him and said, "Lord, if you are willing, you can make me clean." Jesus reached out His hand and touched the man. "I am willing," He said. "Be clean!" Immediately he was cleansed of his leprosy.
—Matthew 8:1–2 (NIV)

When Jesus had entered Capernaum, a centurion came to Him, asking for help. "Lord," he said, "my servant lies at home paralyzed, suffering terribly." Jesus said to him, "Shall I come and heal him?" The centurion replied, "Lord, I do not deserve to have you come under my roof. But just say the word, and my servant will be healed.
—Matthew 8:5–8 (NIV)

Then the woman, seeing that she could not go unnoticed, came trembling and fell at His feet. In the presence of all the people, she told why she had touched Him and how she had been instantly healed. Then He said to her, "Daughter, your faith has healed you. Go in peace."
—Luke 8:48 (NIV)

These stories in the Bible are only a few examples of faith, miracles, and power poured out from Jesus as they believed. They pushed through barriers—venturing out into public, traveling far, pushing through crowds of people. Each had a need. Each believed Jesus could meet their need. Whatever your need, Jesus has the power to provide it for you.

As a little girl I was fascinated by trains, and this fascination carried on through adulthood. Though I don't run and scream anymore when I hear a whistle blow, I will still stop and listen when I hear a train's whistle in the distance; and sometimes even a smile, or a tear will fall. Why? The massive locomotive traveling on the tracks with the wheels clattering and the train whistle blowing reminds me of how God shows His love over and over again. He showed me faith that can push through barriers I thought impossible. I thought I had everything figured out, confident and living a Christian life as best I could. I had lost all desire to live as I sat on the railroad tracks in my town, hoping for a train to come and take away all of the pain. I was so frightened by the thought of living with the pain. That amazing locomotive was not sent for my salvation; it wasn't the train's duty to save me from my despair, but to remind me of the wonder I saw as a child, watching the colorful cars pass by and the sounds that had once brought such joy to my heart, watching in amazement. I remembered the little things in life are what make all the difference and the childlike faith that could help one believe again—live again. My spiritual eyes were opened. My only source of help was to look up, and I thank my heavenly Father for pulling me up out of this pit. With a new heart, new mind transformed by the God of glory Himself, I could live free from the prison of fear! I had crossed over the tracks from this side of tragedy onto the other side of restoration. My tears turned into laughter, my pain into joy. Through faith, love, and hope I found peace and joy.

Push through. Press forward. And you will cross the railroad tracks and leave fear behind.

# December 12

Shaken but Not Moved

"Simon, Simon, Satan has asked to sift all of you as wheat. But I have prayed for you, Simon, that your faith may not fail. And when you have turned back, strengthen your brothers."
—Luke 22:31–32 (NIV)

Satan asks permission to shake you so that you are separated—as sifting of wheat separates. Jesus intercedes for us so that our faith increases. The Son of God is our intercessor. This fact brings peace to our hearts so that our faith will not fail. Did Simon Peter go on to deny Jesus? Yes. But, Jesus prayed for him. And as it turned out, Peter did *turn back* and he preached the gospel to many! Peter was shaken, but he was certainly not moved.

# December 13

> Your eyes saw my unformed body; all the days ordained for me were written in Your book before one of them came to be.
> —Psalm 139:16 (NIV)

Your life, from the moment God thought to bring it about and then from the time you were born, has been carefully planned out. Each day, each moment, He knew what it would consist of. Even the very moment you read these words, He gave to the writer to say—sent as a reminder, He is present, He has plans for you, and He has placed you where He wants you to be. He was there before you were born, and will continue to be there in eternity with you.

# December 14

> Immediately the boy's father exclaimed, "I do believe; help me overcome my unbelief!"
> —Mark 9:24 (NIV)

Are you struggling to believe? The father in this story admitted, "I do believe," but also wanted to *overcome his disbelief.* Is it possible to believe all the while struggling with disbelief? God is able to increase your faith when you ask Him to help you in your doubt. He already knows your heart—that you want to believe and, at the least, believe it is possible. He created you, so be honest with Him.

# December 15

That is what the Scriptures mean when they say,

> "No eye has seen, no ear has heard, and no mind has imagined what God has prepared for those who love Him."
> —1 Corinthians 2:9 (NLT)

It's hard for us to have faith. Things go wrong, and we question our existence—our reason for being. We become frustrated, hopeless and defeated. It's difficult to look up, when the things in our faces are so prominent.

We have this hope, to one day enter into His eternal glory. Until that day, continue to listen and be led by His Spirit. Keep moving forward, even when it doesn't make any sense to believe. Paul reminded the Corinthians of what Isaiah had prayed so many years before. We can't imagine the incredible things that God is doing, and what He has prepared for us.

> For since the world began, no ear has heard and no eye has seen a God like You, who works for those who wait for Him!
> —Isaiah 64:4 (NLT)

# December 16

> Faith shows the reality of what we hope for; it is the evidence of things we cannot see. Through their faith, the people in days of old earned a good reputation.
> —Hebrews 11:1–2 (NLT)

Hebrews 11 has been deemed the chapter of faith. It speaks of many men and women who were commended for their faith. They believed when things didn't make sense; they continued to believe when life was ending; they showed faithfulness in their offerings to God; they pleased God in their faithful walk; even when they didn't know where God's plan would take them, they went forward; and they stepped out in faith. Abraham had faith in a city no one had yet seen—the New Jerusalem. And all of them were waiting for the promise to be fulfilled when they died. "They only saw them and welcomed them from a distance. And they admitted that they were aliens and strangers on earth. People who say such things show that they are looking for a country of their own. They were longing for a better country—a heavenly one." (Hebrews 11:13–16 NIV) The chapter finishes by saying, "God had planned something better for us so that only together with us would they be made perfect." (Hebrews 11:39 NIV) His plan is forever. His plan is of love. His plan is good. His plan is better!

Faith is not given so that God's children can achieve greatness in themselves or obtain riches. Though God may give these gifts to you, the purpose of our faith is to believe there's something bigger about this earthly life, and someone—God—bigger than anything or anyone else. Remember these great examples of faith, when you begin to doubt. Faith offers citizenship into an eternal home. Keep that in mind when things around you are failing, or deteriorating. These sufferings are temporary, but our God—our faith—is eternal.

# December 17

> So never be ashamed to tell others about our Lord. And don't be ashamed of me, either, even though I'm in prison for Him. With the strength God gives you, be ready to suffer with me for the sake of the Good News. For God saved us and called us to live a holy life. He did this, not because we deserved it, but because that was His plan from before the beginning of time—to show us His grace through Christ Jesus. And now He has made all of this plain to us by the appearing of Christ Jesus, our Savior. He broke the power of death and illuminated the way to life and immortality through the Good News.
>
> —2 Timothy 1:8–10 (NLT)

Are you willing and ready to choose God's purpose for your life? Will you share your story as a testimony of God's grace and power? When you look back on this day, you will be able to know your choice made a difference; so let it be a good one. It may not be an easy decision; it may be a time when God will increase your faith through blind trust. God knows your heart; as you walk in faith, believe God will direct your steps.

_____
_____
_____
_____

# December 18

Looking Back and Pressing Forward

> Brothers and sisters, I do not consider myself yet to have taken hold of it. But one thing I do: Forgetting what is behind and straining toward what is ahead, I press on toward the goal to win the prize for which God has called me heavenward in Christ Jesus.
> —Philippians 3:13–14 (NIV)

The year is almost gone, and you may already be reflecting on the past year. "Did I do all I planned to do this year? What *did* I accomplish?" You may be in a place in your *life* where, as you reflect on your past, you are unsure that you have accomplished all you feel you should have by now. It is common to feel unfulfilled at times, because we push ourselves to excellence, success, and sometimes even perfection. Rather than allow the unfulfilled plans of the past frustrate and depress you, simply take one more step. Ask yourself what you're doing *today* to make a difference. What needs to change today; what choices can you make, to change what you can today.

It's not too late. You can start today with a heart to please God and take your next step toward the goal He has called you to. Forget your successes, and failures, and shortcomings of the past; and look forward to what God has called you to do.

# December 19

> What actually took place is this: I tried keeping rules and working my head off to please God, and it didn't work. So I quit being a "law man" so that I could be *God's* man. Christ's life showed me how, and enabled me to do it. I identified myself completely with him. Indeed, I have been crucified with Christ. My ego is no longer central. It is no longer important that I appear righteous before you or have your good opinion, and I am no longer driven to impress God. Christ lives in me. The life you see me living is not "mine," but it is lived by faith in the Son of God, who loved me and gave himself for me. I am not going to go back on that.
>
> Is it not clear to you that to go back to that old rule-keeping, peer-pleasing religion would be an abandonment of everything personal and free in my relationship with God? I refuse to do that, to repudiate God's grace. If a living relationship with God could come by rule-keeping, then Christ died unnecessarily.
> —Galatians 2:19–21 (MSG)

If we could keep all of God's commandments, and follow after righteousness in our own disciplines, we could claim to be perfect in the sight of God and all others. But we can't, so we cannot claim to be perfect in ourselves. This is why we needed a savior, Jesus. Through Him we are made perfect; and through His sacrifice, God sees no sin in us. God sees us as perfect children. He looks at us and sees His perfect Son. He looks through His perfect Son Jesus as a living, breathing lens to filter the imperfections caused by sin. By doing so, He is ultimately seeing us how we will be in our glorified bodies as they will be in eternity. He doesn't see us like we see ourselves. We look in the mirror, and we see how it is with our physical eyes. God looks upon us not with physical eyes that are limited to see what is only material, but with Spiritual eyes that can see the true reality—His kingdom.

It's okay to admit you are not perfect, and need a savior—we are human, you know. So, let go of your failures or disabilities, your successes and achievements, and allow His way to be revealed to you.

_____
_____
_____
_____

# December 20

> Consider it pure joy, my brothers and sisters, whenever you face trials of many kinds, because you know that the testing of your faith produces perseverance. Let perseverance finish its work so that you may be mature and complete, not lacking anything.
> —James 1:2–4 (NIV)

Living a life of faith will require perseverance. And faith will bring courage.

Have you ever started a diet with full vigor and anticipation to succeed, and then after some time, when you had a bad day, you find yourself giving up? Because of that one, poor choice, one day of going off the diet, we tend to repeat it the next day, and the next, leaving us feeling defeated. What if you, instead, decided that the diet is a lifestyle of change to good healthy choices, and not a temporary change in healthy habits? It then could have long term results and success, because it isn't about a ninety day plan, but a change in perspective.

This is how our walk of faith is. You will have difficult days, and you may even make poor choices that result in grim consequences; however, if you have dedicated this faith-walk to be a lifetime commitment, then you will persevere and allow your faith to become stronger through these difficult times. You will be determined to stay committed to the finish. You will show yourself to be faithful by still being in the race when the race is over.

Looking back, what do you see? Do you see He is faithful? Do you realize He delivered you?

Look at where you are now? How do you see God today? Do you know He can be trusted? Do you accept His peace?

Pressing forward, what do you hope for? Do you allow Him to guide you?

_____

_____

_____

# December 21

This is how the birth of Jesus the Messiah came about: His mother Mary was pledged to be married to Joseph, but before they came together, she was found to be pregnant through the Holy Spirit. Because Joseph her husband was faithful to the law, and yet did not want to expose her to public disgrace, he had in mind to divorce her quietly.

But after he had considered this, an angel of the Lord appeared to him in a dream and said, "Joseph son of David, do not be afraid to take Mary home as your wife, because what is conceived in her is from the Holy Spirit. She will give birth to a son, and you are to give Him the name Jesus, because He will save His people from their sins."

All this took place to fulfill what the Lord had said through the prophet: "The virgin will conceive and give birth to a son, and they will call Him Immanuel" (which means "God with us").

When Joseph woke up, he did what the angel of the Lord had commanded him and took Mary home as his wife. But he did not consummate their marriage until she gave birth to a son. And he gave Him the name Jesus.

—Matthew 1:18–25 (NIV)

Joseph had to believe what he had heard in a dream as being true, to be able to move forward in faith. He was faced with a difficult situation—his betrothed wife had become pregnant. How humiliating—He was going to be married, and now believes his soon-to-be-wife, Mary had been unfaithful. Joseph was a kind man, and did not want Mary to be publicly shamed, so he planned to divorce her quietly. Then. Then everything changed. He had a dream. Joseph could have disbelieved the dream. He could have thought it was all in his mind—made excuses or ignored it. But, he didn't. He woke up and did what the angel said to do.

Sometimes doing what God wants you to do will not be easy. You might be afraid. You might wonder if it isn't really what He wants. Have faith and accept the challenge He has presented to you.

# December 22

When God is Silent

> O God, do not remain silent; do not turn a deaf ear, do not stand aloof, O God.
> —Psalm 83:1 (NIV)

Have you ever had a time when you couldn't hear God speak? Maybe you are waiting to hear God's direction and He is quietly waiting. Though you may not see Him, He is still working on your behalf.

There will be days when you experience God's presence and His voice is loud, speaking to your heart. These are times when God knows you need to hear Him. But there will be other times when you will not hear His voice. You might read the Bible and not understand the meaning. In these moments, remember the past experiences when you heard God. It is in these moments when you will grow more spiritually because of the silence as you blindly trust God for the answers. Then keep a keen ear out for when He does speak. In due time, He will answer.

# December 23

Each of you should use whatever gift you have received to serve others, as faithful stewards of God's grace in its various forms. If anyone speaks, they should do so as one who speaks the very words of God. If anyone serves, they should do so with the strength God provides, so that in all things God may be praised through Jesus Christ. To Him be the glory and the power for ever and ever. Amen.
—1 Peter 4:10–11 (NIV)

Each of us has a gift that can be used to serve others. This is an act of faithfulness. God will give us all that we need to be able to serve.

We have different gifts, according to the grace given to each of us. If your gift is prophesying, then prophesy in accordance with your faith; if it is serving, then serve; if it is teaching, then teach; if it is to encourage, then give encouragement; if it is giving, then give generously; if it is to lead, do it diligently; if it is to show mercy, do it cheerfully.
—Romans 12:6–8 (NIV)

Do you believe there is a calling on your life to serve in a certain capacity? Maybe you're not sure what gift you have been given. Wait on the Lord and ask Him for affirmation of your gift, and then you will be able to know what He is doing or will do for you. Make sure your ideas do not contradict the Bible and His plan. Be careful to know what is true, before you claim what you believe is to be your next move. *Then*, move forward with boldness, knowing God is with you!

So let's say you've failed. Does that mean you are unworthy to serve God? Are you finished? Washed up? No! Jesus is greater than your failures. Jesus is greater than sickness, disease, divorce, or death or life! His name is higher than the darkness we face. His name defeats the enemy and brings victory even in and through great loss. We can't earn the right to serve God in the first place. It's not about our power, but about God's power. We are already unworthy in our sinful state—no matter how good you may think you are until you fail. It is Jesus who makes us worthy, not anything of ourselves. Paul served God and confessed that what he wanted to do, he didn't do, and what he didn't want to do, he did.

We must keep our focus on the foundation that keeps us grounded in the truth—that is, Jesus. Keep your eyes on "the trunk" of the tree. The branches and leaves may change and even blow away in a season of your life—you may lose more than you ever expected could be lost—but you are still a child loved by God. That's who you are. And you cannot be moved when you are firmly planted in the Word of God, which is Jesus Himself. God will equip you to do what He has asked of you. Your response to what God asks of you is critical.

---------------------------------------------------------------
---------------------------------------------------------------
---------------------------------------------------------------
---------------------------------------------------------------

# December 24

> But to those called by God to salvation, both Jews and Gentiles, Christ is the power of God and the wisdom of God. This foolish plan of God is wiser than the wisest of human plans, and God's weakness is stronger than the greatest of human strength.
>
> Remember, dear brothers and sisters, that few of you were wise in the world's eyes or powerful or wealthy when God called you. Instead, God chose things the world considers foolish in order to shame those who think they are wise. And He chose things that are powerless to shame those who are powerful. God chose things despised by the world, things counted as nothing at all, and used them to bring to nothing what the world considers important. As a result, no one can ever boast in the presence of God.
>
> God has united you with Christ Jesus. For our benefit God made Him to be wisdom itself. Christ made us right with God; He made us pure and holy, and He freed us from sin. Therefore, as the Scriptures say, "If you want to boast, boast only about the LORD."
> —1 Corinthians 1:25–31 (NLT)

You do not have to be perfect, wise, wealthy or powerful to come to God for forgiveness and salvation. God's wisdom, power and wealth is not of this world. Neither do you need the approval of others to serve Him.

Think of what you were when God found you. Were you a scholar of the Bible? Wise by societies standards? Are you influential, or of noble heritage? But God chose *you*!

God will use the weak, the broken, the unexpected, the uneducated, the young and old to confound the wisest. Society will claim that the fittest, strongest, most wise and educated, and most beautiful will succeed—that these are the people to listen to when you need good advice. Be careful not to place God in a box—God can work in the small details and in the storms.

Others say, "Who is she to think she can tell others how to live? Look at her!" Ridiculed by others as being the wrong choice to speak on His behalf, and God chose me and you! Be strong and brave.

We cannot ascertain the fullness of God and His strength and wisdom. Our God is much higher that all that. Yet, even Jesus came to us as a baby, born is a humble place—an animal's stable.

> Since God in His wisdom saw to it that the world would never know Him through human wisdom, He has used our foolish preaching to save those who believe.
> —1 Corinthians 1:21 (NLT)

# December 25

> Again the LORD spoke to Ahaz, "Ask the LORD your God for a sign, whether in the deepest depths or in the highest heights."
>
> But Ahaz said, "I will not ask; I will not put the LORD to the test."
>
> Then Isaiah said, "Hear now, you house of David! Is it not enough to try the patience of humans? Will you try the patience of my God also? Therefore the Lord Himself will give you a sign: The virgin will conceive and give birth to a son, and will call him Immanuel.
> —Isaiah 7:10–14 (NIV)

With rumors of war headed his way, King Ahaz began to panic. But when the Lord told Ahaz to ask for a sign from God to comfort him and show him that there was no need to fear, Ahaz refused the Lord's instruction and didn't want to ask for a sign from God. Even though he refused, God said He would give Ahaz a sign anyway. And it was the sign of the coming of the Lord Jesus, the Messiah. And He would be born of a virgin.

God may want to show you signs—signs to show He is in control and that His will is working on your behalf. He might just be causing that job offer to come your way, or make available the best deal on a car. He might be speaking and you don't even notice it. Just as Jesus was born as a sign to the world, and named Immanuel (God with us), Jesus continues to send signs our way to show us that He is still with us, just as He promised.

_____
_____
_____
_____

# December 26

> Then He said to Thomas, "Put your finger here; see My hands. Reach out your hand and put it into My side. Stop doubting and believe."
>
> Thomas said to Him, "My Lord and my God!"
>
> Then Jesus told him, "Because you have seen Me, you have believed; blessed are those who have not seen and yet have believed."
>
> —John 20:27–29 (NIV)

If I were only to believe in what I can touch, feel, and see, the belief that nothing exists apart from the material world would become my only reality. Nothing past the material world would have meaning or sustenance.

Jesus was born here on earth; He once walked with men as a human. After Jesus died on the cross and rose from the dead, Thomas, forever to be remembered as doubting Thomas, said he would not believe Jesus rose from the dead unless he saw and touched Jesus. We don't have the physical body of Jesus to see and touch, but in faith we can believe He is real. We can celebrate His birth, and know He died for us and rose again, as the Holy Spirit reveals Him to us.

_____
_____
_____
_____

# December 27

> "Be careful, or your hearts will be weighed down with carousing, drunkenness and the anxieties of life, and that day will close on you suddenly like a trap. For it will come on all those who live on the face of the whole earth. Be always on the watch, and pray that you may be able to escape all that is about to happen, and that you may be able to stand before the Son of Man."
> —Luke 21:34–36 (NIV)

Holidays seem to bring out the carousing and drunkenness. A time to party becomes a reason to drink, and I've watched people unable to know when too much is too much. I watch as they allow themselves to become drunk and be the person they wouldn't be sober. Sadly, many things happen when their guard is dropped and common sense is cast away like the beer bottle they just chugged.

Like railroad crossings and the signs and lights, we are given signs in life to announce danger. At times we may not be aware of the danger ahead—as Jesus warned of those days to come in the end times. If we have no warning signs, it can be traumatic when we arrive at the place where danger exists. Keep a keen eye out and always be on watch for signs that can help protect you. For example, signs of depression or sleeplessness may indicate the need to resolve an issue and look to God for healing and renewal. Signs of insecurity may cause a person to look to others to make them feel important and end up doing things they ought not to do.

Around the holidays, people may have sorrows for many reasons. They may miss a loved one, or feel lonely. They can become depressed and the anxieties of life could cause them to want to drink away the reminders of their pain. All of us will experience anxieties of life, but rather than turn to alcohol or any other substance, turn to the God who can give peace. Pray. If not addressed, these warning signs may turn to disaster as you fall farther down into the trap.

# December 28

> And now these three remain: faith, hope and love. But the greatest of these is love.
> —1 Corinthians 13:13 (NIV)

Faith ~ Faith is conviction and belief in God. Though the divine things are not seen, we believe it.

Hope ~ In trust, we believe and long for what we cannot see; hope gives us perseverance and makes life worth living.

Love ~ Pure love is the affection for God and others; God's perfect love flows in us and through us.

And yes, the greatest of these is love. It takes root, and springs forth life from God's love which is in us and forever for us. In the beginning, Jesus was with God and was God. His love created us. Jesus came to earth, born in human form, to save us from our sin and open the doors to eternal life—His love saved us. Jesus taught us how to live a godly life, preparing us for eternity. His love brought us faith. Jesus promises a future that has no pain, no tears, no sickness, no sin. His love gives us hope and life. It's all about Jesus; His love covers it all.

_____
_____
_____
_____

# December 29

> But when Jesus heard what had happened, He said to Jairus, "Don't be afraid. Just have faith, and she will be healed."
>
> —Luke 8:50 (NLT)

Believing—faith—will open the doors to healing, and a life of God's grace and power. Blessed is the believer, for there is peace in the life of faith.

When God is silent, remember His instruction and promises from the time when you knew and heard His voice. Remember what is true—the love He has demonstrated and the grace He has bestowed upon you. Though you may not see God or hear His voice, He is still working His brilliant plan. Even in the silence you can learn from Him and increase your faith.

If you believe the Word of God is true and believe God speaks to you and has a plan for your life, there is nothing to fear. You surely can live a life of peace, love, truth, hope and faith. As Jesus told Jairus, "Don't be afraid. Just have faith."

___
___
___
___

# December 30

Jesus answered, "Neither this man nor his parents sinned, but it was so that the works of God might be displayed *and* illustrated in him.
—John 9:3 (AMP)

Your inadequacies, disabilities, any sickness—your story—can give glory to God. Whether in your broken state as God gives you the ability to persevere, or by God's miraculous healing in your circumstance, your story can magnify and glorify God. You can give glory to God in your broken state by testifying of His sustaining power to bring you through the pain; and you can give Him glory when you receive miraculous victory over the trial. No matter what state you are in, you can testify of His grace and power to persevere and overcome.

You don't know what you can do with your broken pieces until you give God your broken pieces.
—Nick Vujicic, Evangelist, "Life Without Limbs"

Remember what God has done. Remember you are a child of God. Build your stones, write your story, your song, your poem.

Look back and see the power and love of God that shined bright in your darkest hours, so that you can give Him the glory.

Forget the past—past failures, hopelessness and losses. Replace painful memories with thoughts that bring hope and peace.

Press forward—persevere, stand strong and brave.

_____
_____
_____
_____

# December 31

> Don't you realize that in a race everyone runs, but only one person gets the prize? So run to win! All athletes are disciplined in their training. They do it to win a prize that will fade away, but we do it for an eternal prize. So I run with purpose in every step. I am not just shadowboxing. I discipline my body like an athlete, training it to do what it should. Otherwise, I fear that after preaching to others I myself might be disqualified.
> —1 Corinthians 9:24–27 (NLT)

Run with purpose. When the race is over, will you be on the side-lines, or will you be in the race? God's grace is sufficient to see you through to the end of the race. So many things can distract—and while in the race, you can be tripped up if you do not stay focused. Keep the faith as you live this life of purpose. Don't let fear disable you. Run. Keep in mind, always, it's not about me; it's not about you; it's not about your ability, or what you have or don't have. It's all about Jesus. If I have Jesus, I have everything I need! All things are possible—only believe.

If you don't receive a miracle you are asking for, then be a living miracle—an example of God's grace under fire!

I pray that this book has been an encouragement to you and has brought you to a place of confidence in who you are in God. Stand firm in your faith. Never give up. Believe what the Lord has said, because that's all that matters. You are broken, and restored, so that you can believe. Living for Jesus brings peace and joy, and that's all the joy we need.

Spiritual growth through the filling of the Holy Spirit and learning the Word of God enables us to have a strong relationship with the Lord, taking on His attributes of selflessness and humility.

Once we understand that life does not exist within the abundance of "things," we will better understand life's abundance. This abundant life that Jesus spoke of is not found in things we obtain for arrogance's sake—by loving ourselves and the things of the world, which is the *pride of life*—but by loving Jesus.

# Endnotes

1. Why Our Kids Are Out of Control Psychologytoday.com. https://www.psychologytoday.com/articles/200109/why-our-kids-are-out-control. Published by Jacob Azerrad, Paul Chance on September 1, 2001. Accessed November 15, 2017
2. Collins English Dictionary. https://www.collinsdictionary.com/dictionary/english/resort Collins: Pioneers in dictionary publishing since 1819. Accessed December 21, 2017.
3. Merriam-Webster Dictionary. https://www.merriam-webster.com/dictionary/almighty Accessed December 29, 2017.
4. The English Oxford Living Dictionary. https://en.oxforddictionaries.com/definition/humility Accessed January 24, 2018.

Editorial Services provided by Christopher Sanford